THE DAILY STUDY BIBLE

THE GOSPEL OF LUKE

D—I

THE GOSPEL OF LUKE

The Rev. WILLIAM BARCLAY, D.D.

*Lecturer in New Testament Language and Literature,
and in Hellenistic Greek, in the University of Glasgow*

THE SAINT ANDREW PRESS
EDINBURGH

Published by The Saint Andrew Press
121 George Street, Edinburgh 2
and printed in Scotland by
McCorquodale & Co., Ltd., Glasgow

First Edition	-	*September,*	1953
Second Edition	-	*February,*	1956
Third Edition	-	*September,*	1956
Second Impression	-	*May,*	1957
Third Impression	-	*January,*	1958
Fourth Impression	-	*November,*	1958
Fifth Impression	-	*May,*	1960
Sixth Impression	-	*April,*	1961
Seventh Impression	-	*November,*	1962

TO THE KIRK SESSION OF
TRINITY CHURCH, RENFREW,
OVER WHOM GOD CALLED ME TO PRESIDE
FROM 1933 TO 1946
AND IN PARTICULAR TO
M. R. AND J. B. K.,
MEN OF GOD.

GENERAL INTRODUCTION

It may truly be said that this series of Daily Bible Studies began almost accidently. A series which the Church of Scotland was using came to an end, and another series was immediately required. I was asked to write a volume on *Acts*, and, at the moment, had no intention beyond that. But one volume followed another, until the demand for one volume became a plan to write on the whole New Testament.

The translation which is given in each volume claims no special merit. It was included in order that the reader might be able to carry both the text of the New Testament and the comments on it wherever he went, and that he might be able to read it anywhere. While I was making the translation, the translations of Moffatt, Weymouth, and Knox were ever beside me. *The American Revised Standard Version*, *The Twentieth Century New Testament*, and *The New Testament in Plain English*, by Charles Kingsley Williams, have been in constant use. Since its publication, I have consistently consulted *The Authentic New Testament*, translated by Hugh J. Schonfield.

I cannot see another edition of these books going out to the public without expressing my very deep and sincere gratitude to the Church of Scotland Publications Committee for allowing me the privilege of first beginning, and then continuing, this series. And in particular I wish to express my very great gratitude to the convener, Rev. R. G. Macdonald, O.B.E., M.A., D.D., and to the committee's secretary and manager, Rev. Andrew McCosh, M.A., S.T.M., for constant encouragement and never-failing sympathy and help.

As these volumes went on, the idea of the whole series developed. The aim is to make the results of modern scholarship available to the non-technical reader in a form that it does not require a theological education to understand; and then to seek to make the teaching of the New Testament books relevant to life and work to-day. The whole aim of these books is summed up in Richard of Chichester's famous prayer; they are meant to enable men and women to know Jesus Christ more clearly, to love Him more dearly, and to follow Him more nearly. It is my prayer that they may do something to make that possible.

FOREWORD

ANYONE who writes a book like this has necessarily many debts. The commentaries on *Luke* by Alfred Plummer, in the International Critical Commentary, and by J. M. Creed in the Macmillan Commentary, have been constantly beside me. These are commentaries on the Greek text. The commentaries on the English text by H. Balmforth, in the Clarendon Bible, and by W. Manson, in the Moffatt Commentary, have been in constant use.

It is my hope and my prayer that something of the loveliness of what is to many the loveliest of all the gospels may shine through this book.

WILLIAM BARCLAY

TRINITY COLLEGE, GLASGOW
November, 1955

CONTENTS

THE GOSPEL OF LUKE

CONTENTS

THE GOSPEL OF LUKE

CONTENTS

CONTENTS

THE GOSPEL OF LUKE

INTRODUCTION

A lovely Book and its Author

The gospel according to St. Luke has been called the loveliest book in the world. Once an American asked Denney if he could recommend a good life of Christ, and Denney answered, " Have you tried the one that Luke wrote? " There is a legend that Luke was a skilled painter; there is even a painting of Mary in a Spanish cathedral to this day which purports to be by him. Certainly he had an eye for vivid things. It would not be far wrong to say that the third gospel is the best life of Christ ever written. Tradition has always believed that Luke was the author and we need have no qualms in accepting tradition in this case. In the ancient world it was the regular thing to attach books to famous names; no one thought it wrong. But Luke was never one of the famous figures of the early Church. If he had not written the gospel very certainly no one would have attached it to his name. Luke was a Gentile; and he has the unique distinction of being the only New Testament writer who was not a Jew. He was a doctor to profession (Colossians 4: 14) and maybe that very fact gave him the wide sympathy that he possessed. It has been said that a minister sees men at their best; a lawyer sees men at their worst; and a doctor sees men as they are. Luke saw men and loved them all. The book was written to a man called Theophilus. He is called most excellent Theophilus and the title given to him is the normal title for a high official in the Roman government. No doubt Luke wrote it to tell an earnest inquirer more about Jesus; and he succeeded in giving Theophilus a picture which must have thirled his heart even closer to the Jesus of whom he had heard.

The Symbols of the Gospels

Every one of the four gospels was written from a certain point of view. Very often on stained glass windows the writers of the gospels are pictured; and usually to each of them there is attached a symbol. The symbols vary but one of the commonest allocations of them is this. The emblem of *Mark* is a *man*. Mark is the simplest and the most straightforward of the gospels. It has been well said that its characteristic is *realism*. It is the nearest to being a report of Jesus' life. The emblem of *Matthew* is a *lion*. Matthew was a Jew writing for Jews and he saw in Jesus the Messiah, the Lion of the tribe of Judah, the one whom all the prophets had predicted. The emblem of *John* is the *eagle*. The eagle can fly higher than any other bird. It is said that of all creatures only the eagle can look straight into the sun. John is the theological gospel; its flights of thought are higher than those of any of the others. It is the gospel where the philosopher can find themes to think about for a lifetime and to solve only in eternity. But the symbol of *Luke* is the *calf*. The calf is the animal for sacrifice; and Luke saw in Jesus the sacrifice for all the world. In Luke above all the barriers are broken down and Jesus is for Jew and Gentile, saint and sinner alike. He is the Saviour of the World. Keeping that in mind, let us now set down the characteristics of Luke's gospel.

An Historian's Care

First and foremost, Luke's gospel is an exceedingly careful bit of work. His Greek is notably good. The first four verses are well-nigh the best Greek in the New Testament. In these verses he claims that his work is the product of the most careful research. His opportunities were ample and his sources must have been good. As the trusted companion of Paul he must have known all the great figures of the Church, and we may be sure that he made them tell their story to him. For two years he was Paul's companion in imprisonment in Caesarea. In the long days Luke had every opportunity for study and research and he must have used them well. An example of Luke's care is the way in which he dates the emergence of John the

Baptist. He dates it by no fewer than six contemporary datings. " Now in the fifteenth year of Tiberius Caesar (1), Pontius Pilate being governor of Judaea (2), Herod being tetrarch of Galilee (3), and his brother Philip being tetrarch of Ituraea and of the regions of Trachonitis (4), and Lysanias the tetrarch of Abilene (5), Annas and Caiaphas being the high priests (6), the word of God came unto John " (Luke 3: 1, 2). Here is a man who is writing with care and who will be as accurate as it is possible for him to be.

The Gospel for the Gentiles

It is clear that Luke wrote mainly for Gentiles. Theophilus was a Gentile, as was Luke himself, and there is nothing in the gospel that a Gentile could not grasp and understand. (a) As we have seen Luke begins his dating from the reigning *Roman* Emperor and the current *Roman* governor. The *Roman* date comes first. (b) Unlike Matthew, he is not greatly interested in the life of Jesus as the fulfilment of Jewish prophecy. (c) He very seldom quotes the Old Testament at all. (d) He has a habit of giving Hebrew words in their Greek equivalent so that a Greek would understand. Simon the *Cananaean* becomes Simon the *Zealot.* (cp. Luke 6: 15 and Matthew 10: 4, where *Canaanite* should be *Cananaean*). In Luke *Calvary* is called not by its Hebrew name, *Golgotha*, but by its Greek name, *Kranion.* Both mean *the place of a skull.* He never uses the Jewish term *Rabbi* of Jesus but always a Greek term meaning *Master.* When he is tracing the descent of Jesus, he traces it not to Abraham, the founder of the Jewish race, as Matthew does, but to Adam, the founder of the human race. (cp. Matthew 1: 2 and Luke 3: 38). It is just because of this that Luke is the easiest of all the gospels to read. He was writing, not for Jews, but for people very like ourselves.

The Gospel of Prayer

Luke's gospel is specially the gospel of prayer. At all

the great moments of His life, Luke shows us Jesus at prayer. Jesus prayed at His Baptism (3: 2); before His first collision with the Pharisees (5: 16); before He chooses the Twelve (6: 12); before He questions His disciples as to who they think He is and before His first prediction of His own death (9: 18); at the Transfiguration (9: 29); and upon the Cross (23: 40). Only Luke tells us that Jesus prayed for Peter in his hour of testing (22: 32). Only he tells us the prayer parables of the Friend at Midnight (11: 5-13) and the Unjust Judge (18: 1-8). To Luke the unclosed door of prayer was one of the most precious doors in all the world.

The Gospel of Women

In Palestine the place of women was low. In the Jewish morning prayer a man thanks God that God has not made him " a Gentile, a slave or a woman." But Luke in his gospel gives a very special place to women. The Birth narrative is told from Mary's point of view. It is in Luke that we read of Elizabeth, of Anna, of the widow at Nain, of the woman who anointed Jesus' feet in the house of Simon the Pharisee. It is Luke who makes vivid the picture of Martha and of Mary, and of Mary Magdalene. It is very likely that Luke was a native of Macedonia. In Macedonia women held a more emancipated position than anywhere else, and that may have something to do with it.

The Gospel of Praise

In the gospel of Luke the phrase *praising God* occurs oftener than in all the rest of the New Testament put together. This praise reaches its peak in the three great hymns that the Church has sung throughout all her generations—*The Magnificat* (1: 46-55); the *Benedictus* (1: 68-79); and the *Nunc Dimittis* (2: 29-32). There is a radiance in Luke's gospel which is a lovely thing, as if the sheen of heaven had touched the things of earth.

The Universal Gospel

But the outstanding characteristic of Luke is that his is the universal gospel. All the barriers are down; Jesus Christ is for all men without distinction. (*a*) The Kingdom of Heaven is not shut to the Samaritans (Luke 9: 51-56). Luke alone tells the parable of the Good Samaritan (10: 30-37). The one grateful leper was a Samaritan (Luke 17: 11-19). John can record a saying that the Jews have no dealings with the Samaritans (John 4: 9). But Luke refuses to shut the door on any man. (*b*) Luke shows Jesus speaking with approval of Gentiles whom the orthodox Jew would have considered unclean. He shows us Jesus citing the widow of Sarepta and Naaman the Syrian as shining examples (4: 25-27). The Roman centurion is praised for the greatness of his faith (7: 9). Luke tells us of that great word of Jesus, " They shall come from the east and from the west and from the north and from the south, and shall sit down in the Kingdom of God " (13: 29). (*c*) Luke is supremely interested in the poor. When Mary brought her offering for her purification it was the offering of the poor (2: 24). When Jesus is, as it were, setting out His credentials to the emissaries of John, the climax is, " The poor have the gospel preached to them " (7: 22). He alone tells the Parable of the Rich Man and the Poor Man (16: 19-31). In Luke's account of the Beatitudes the saying of Jesus runs, not, as in Matthew (5: 3), " Blessed are the poor in spirit," but simply, " Blessed are ye poor " (Luke 6: 20). Luke's gospel has been called " the gospel of the underdog." His heart ran out to everyone for whom life was an unequal struggle. (*d*) But above all Luke shows Jesus as the friend of outcasts and sinners. He alone tells the story of the woman who anointed Jesus' feet and bathed them with her tears and wiped them with her hair in the house of Simon the Pharisee (7: 36-50); of Zacchaeus, the quisling tax-gatherer (19: 1-10); the parable of the Pharisee and the Tax-gatherer (18: 9-14). Luke alone tells the story of the Penitent Thief

(23: 43); and Luke alone has the immortal story of the Prodigal Son and the Loving Father (15: 11-32). When Matthew tells how Jesus sent His disciples out to preach, he says that Jesus told them not to go to the Samaritans or the Gentiles (Matthew 10: 5); but Luke omits that altogether. All the four gospel writers quote from Isaiah 40 when they give the message of John the Baptist, " Prepare ye the way of the Lord; make straight in the desert a highway for our God "; but only Luke continues the quotation to its triumphant conclusion, " And all flesh shall see the salvation of God " (Isaiah 40: 3-5; Matthew 3: 3; Mark 1: 3; John 1: 23; Luke 3: 4). Luke of all the gospel writers saw no limits to the love of God.

The Book Beautiful

As we study this book we must look for these characteristics. Somehow of all the gospel writers one would have liked to meet Luke best of all, for this Gentile doctor who had the tremendous vision of the infinite sweep of the love of God must have been a lovely soul. Faber wrote the lines,

> There's a wideness in God's mercy,
>   Like the wideness of the sea;
> There's a kindness in His justice,
>   Which is more than liberty.

> For the love of God is broader
>   Than the measures of man's mind;
> And the heart of the Eternal
>   Is most wonderfully kind.

And Luke's gospel is the demonstration that that is true.

ST. LUKE

AN HISTORIAN'S INTRODUCTION

Luke I: I-4

> Since many have set their hands to the task of drawing
> up an account of the events which were completed
> amongst us, telling the story just as those who were
> the original eye-witnesses and who became the servants
> of the word handed it down to us, I too made up my
> mind to carry out a careful investigation of all things
> from the beginning, and to write to you, Theophilus,
> your excellency, an orderly account of them, so that
> you might have in your mind a full and reliable account
> of the things in which you have been instructed.

LUKE'S introduction is unique in the first three gospels
because it is the only place in them where the author
steps out upon the stage and when the writer uses the
pronoun " I." There are three things to note in this passage.
(i) It is the best bit of Greek in the New Testament.
Luke uses here the very form of introduction which the
great Greek historians all used. Herodotus, the famous
writer of Greek history, begins, " These are the researches
of Herodotus of Halicarnassus." A much later historian,
Dionysius of Halicarnassus, tells us at the beginning of his
history, " Before beginning to write I gathered information,
partly from the lips of the most learned men with whom
I came into contact, and partly from histories written by
Romans of whom they spoke with praise." So Luke, as
he began his gospel story, in the most sonorous Greek
followed the highest models he could find. It is as if Luke
said to himself, " I am writing the greatest story in the
world, and nothing but the best is good enough for that
story." Some of the ancient manuscripts are very beautiful
productions, written in silver ink on purple vellum; and
often the scribe, when he came to the name of God or of
Jesus, wrote it in gold. Dr. Boreham tells of an old workman
who, every Friday night, took the newest and the shiniest

coins out of his pay packet for Sunday's offering in Church. The historian, the scribe and the workman were all filled with the same idea—only the best is good enough for Jesus. They would always give their utmost for the highest. (ii) It is a most significant thing that Luke was not satisfied with anyone else's story of Christ He must have his own. Real religion is never a second hand thing, a carried story, a repeated tale. It is a personal discovery. Dr. Gossip used to say that the four gospels are important, but beyond them all comes the gospel of personal experience. Luke had to rediscover Jesus Christ for himself. (iii) There is no passage of the Bible which sheds such a flood light on the doctrine of the inspiration of scripture. No one will deny that the gospel of Luke is an inspired document; and yet Luke begins by affirming that it is the product of the most careful historical research. God's inspiration does not come to the man who sits with folded hands and lazy mind and only waits, but to the mind which thinks and seeks and searches. True inspiration comes when the seeking mind of man meets the revealing Spirit of God. The word of God is given, but it is given to the man who is seeking for it. " Seek and ye shall find."

A SON IS PROMISED

Luke I: 5-25

In the time of Herod, the king of Judaea, there was a priest called Zacharias, who belonged to the section of Abia. His wife was also a direct descendant of Aaron and her name was Elizabeth. Both of them were good people before God, for they walked blamelessly in all the commandments and ordinances of the Lord. They had no child because Elizabeth was barren and both of them were far advanced in years. When he was acting as priest before God, when his section was on duty, in accordance with the custom of priestly duty, it fell to him by lot to go into the Temple of the Lord to burn the incense. The whole congregation of the people was praying outside at the hour when incense was offered. The angel of the Lord appeared to him, standing at the right side of the altar of incense. When Zacharias saw him he was deeply moved and awe fell upon him. The angel said to him, " Do not be afraid, Zacharias, because your request has been heard and your wife Elizabeth will bear you a son and you must call him by the name of John. You will have joy and exultation and many will rejoice at his birth. He will be great in God's sight; he must not drink wine or strong drink and, even from the time he is in his mother's womb, he will be filled with the Holy Spirit. He will turn many sons of Israel to the Lord their God; and he himself will go before His face in the spirit and the power of Elijah, to turn the hearts of the fathers to the children, and the disobedient to the wisdom of the just, to get ready a people prepared for the Lord." Zacharias said to the angel, " How will I know that this is going to happen? For I am an old man and my wife is far advanced in years." " I am Gabriel," the angel answered, " who stands before God, and I have been sent to speak to you and to tell you this good news. And—look you— you will be silent and unable to speak until the day these things happen, because you did not believe my words which will be fulfilled in their own time." The people were waiting for Zacharias and they were surprised that he was lingering so long in the Temple. When he came out he was not able to speak to them and they realized that he had seen a vision in the Temple. He kept making signs to them but he remained unable to speak. When the days of his time of service were completed he went away to his own home. After these days Elizabeth his wife conceived; and she hid herself for five months. " This is God's doing for me," she said, " when He looked upon me to take away my shame among men."

ZACHARIAS, the central character in this scene, was a priest. He belonged to the section of Abia. Every direct descendant of Aaron was automatically a priest. That meant that for all ordinary purposes, there were far too many priests. They were therefore divided into twenty-four sections. Only at the Passover, at Pentecost and at the Feast of Tabernacles did all the priests serve. For the rest of the year each course served one week twice a year. Priests who loved their work looked forward to that week of service above all things; it was the high-light of their lives. A priest might only marry a woman of absolutely pure Jewish lineage. It was specially meritorious to marry a woman who was also a descendant of Aaron, as Elizabeth, the wife of Zacharias, was. There were as many as twenty thousand priests altogether and so there were not far short of a thousand in each section. So within the sections all the duties were allocated by lot. Every morning and evening, sacrifice was made for the whole nation. A burnt offering of a male lamb, one year old, without spot or blemish was offered, together with a meat offering of flour and oil and a drink offering of wine. Before the morning sacrifice and after the evening sacrifice incense was burned on the altar of incense so that, as it were, the sacrifices might go up to God wrapped in an envelope of sweet-smelling incense. It was quite possible that many a priest would never have the privilege of burning incense all his life; but if the lot did fall on any priest that day was the greatest day in all his life, the day he longed for and dreamed of. On this day the lot fell on Zacharias and very certainly he would be thrilled to the core of his being. But in Zacharias' life there was a tragedy. He and Elizabeth were childless. The Jewish Rabbis said that seven people were excommunicated from God and the list began, " A Jew who has no wife, or a Jew who has a wife and who has no child." Childlessness was a valid ground for divorce. Not unnaturally Zacharias, even on his great day, was thinking of his personal and domestic tragedy and was praying about it. And then the wondrous vision came and the glad message that, even when hope was dead, a son would be born to him. The incense was burned and the offering made in the inmost court of the Temple, the Court of the Priests. While the sacrifice was being made, the congregation thronged the next court, the Court of the Israelites. It was the privilege of the priest at the evening

sacrifice to come to the rail between the two courts after
the incense had been burned to bless the people. And the
people marvelled that Zacharias was so long delayed.
When he came he could not speak and the people knew
that he had seen a vision. So in a wordless daze of joy
Zacharias finished his week's duty and went home; and
then the message of God came true and Elizabeth knew
that she was going to have a child. One thing stands out
here. *It was in God's house that God's message came to
Zacharias.* We often wish that a message from God would
come to us. In Shaw's play, *Saint Joan,* Joan hears the
voices from God. The Dauphin is annoyed. " Oh, your
voices, your voices," he said, " Why don't your voices
come to me ? I am the king not you." " They do come,"
said Joan, " but you do not hear them. You have not
sat in the field in the evening listening for them. When
the angelus rings you cross yourself and have done with it,
but if you prayed from your heart and listened to the
thrilling of the bells in the air after they stopped ringing,
you would hear the voices as well as I do." Joan gave
herself the chance to hear God's voice. Zacharias was in
the Temple waiting on God. God's voice comes to those
who listen for it—as Zacharias did—in God's house.

GOD'S MESSAGE TO MARY

Luke I: 26-38

In the sixth month the angel Gabriel was sent from
God to a town of Galilee called Nazareth, to a maiden
who was betrothed to a man called Joseph, who belonged
to the house of David. The maiden's name was Mary.
He came in to her and said, " Greetings, most favoured
one. The Lord is with you." She was deeply moved
at this word and wondered what a greeting like that
could mean. The angel said to her, " Do not be afraid,
Mary, for you have found favour in God's sight.
Look you—you will conceive and you will bear a
son and you must call him by the name of Jesus.

He will be great and He will be called the Son of the Most High; and the Lord God will give Him the throne of David His father; and He will rule over the house of Jacob forever, and there will be no end to His Kingdom." Mary said to the angel, " How can this be since I do not know a man ? " The angel answered, " The Holy Spirit will come upon you and the Spirit of the Most High will overshadow you, and so the child who will be born will be called holy, the Son of God, and—look you—Elizabeth, too, your kinswoman has also conceived in her old age; and this is now the sixth month for her who is called barren, because there is nothing which is impossible with God." Mary said, " I am the Lord's servant. Whatever He says, I accept." And the angel went away from her.

MARY was betrothed to Joseph. Betrothal lasted for a year, and it was quite as binding as marriage. It could only be dissolved by divorce. Should the man to whom a girl was betrothed die, in the eyes of the law she was a widow. In the law there occurs the strange-sounding phrase, " a virgin who is a widow." Once two people were betrothed there was a bond between them which nothing but death could break. Here in this passage we are face to face with one of the great controversial doctrines of the Christian faith—the Virgin Birth. The Church does not insist that we believe in this doctrine. Let us look at the reasons for and against believing in it, and then we may make our own decision. There are two great reasons for accepting it literally. (i) If we read this passage, and still more if we read Matthew I: 18-25, the literal meaning is that Jesus was to be born of Mary, without a human father. (ii) It is very natural to argue that if Jesus was, as we believe, so very special a person, He would have a special entry into the world. And now let us look at the things which may make us wonder if the story of the Virgin Birth is to be taken as literally as all that. (i) The geneal-ogies of Jesus both in Luke and in Matthew (Luke 3: 23-38; Matthew I: I-17) both trace the genealogy of Jesus through Joseph, which is strange if Joseph was not His real father.

(ii) When Mary was looking for Jesus on the occasion that He lingered behind in the Temple, she said, " Your father and I have been searching for you and we were very worried " (Luke 2: 48). There the name *father* is very definitely given by Mary to Joseph. (iii) Repeatedly Jesus is referred to as Joseph's son (Matthew 13: 35; John 6: 42). (iv) The rest of the New Testament knows nothing of the Virgin Birth. True, in Galatians 4: 4 Paul speaks of Jesus as " born of a woman." But this is the natural phrase for any mortal man. (cp. Job 14: 1; 15: 14; 25: 4). But let us ask, " If we do not take the story of the Virgin Birth literally, how did it arise?" The Jews had a saying that in the birth of *every* child there are three partners—the father, the mother and the Spirit of God. They believed that no child could ever be born without the Spirit. And it may well be that the New Testament stories of the Birth of Jesus are lovely, poetical ways of saying that, even if He had a human father, the Holy Spirit of God was operative in His Birth in the most unique and special way. In this matter we may make our own decision. It may be that we will desire to cling to the literal doctrine of the Virgin Birth; it may be that we will prefer to think of it as a beautiful way of stressing the presence of the Spirit of God in family life.

Mary's submission is a very lovely thing. " Whatever God says, I accept." Mary had learned to forget the world's commonest prayer—" Thy will be *changed* "—and to pray the world's greatest prayer—" Thy will be *done*."

THE PARADOX OF BLESSEDNESS

Luke 1: 39-45

> In those days Mary arose and went eagerly to the hill country, to a city of Judah, and went into the house of Zacharias and greeted Elizabeth. When Elizabeth heard Mary's greeting the babe leaped in

her womb and Elizabeth was filled with the Holy Spirit, and she lifted up her voice with a great cry and said, " Blessed are you among women and blessed is the fruit of your womb. Why has this been granted to me—that the mother of my Lord should come to me? For—look you—when the voice of your greeting came to my ears the babe in my womb leaped with exultation. Blessed is she who believed that the things spoken to her from the Lord would find their fulfilment."

THIS whole passage is a kind of lyrical song on the blessedness of Mary. Nowhere can we better see the paradox of blessedness than in the life of Mary. To Mary was granted the blessedness of being the mother of the Son of God. Well might her heart be filled with a wondering, tremulous, amazed joy at so great a privilege. And yet that very blessedness was to be a sword to pierce her heart. That very glory was to break her heart. She was blessed and that very blessedness meant that some day she would see that Son of hers hanging on a cross. To be chosen by God so often means at one and the same time a crown of joy and a cross of sorrow. The piercing truth is that God does not choose a person for ease and comfort and selfish joy but for a great task that will take all that head and heart and hand can bring to it. *God chooses a person to use that person.* When Joan of Arc knew that her time was short she prayed, " I shall only last a year; use me as you can." When that is realized then the sorrows and the hardships that serving God may bring are not matters for lamentation; they are our glory, for all is done and suffered for God. When Richard Cameron was caught by the dragoons they killed him. He had very beautiful hands and they cut off these hands and sent them to his father with a message asking if he recognized them. " They are my son's," he said, " my own dear son's. Good is the will of the Lord who can never wrong me or mine." The tears of life were lit by the sense that this too was in the plan of God. A great Spanish saint prayed for his people, " May God deny you peace and give you glory." A great modern preacher said, " Jesus Christ came not to make life easy but to make men great." It is the paradox of blessedness that it confers on a person at one and the same time the greatest joy in all the world and the greatest task in all the world.

A WONDROUS HYMN

Luke I: 46-56

And Mary said, " My soul magnifies the Lord, and my spirit has exulted in God, my Saviour, because He looked graciously on the humble estate of His servant. For—look you—from now on all generations shall call me blessed, for the Mighty One has done great things for me and His name is holy. His mercy is from generation to generation to those who fear Him. He demonstrates His power with His arm. He scatters the proud in the plans of their hearts. He casts down the mighty from their seats of power. He exalts the humble. He fills those who are hungry with good things and He sends away empty those who are rich. He has helped Israel, His son, in that He has remembered His mercy—as He said to our fathers that He would—to Abraham and to his descendants forever."

HERE we have a passage which has become one of the great hymns of the Church—the *Magnificat*. It is a passage which is saturated in the Old Testament. It is specially kin to Hannah's song of praise in I Samuel 2: I-IO. It has been said that religion is dope, the opiate of the people; but, as Stanley Jones said, " the *Magnificat* is the most revolutionary document in the world." The *Magnificat* speaks of three of the revolutions of God. (i) *He scatters the proud in the plans of their hearts.* That is a *moral* revolution. Christianity is the death of pride. Why? Because if a man sets his life beside the life of Christ it tears the last vestiges of pride from him. Sometimes something

9

happens to a man which with a vivid, blinding, revealing light shames him. O. Henry has a short story like this. There was a lad who was brought up in a village. In school he used to sit beside a girl and they were fond of each other. He went to the city and he fell on evil ways. He became a pickpocket and a petty thief. One day he had just snatched an old lady's wallet. It was clever work, and he was pleased. And then he saw coming down the street the girl whom he used to know, still sweet with the radiance of innocence. And suddenly he saw himself for the cheap, vile thing he was. Burning with shame, he leaned his head against the cool iron of a lamp standard. " God," he said, " I wish I could die." He saw himself. Christ enables a man to see himself. It is the deathblow to pride. The moral revolution has begun. (ii) *He casts down the mighty—he exalts the humble*. That is a social revolution. Christianity puts an end to the world's labels and prestige. Muretus was a wandering scholar of the middle ages. He was poor. In an Italian town he took ill and was taken to a hospital for waifs and strays. The doctors were discussing his case in Latin, never dreaming he could understand. They suggested that since he was such a worthless wanderer they might use him for medical experiments. He looked up and answered them in their own learned tongue, " Call no man worthless for whom Christ died." When we have realized what Christ did for all men, it is no longer possible to speak about a *common* man. The social grades and ranks are gone. (iii) *He has filled those who are hungry . . . those who are rich he has sent empty away*. That is an *economic* revolution. A non-Christian society is an acquisitive society where each man is out to amass as much as he can get. A Christian society is a society where no man dares to have too much while others have too little, where every man must get only to give away. There is loveliness in the *Magnificat* but in that loveliness there is dynamite. Christianity begets a revolution in each man, and a revolution in the world.

HIS NAME IS JOHN

Luke 1: 57-66

When Elizabeth's time to bear the child was completed she brought forth a son. When her neighbours and kinsfolk heard that the Lord had shown great mercy to her they rejoiced with her. On the eighth day they went to circumcise the child and it was their intention to call him Zacharias after his father. But his mother said, " No; he must be called John." They said to her, " There is no one in your connection who is called by this name." They asked his father by signs by what name he wished him to be called. He asked for a writing tablet and wrote, " John is his name." Immediately his mouth was opened and his tongue was loosed and he kept on praising God. And great awe fell upon all the neighbours, and all these events were talked about in all the hill country of Judaea; and all those who heard them kept them in their hearts and said, " What will this child turn out to be, for the hand of the Lord is with him? "

IN Palestine the birth of a child was an occasion of great joy, especially if the child was a boy. When the time of the birth was near at hand, the friends and the local musicians gathered near the house. When the birth was announced, if it was a boy, the musicians broke into music and song, and there was universal congratulation and rejoicing. If it was a girl the musicians went silently and regretfully away! There was a saying, " The birth of a male child causes universal joy, but the birth of a female child causes universal sorrow." So in Elizabeth's house there was a double joy. At last she had a child and that child was a son. On the eighth day the boy was circumcised and on that day he received his name. Girls could be named any time within thirty days of their birth. In Palestine names were descriptive. They sometimes described a circumstance attending the birth as *Esau* and *Jacob* do (Exodus 25: 26). They sometimes describe the child. *Laban,* for instance, means *white* or *blonde*. Sometimes the child received the parental name. Often

11

the name describes the parents' joy. *Saul* and *Samuel*, for instance, both mean *asked for*. Sometimes the name was a declaration of the parents' faith. *Elijah* for instance, means *Jehovah is my* God. Thus in a time of Baal worship Elijah's parents asserted their faith in the true God. Elizabeth, to the neighbours' surprise, said that her son must be called John and Zacharias indicated that that was also his desire. *John* is a shorter form of the name *Jehohanan,* which means *Jehovah's gift* or *God is gracious*. It was the name which God had ordered to be given to the child and it described the parents' gratitude for an all-unexpected joy. It was the question of the neighbours and of all who had heard the amazing story, " What will this child turn out to be? " Every child is a bundle of possibilities. There was an old Latin schoolmaster who always bowed gravely to his class before he taught them. When he was asked why, he answered, " Because you never know what one of these lads will turn out to be." The entry of a child into a family is two things. First, it is the greatest privilege which life can offer a man and a wife. It is something for which to thank God. Second, it is one of life's supreme responsibilities, for that child is a bundle of possibilities, and on parents and teachers depends how these possibilities will or will not be realized.

A FATHER'S JOY

Luke I: 67-80

His father Zacharias was filled with the Holy Spirit and prophesied like this: " Blessed be the Lord, the God of Israel, because He has graciously visited His people and wrought deliverance for them. He has raised the horn of salvation for us in the house of David, His servant—as long ago He said He would through the mouth of His holy prophets—even deliverance from our enemies and from the hand of all who hate us, in that He has shown mercy to us as He did to our fathers and has remembered His

holy covenant, the pledge which He gave to Abraham
our father, to grant to us that we, being delivered
from the hands of our enemies, should fearlessly
serve Him, in holiness and righteousness before Him,
all our days. And you, child, shall be called the
prophet of the Most High; for you will walk before
the Lord to prepare His ways, in order to give the
knowledge of salvation to His people together with
forgiveness of their sins, through the mercy of our
God, in which the dawn from on high has graciously
visited us, to shine upon those who sit in darkness
and in the shadow of death, and to direct our feet
in the way of peace."

And the child grew and was strengthened by the
Spirit; and he lived in the desert places until the day
when he was displayed to Israel.

ZACHARIAS had a great vision for his son. He thought of
him as the prophet and the forerunner who would prepare
the way of the Lord. All devout Jews hoped and longed
for the day when the Messiah, God's Anointed King,
would come. Most of them believed that, before He came,
a forerunner would come to announce His coming and to
prepare His way. The usual belief was that Elijah would
return to do so (Malachi 4: 5). Zacharias saw in his son
the one who would prepare the way for the coming of
God's King. Verses 75-77 give a great picture of the steps
of the Christian way. (i) There must be a *preparation*.
All life is a preparation to lead us to Christ. When Sir
Walter Scott was young his aim was to be a soldier. An
accident made him slightly lame and that dream had to
be abandoned. He took to reading the old Scottish histories
and romances and he so became the master novelist.
An old man said of him, " He was makin' himsell a' the
time; but he didna ken maybe what he was about till
years had passed." In life God is working all things together
to bring us to Christ. (ii) There must be *knowledge*. It
is the simple fact that men did not know what God was
like until Jesus came. The Greeks thought of a passionless
God, beyond all joy and sorrow, looking on men in calm

unmoved detachment—no help there. The Jews thought of a demanding God, whose name was law and whose function was that of judge—nothing but terror there. Jesus came to tell of a God who was love, and in staggered amazement men could only say, " We never knew that God was like that." One of the great functions of the incarnation is to bring to men the knowledge of God. (iii) There is *forgiveness*. We must be clear about one thing regarding forgiveness. Forgiveness is not so much the remission of penalty as the restoration of a relationship. Nothing can deliver us from certain consequences of our sins; the clock cannot be put back; but the estrangement from God is turned to friendship. The distant God is become near and the God we feared has become the lover of the souls of men. (iv) There is a *new walk in life* in the ways of peace. *Peace* in Hebrew does not mean merely freedom from trouble; it means all that makes for a man's highest good; and through Christ a man is enabled to walk in the ways that lead to everything that means life, and no longer to all that means death.

JOURNEY TO BETHLEHEM

Luke 2: 1-7

In these days a decree went out from Caesar Augustus that a census should be taken of all the world. The census first took place when Quirinius was governor of Syria; and everyone went to enrol himself, each man to his own town. So Joseph went up from Galilee, from the town of Nazareth, to Judaea, to David's town, which is called Bethlehem, because he belonged to the house and the line of David, to enrol himself with Mary who was betrothed to him and she was with child. When they arrived there her time to bear the child was completed; and she bore her first-born son and wrapped him in swaddling clothes and laid him in a manger because there was no room for them in the place where they had meant to lodge.

IN the Roman Empire periodical censuses were taken with the double object of assessing taxation and discovering those who were liable for compulsory military service. The Jews were exempt from military service, and, therefore, in Palestine a census would be predominantly for taxation purposes. Regarding these censuses, we have definite information as to what happened in Egypt; and almost certainly what happened in Egypt happened in Syria too and Judaea was part of the province of Syria. The information we have comes from actual census documents written on papyrus and then discovered in the dust-heaps of Egyptian towns and villages and in the sands of the desert. Such censuses were taken every fourteen years. And from A.D. 20 until about A.D. 270 we possess actual documents from every census taken. If the fourteen year cycle held good in Syria then this census must have been in 8 B.C. and that year was the year in which Jesus was born. It may be that Luke has made one slight mistake. Quirinius did not actually become governor of Syria until A.D. 6; but he held an official post previously in those regions from 10 B.C. until 7 B.C. and it was during that first period that this census must have been taken. Critics used to question the fact that every man had to go to his own city to be enrolled; but here is an actual government edict from Egypt:

> " Gaius Vibius Maximus, Prefect of Egypt orders: ' Seeing that the time has come for the house to house census, it is necessary to compel all those, who for any cause whatsoever are residing outside their districts to return to their own homes, that they may both carry out the regular order of the census, and may also diligently attend to the cultivation of their allotments.' "

If that was the case in Egypt, it may well be that in Judaea, where the old tribal ancestries still held good, men had to go to the headquarters of their tribe. Here is an instance where further knowledge has shown the accuracy of the New Testament.

The journey from Nazareth to Bethlehem was 80 miles in length. The accommodation for travellers was in any case most primitive. The eastern khan was like a series of stalls opening off a common courtyard. Travellers brought their own food; all that the innkeeper provided was fodder for the animals and a fire to cook. The town was crowded and there was no room for Joseph and Mary. So it was in the common courtyard that Mary's child was born. Swaddling clothes were like this—they consisted of a square of cloth with a long, bandage-like strip coming diagonally off from one corner. The child was first wrapped in the square of cloth and then the long strip was wound round and round about him. The word which is translated *manger* means, quite generally, a place where animals feed; and therefore it can be either the stable or the manger which is meant. That there was no room in the inn was symbolic of what was to happen to Jesus. The only place where there was room for Him was on a cross. He sought an entry to the over-crowded hearts of men; He could not find it; and still His search—and His rejection—go on.

SHEPHERDS AND ANGELS

Luke 2: 8-20

In this country there were shepherds who were in the fields, keeping watch over their flock by night. An angel of the Lord appeared to them and the glory of the Lord shone round about them and they were much afraid. The angel said to them, " Do not be afraid; for—look you—I am bringing you good news of great joy, which will be to every people, for to-day a Saviour has been born for you, in David's town, who is Christ the Lord. You will recognize Him by this sign. You will find the Babe wrapped in swaddling clothes and laid in a manger." And suddenly with the angel there was a crowd of heaven's host, praising God and saying, " In the highest heights glory to God; and on earth peace to the men whose welfare He ever seeks." When the angels had left them and gone away to heaven, the shepherds said to each other, "Come! Let us go across to Bethlehem and let us see this thing which has happened which the Lord has made known to us." So they hurried on and they discovered Mary and Joseph, and the Babe lying in a manger. When they had seen Him they told everyone about the word which had been spoken to them about this child; and all who heard were amazed at what was told them by the shepherds. But Mary stored up these things in her memory and in her heart kept wondering what they meant. So the shepherds returned glorifying and praising God for all that they had seen, just as it had been told to them.

IT is a wonderful thing that the story should tell that the first announcement of God should come to the shepherds. The shepherds were despised by the orthodox good people of the day. Shepherds were quite unable to keep the details of the ceremonial law; they could not observe all the meticulous hand-washings and rules and regulations. Their flocks made far too constant demands on them; and so the orthodox looked down on them as very common people. It was to simple men of the fields that God's message first came. But these shepherds were in all likelihood very special shepherds. We have already seen how in the Temple, morning and evening, an unblemished lamb was offered as a sacrifice to God. To see that the supply of perfect and unblemished offerings was always available the Temple authorities had their own private sheep flocks; and we know that these flocks were pastured near Bethlehem. It is most likely that these shepherds were in charge of the flocks from which the Temple offerings were chosen. It is a lovely thought that the shepherds who looked after the Temple lambs were the first to see the Lamb of God who takes away the sin of the world.

We have already seen that when a child was born the local musicians congregated at the house to greet him with simple music. Jesus was born in a stable in Bethlehem and therefore that ceremony could not have been carried out. It is a lovely thought that the minstrelsy of heaven took the place of the minstrels of earth, and angels sang the songs for Jesus that it was impossible for the earthly singers to sing.

All through these readings we must have been thinking of the rough simplicity of the birth of the Son of God. We might have expected that, if the Son of God had to be born into this world at all, it would be in a palace or a mansion. There was a European monarch who worried his court by often disappearing and walking incognito amongst his people. When he was asked not to do so for security's sake, he answered, " I cannot rule my people unless I know how they live." It is the great thought of the Christian faith that we have a God who knows this life we live because He too lived it, and claimed no special advantage over common men.

THE ANCIENT CEREMONIES ARE OBSERVED

Luke 2: 21-24

> When the eight days necessarily prior to circumcision had elapsed, He was called by the name of Jesus, the name by which He had been called by the angel before He had been conceived in the womb. When the time which, according to the law of Moses, must precede the ceremony of purification had elapsed, they brought Him up to Jerusalem to present Him to the Lord (in accordance with the regulation in the Lord's law, " Every male creature which opens the womb must be called sacred to the Lord ") and to make the sacrifice which the regulation in the Lord's law lays down, that is, a pair of doves or two young pigeons.

IN this passage we see Jesus undergoing three ancient ceremonies which every Jewish boy had to undergo. (i) *Circumcision.* Every Jewish boy was circumcised on the eighth day after his birth. So sacred was that ceremony that it could be carried out even on a Sabbath when the law forbade almost every act which was not absolutely essential; and, as we have seen, on that day a boy received his name. (ii) *The Redemption of the First-born.* According to the law (Exodus 3: 2) every firstborn male, both of human beings and of cattle, was sacred to God. That law may have been a recognition of the gracious power of God in giving human life, or it may even have been a relic of the day when children were sacrificed to the gods. Clearly if it had been carried out literally life would have been disrupted. There was therefore a ceremony called the Redemption of the Firstborn (Numbers 18: 16). It is laid down that for the sum of five shekels—approximately fifteen shillings—parents could, as it were, buy back their son from God. The sum had to be paid to the priests. It could not be paid sooner than thirty-one days after the birth of the child and it might not be long delayed after that. (iii) *The Purification after Childbirth.* When a woman had borne a child, if it was a boy she was unclean for forty days, if it was a girl, for eighty days. She could go about her household and her daily business but she could not enter the Temple or share in any religious ceremony (Leviticus 12). At the end of that time she had to bring to the Temple a lamb for a burnt offering and a young pigeon for a sin offering. That was a somewhat expensive sacrifice, and so the law laid it down (Leviticus 12: 8) that if she could not afford the lamb she might bring another pigeon. The offering of the two pigeons instead of the lamb and the pigeon was technically called *The Offering of the Poor.* It was the offering of the poor which Mary brought. Again we see that it was into an ordinary home that Jesus was born, a home where there were no luxuries, a home where every penny had to be looked at twice, a home where the members of the family knew all about the difficulties of making a living and the haunting insecurity of life. When life is worrying for us we must remember that Jesus knew what the difficulties of making ends meet can be.

These three ceremonies are strange old ceremonies; but all three have at the back of them the conviction that a child is a gift of God. The Stoics used to say that a child was not *given* to a parent but only *lent* by God. Of all God's gifts there is none for which we shall be so answerable as the gift of a child.

A DREAM REALIZED

Luke 2: 25-35

Now—look you—there was a man in Jerusalem called Simeon. This man was good and pious. He was waiting for the comforting of Israel and the Holy Spirit was upon him. He had received a message from the Holy Spirit that he would not see death until he had seen the Lord's Anointed One. So he came in the Spirit to the Temple precincts. When His parents brought in the child Jesus, to do regarding Him the customary ceremonies laid down by the law, he took Him into his arms and blessed God and said, " Now, O Lord, as you said, let your servant depart in peace, because my eyes have seen your instrument of salvation, which you have prepared before all the people, a light to bring your revelation to the Gentiles, and the glory of your people Israel." His father and mother were amazed at what was said about Him. Simeon blessed them and said to Mary His mother, " Look you, this child is appointed to be the cause whereby many in Israel will fall and many rise and for a sign which will meet with much opposition. As for you— a sword will pierce your soul—and all this will happen that the inner thoughts of many hearts may be revealed."

THERE was no Jew who did not regard his own nation as the chosen people. But the Jews saw quite clearly that by human means their nation could never attain to the supreme world greatness which they believed that their destiny involved. By far the greater number of them believed that because the Jews were the chosen people they were bound some day to become masters of the world and lords of all the nation. To bring in that day some believed that some great, celestial champion would descend upon the earth; some believed that there would arise another king of David's line and that all the old glories would revive; some believed that God Himself would break directly into history by supernatural means. But in contrast to all that there were some few people who were known as *the Quiet in the Land*. They had no dreams of violence and of power and of armies with banners; they believed in a life of constant prayer and quiet watchfulness until God should come. All their lives they waited quietly and patiently upon God. Simeon was like that; in prayer, in worship, in humble and faithful expectation he was waiting for the day when God would comfort His people. God had promised to him through the Holy Spirit that life would not end for him before he had seen God's own Anointed King. In the baby Jesus he recognized that King and he was glad. Now he was ready to depart in peace and his words have become the *Nunc Dimittis*, another of the great and precious hymns of the Church.

In verse 34 Simeon gives a kind of summary of the work and fate of Jesus. (i) Jesus will be the cause whereby *many will fall*. This is a strange and a hard saying but it is true. It is not so much God who judges a man; a man judges himself; and his judgment is his reaction to Jesus Christ. If, when he is confronted with that goodness and that loveliness, his heart runs out in answering love he is within the Kingdom. If, when so confronted, he remains coldly unmoved or actively hostile, he is condemned. There is a great refusal just as there is a great acceptance. (ii) Jesus will be the cause whereby *many will rise*. Long ago Seneca said that what men needed above all was a hand let down to lift them up. It is the hand of Jesus which lifts a man out of the old life and into the new, out of the sin into the goodness, out of the shame into the glory. (iii) Jesus would meet with *much opposition*. Towards Jesus Christ there can be no neutrality. We either surrender to Him or are at war with Him. And it is the tragedy of life that the pride of man keeps us from making that surrender wherein is victory.

21

A LOVELY OLD AGE

Luke 2: 36-40

> There was a prophetess called Anna. She was the
> daughter of Phanuel and she belonged to the tribe
> of Asher. She was far advanced in years. She had
> lived with her husband ever since seven years after
> she came to womanhood; and now she was a widow
> of eighty-four years of age. She never left the Temple
> and day and night she worshipped with fastings and
> with prayers. At that very time she came up and she
> began to give thanks to God and she kept speaking
> about Him to all those who were waiting expectantly
> for the deliverance of Jerusalem. When they had
> completed everything which the Lord's law lays down
> they returned to Galilee to their own town of Nazareth.
> And the child grew bigger and stronger and He was
> filled with wisdom, and God's grace was on Him.

ANNA, too, was one of the Quiet in the Land. We know
nothing about her except what these verses tell but even
in this brief compass Luke has drawn us a complete character sketch. (i) Anna was a widow. *She had known sorrow
and she had not grown bitter.* Sorrow can do one of two
things to us. It can make us hard, bitter, resentful, rebellious
against God. Or, it can make us kinder, softer, more
sympathetic. It can despoil us of our faith. Or, it can
root faith ever deeper and more immovable. It all depends
how we think of God. If we think of God as a tyrant we
will resent God. If we think of God as Father we too will
be sure that

> A Father's hand will never cause
> His child a needless tear.

(ii) She was eighty-four years of age. *She was old and she
had never ceased to hope.* Age can take away the bloom and
the strength of our bodies; but age can do worse—the
years can take away the life of our hearts until the hopes
that once we cherished die and we become dully contented
and grimly resigned to things as they are. Again it all
depends on how we think of God. If we think of God as

22

distant and remote and detached we may well despair;
but if we think of God as intimately connected with life,
as having His hand on the helm of life we too will be sure
that the best is yet to be, and the years will never kill
our hope. How then was Anna such as she was? (i) *She
never ceased to worship.* She spent her life in God's house
with God's people. God gave us His Church to be our
mother in the faith. We rob ourselves of a priceless treasure
when we neglect to be one with God's worshipping people.
(ii) *She never ceased to pray.* Public worship is great;
but private worship is also great. As someone has truly
said, " They pray best together who first pray alone."
The years had left Anna without bitterness and in unshak-
able hope because day by day she kept her contact with
Him who is the source of strength and in whose strength
our weakness is made perfect.

THE DAWNING REALIZATION

Luke 2: 41-52

Every year His parents used to go to Jerusalem for
the feast of the Passover. When He was twelve years
of age, when they went up according to the custom
of the feast, and when they had completed the days
of the feast, when they returned home the child Jesus
stayed on in Jerusalem. His parents were not aware
of this. They thought He was in the caravan and when
they had gone a day's journey they looked for Him
amongst their kinsfolk and acquaintances. When
they did not find Him they turned back to Jerusalem,
looking for Him all the time. After three days they
found Him in the Temple precincts, sitting in the
middle of the Rabbis, listening to them and asking
them questions. All who were listening were astonished
at His understanding and at His answers. When
they saw Him they were amazed. His mother said
to Him, " Child, why did you do this to us? Look
you, your father and I have been looking for you and
we have been very worried." He said to them, " Why
were you looking for me? Did you not know that I
was bound to be in my Father's house? " They did

not understand the meaning of what He said to them. So He came home with them and went to Nazareth and He was obedient to them. His mother kept all these things in her heart. And Jesus grew wise and grew bigger and increased in favour with God and man.

THIS is one of the supremely important passages in the gospel story. It was laid down by law that every adult male Jew who lived within twenty miles of Jerusalem must attend the Passover. In point of fact it was the aim of every Jew in all the world at least once in a lifetime to attend that feast. A Jewish boy became a man when he was twelve years of age. Then he became *a son of the law* and had to take the obligations of the law upon him. So at twelve Jesus for the first time went to the Passover. We may well imagine how the holy city and the Temple and the sacred ritual fascinated Him. When His parents returned He lingered behind. It was not through carelessness that they did not miss Him. Usually the women in a caravan started out much earlier than the men for they travelled more slowly. The men started later and travelled faster and the two sections would not meet until the evening encampment was reached. It was Jesus' first Passover. No doubt Joseph thought He was with Mary and Mary thought that He was with Joseph and not till the evening camp did they miss Him. They returned to Jerusalem to search for Him. For the Passover season it was the custom for the Sanhedrin to meet in public in the Temple court to discuss, in the presence of all who would listen, religious and theological questions. It was there that they found Jesus. We must not think of it as a scene where a precocious boy was dominating a crowd of his seniors. *Hearing and asking questions* is the regular Jewish phrase for a student learning from his teachers. Jesus was listening to the discussions and eagerly searching for knowledge like an avid student. And now there comes one of the key passages in the life of Jesus. " *Your father* and I," said Mary, " have been searching for you." " Did you not realize," said Jesus, " that you would find me in *my Father's* house "?

See how very gently but very definitely Jesus takes the name *father* from Joseph and gives it to God. At some time Jesus must have discovered His own unique relationship to God. He cannot have known it when He was a child in the manger and a baby at His mother's breast or He would be a monstrosity and an abnormality. As the years went on He must have thought; and then at this first Passover, with manhood dawning on Him, there came in a sudden blaze of realization the consciousness that He was not as other men are, that in a unique and special sense He was the Son of God. Here we have the story of the day when Jesus discovered who He was. And mark one thing—the discovery did not make Him proud. It did not make Him look down on His humble parents, the gentle Mary and the hard-working Joseph. He went home and *He was obedient to them.* The very fact that He was God's Son made Him the perfect son of His human parents. The real man of God does not despise earthly ties; just because he is God's man he discharges human duties with supreme fidelity.

THE COURIER OF THE KING

Luke 3: 1-6

In the fifteenth year of the reign of Tiberius Caesar, when Pontius Pilate was governor of Judaea, and when Herod was tetrarch of Galilee, his brother Philip, tetrarch of Ituraea and the district of Trachonitis, and Lysanias, tetrarch of Abilene, in the high-priesthood of Annas and Caiaphas, the word of God came to John, the son of Zacharias, when he was in the desert. So he came into the territory around Jordan, preaching a baptism of repentance whereby sins might be forgiven—as it stands written in the book of the words Isaiah, the prophet, " The voice of one crying in the wilderness, ' Get ready the road of the Lord, make His paths straight; every ravine shall be filled up; every mountain and hill will be made low; the twisted places will be made into straight roads and the rough places into smooth; and all flesh shall see God's instrument of salvation.' "

To Luke the emergence of John the Baptist was one of the hinges on which history turned. So much so is that the case that he dates it in no fewer than six different ways. (i) Tiberius was the successor of Augustus and therefore the second of the Roman Emperors. As early as A.D. 11 or 12 Augustus had made him his colleague in the imperial power but he did not become sole emperor until A.D. 14. The fifteenth year of his reign would therefore be A.D. 28-29. Luke then begins by setting the emergence of John against a world background, the background of the Roman Empire. (ii) The next three dates Luke gives are connected with the political organisation of Palestine. The title tetrarch literally means *governor of a fourth part*. In such provinces as Thessaly and Galatia, which were divided into four sections or areas, the governor of each part was known as a *tetrarch*; but later the word widened its meaning and came to mean the governor of any part. Herod the Great died in 4 B.C. after a reign of about forty years. He divided his kingdom between three of his sons and in the first instance the Romans approved the decision. (*a*) To Herod Antipas he left Galilee and Peraea. He reigned from 4 B.C. to A.D. 39 and therefore Jesus' life was lived in Herod's reign and very largely in Herod's dominions in Galilee. (*b*) To Herod Philip he left Ituraea and Trachonitis. He reigned from 4 B.C. to A.D. 33. Caesarea Philippi was called after him and was actually built by him. (*c*) To Archelaus he left Judaea, Samaria and Edom. He was a thoroughly bad king. The Jews in the end actually petitioned Rome for his removal; and Rome, impatient of the continual troubles in Judaea, installed a procurator or Roman governor. That is how the Romans came directly to rule Judaea. At this time Pilate, who was in power from A.D. 25 until A.D. 37, was the Roman governor. So in this one sentence Luke gives us a panoramic view of the division of the Kingdom which had once belonged to Herod the Great. (iii) Of Lysanias we know practically nothing. (iv) Having dealt with the world situation and the

Palestinian political situation, Luke turns to the religious situation and he dates John's emergence as being in the priesthood of Annas and Caiaphas. There never at any time were two high-priests at the one time. What then does Luke mean by giving these two names? The high-priest was at one and the same time the civil and the religious head of the community. In the old days the office of high-priest had been hereditary and for life. But with the coming of the Romans the office was the object of all kinds of intrigue. The result was that between 37 B.C. and A.D. 26 there were no fewer than twenty-eight different high-priests. Now Annas was actually high-priest from A.D. 7 until A.D. 14. He was therefore at this time out of office; but he was succeeded by no fewer than four of his sons and Caiaphas was his son-in-law. Therefore, although Caiaphas was the reigning high-priest, Annas was the power behind the throne. That is in fact why Jesus was brought first to him after His arrest (John 18: 13) although at that time he was not in office at all. Luke associates his name with Caiaphas because, although Caiaphas was actually high-priest, Annas was still the most influential priestly figure in the land.

Verses 4-6 are a quotation from Isaiah 40: 3-5. When a king proposed to tour a part of his dominions in the east, he sent a courier before him to tell the people to prepare the roads. During the Coronation Service in Westminster Abbey there happened a kind of modern parallel to this. When all the congregation was seated, a squad of cleaners unexpectedly emerged with brushes and vacuum cleaners and proceeded to sweep the carpets so that they would be absolutely clean for the coming of the Queen. So John is regarded as the courier of the King. But the preparation on which he insisted was a preparation of the heart and of the life. " The King is coming," he said. " Mend, not your roads, but your lives." There is laid on everyone of us the perennial duty of seeking to make life fit for the King to see.

JOHN'S SUMMONS TO REPENTANCE

Luke 3: 7-18

To the crowds who came out to be baptized by him, John used to say, " You spawn of vipers, who put it into your heads to flee from the coming wrath? Produce fruits to match repentance. Do not begin to say among yourselves, ' We have Abraham as our father.' I tell you that God is able to raise up children to Abraham from these stones. Even now the axe is laid at the root of the trees. Every tree that does not bear good fruit is cut down and thrown into the fire." The crowds asked him, " What are we to do?" He answered them, " Let him who has two robes give one to one who has none and let him who has food do likewise." The tax-collectors came to be baptized and said to him, " Teacher, what are we to do?" He said to them, " Exact no more beyond what your instructions lay down." The soldiers, too, asked him, " What are we to do?" He said to them, " Treat no man with violence and do not play the false informer and be content with your pay."

When the people were in a state of expectancy and when they were all wondering in their hearts about John, as to whether he could be the Anointed One, John answered them all, " I baptize you with water, but the One who is stronger than I is coming, the latchet of whose sandals I am not worthy to unloose. He will baptize you with the Holy Spirit and with fire. His winnowing fan is in His hand to cleanse His threshing floor and He will gather the corn into His store but He will burn the chaff with unquenchable fire."

HERE we have the message of John to the people. Nowhere does the difference between John and Jesus stand out so clearly because, whatever the message of John was it was not a gospel. It was not good news; it was news of terror. John had lived in the desert. The face of the desert was covered with stubble and brushwood, as dry as tinder. Sometimes a spark set the face of the desert alight and out from their crannies came the vipers and the snakes, scurrying in terror from the menacing flames. It was to them that John likened the people who came to

be baptized. The Jews had not the slightest doubt that in
God's economy there was a most favoured nation clause.
They held that God would judge the nations with one
standard but the Jews with another. They, in fact, held
that a man was safe from judgment simply in virtue of
the fact that he was a Jew. A son of Abraham was exempt
from judgment. John told them that racial privilege
meant nothing; that life not lineage was God's standard
of judgment. There are three outstanding things about
John's message. (i) It began by demanding that men should
share with one another. It was a social gospel which
laid it down that God will never absolve the man who is
content to have too much while others have too little.
(ii) It ordered a man, not to leave his job, but to work
out his own salvation by doing that job as it should be
done. Let the tax-collector be a good tax-collector; let
the soldier be a good soldier. It was a man's duty to serve
God where God had set him. There is a negro spiritual
like this:

There's a king and captain high,
And he's coming by and by,
And he'll find me hoeing cotton when he comes.
You can hear his legions charging in the regions of the
    sky,
And he'll find me hoeing cotton when he comes.
There's a man they thrust aside,
Who was tortured till he died,
And he'll find me hoeing cotton when he comes.

He was hated and rejected,
He was scorned and crucified,
And he'll find me hoeing cotton when he comes.
When he comes ! when he comes !
He'll be crowned by saints and angels when he comes,
They'll be shouting out Hosanna ! to the man that
    men denied,
And I'll kneel among my cotton when he comes.

It was John's conviction that nowhere can a man serve God better than in his day's work. (iii) John was quite sure that he himself was only the forerunner. The King was still to come and with Him there would come judgment. The winnowing fan was a great flat wooden shovel; with it the grain was tossed into the air; the heavy grain fell to the ground and the chaff was blown away. And just as the chaff was separated from the grain so the King would separate the good and bad. So John painted a picture of judgment, but it was a judgment which a man could meet with confidence if he had discharged his duty to his neighbour and if he had faithfully done his day's work.

John was one of the world's supremely effective preachers. Once Chalmers was congratulated on a sermon. " Yes," he said, " *but what did it do?* " It is clear that John preached for action and produced action. He did not deal in theological subtleties but in life.

THE ARREST OF JOHN

Luke 3: 19, 20

> So then, urging the people with many other pleas, John preached the gospel to them. But, when Herod the tetrarch was rebuked by him concerning the matter of Herodias, his brother's wife, and concerning all the other wicked things he had done, he added this also to them all—he shut up John in prison.

JOHN was so plain and blunt a preacher of righteousness that he was bound to run into trouble. In the end Herod arrested him. Josephus, the Jewish historian, says that the reason of the arrest was that Herod " feared lest the great influence John had over the people might put it in his power and inclination to raise a rebellion; for they seemed ready to do anything he should advise." That is no doubt true but the New Testament writers give a much more personal and immediate cause. Herod Antipas had married Herodias and John rebuked him for it. Now the relationships involved in this marriage are extremely complicated. Herod the Great was a much-married man. Herod Antipas, who married Herodias and who arrested John, was the son of Herod the Great by a woman called Malthake. Herodias herself was the daughter of Aristobulus, who was also the son of Herod the Great by Mariamne, commonly called the Hasmonean. Now, as we have seen, Herod had divided up his realm between Archelaus, Herod Antipas and Herod Philip. He had another son, also called Herod, who was his son by another Mariamne, the daughter of a high priest. This Herod had no share in his father's realms and lived as a private citizen in Rome. This Herod married Herodias. He was in fact her half-uncle, because her father, Aristobulus, and he were both sons of Herod by different wives. Herod Antipas, on a visit to Rome, seduced her from his half-brother and married her. She was at one and the same time his sister-in-law, because she was married to his half-brother, and his niece because she was the daughter of Aristobulus, another half-brother. The whole proceeding was utterly revolting to Jewish opinion and quite contrary to Jewish law, and indeed improper on any standards. It is a dangerous thing to rebuke an eastern tyrant, but John did so. The result was that he was arrested and imprisoned in the dungeon castle of Machaerus on the shores of the Dead Sea. There could be no greater cruelty than to take this child of the desert and shut him up in the confines of a dungeon cell. Ultimately he was beheaded to gratify the resentment of Herodias (Matthew 14: 5-12; Mark 6: 17-29).

It is always a dangerous thing to speak the truth; and yet the man who allies himself with the truth, may for the moment end in gaol or on the scaffold, but in the final count he is the victor. Once the Earl of Morton, who was the regent of Scotland, threatened Andrew Melville, the reformer. "There will never," he said menacingly, " be quietness in this country till half a dozen of you be hanged or banished the country." Melville answered him, " Tush! sir, threaten your courtiers in that fashion. It is the same to me whether I rot in the air or in the ground . . . God be glorified, it will not lie in your power to hang nor exile His truth." Plato once said that the wise man will always choose to suffer wrong rather than to do wrong. We need only ask ourselves whether in the last analysis and at the final assize we would prefer to be Herod Antipas or John the Baptist.

THE HOUR STRIKES FOR JESUS

Luke 3: 21, 22

> When all the people had been baptized and when Jesus too had been baptized, as He was praying, the heaven was opened and the Holy Spirit in bodily form like a dove came down upon Him and there was a voice from heaven, " You are my beloved son; in you I am well pleased."

THE thinkers of the Church have always sought an answer to the problem, " Why did Jesus go to John to be baptized?" The baptism of John was a baptism of repentance and it is our conviction that Jesus was without sin. Why then did He offer Himself for this baptism? In the early Church it was sometimes suggested, with a homely touch, that He did it to please Mary, His mother, and in answer to her entreaties; but we would need a better reason than that. In the life of every man there are certain definite stages, certain hinges on which his whole life turns. It was so in the life of Jesus and, every now and again, we must stop and try to see the life of Jesus as a whole. The first great hinge, as we have already seen, was the visit to the Temple when He was twelve, when He discovered His unique relationship to God. By the time of the emergence of John Jesus was about thirty (Luke 3: 23). That is to say at least eighteen years had passed. All through these years Jesus must have been thinking and realizing

more and more His own uniqueness. But still He remained
the village carpenter of Nazareth. He must have known
that a day must come when He must say good-bye to
Nazareth and go out upon His larger task. He must have
waited for some sign that that day had come. Now when
John emerged the people flocked out to hear him and to be
baptized. That is to say, throughout the whole country
there was an unprecedented *movement towards God*. When
Jesus saw that He knew that *His hour had struck*. It was
not that He was conscious of sin and of the need of repentance. It was that He knew that now He too must identify
Himself with this movement towards God. For Jesus
the emergence of John was God's call to action; and
His first action was to identify Himself with the people
in their search for God.

But in Jesus' baptism something happened. Before
He could take this tremendous step He had to be sure
that He was right; and in the moment of the baptism
God spoke to Him. Make no mistake, what happened in
the baptism was an experience personal to Jesus. The
voice of God came to Him and the voice of God told
Him that He had taken the right decision. But more—
far more—that very same voice of God mapped out all
His course for Him. God said to Him, " You are my beloved
Son; in you I am well pleased." That saying is composed
of two texts. *You are my beloved Son*—that is from Psalm
2: 7 and was always accepted as a description of the
Messianic King. *In whom I am well pleased*—that is part
of Isaiah 42: 1 and is from a description of the servant
of the Lord whose portrait culminates in the sufferings of
Isaiah 53. Therefore in His baptism Jesus realized, first,
that He was the Messiah, God's Anointed King; and,
second, that that involved not power and glory, but
suffering and a Cross. The Cross did not come on Jesus
unawares; from the first moment of realization He saw
that Cross ahead. The baptism shows us Jesus asking for
God's approval and receiving the destiny of the Cross.

33

THE LINEAGE OF JESUS

Luke 3: 23-38

When Jesus began His ministry He was about thirty years of age. He was the son (as it was supposed) of Joseph, the son of Heli, the son of Matthat, the son of Levi, the son of Melchi, the son of Jannai, the son of Joseph, the son of Mattathias, the son of Amos, the son of Nahum, the son of Esli, the son of Naggai, the son of Maath, the son of Mattathias, the son of Semein, the son of Josech, the son of Joda, the son of Joanan, the son of Rhesa, the son of Zerubbabel, the son of Shealtiel, the son of Neri, the son of Melchi, the son of Addi, the son of Cosam, the son of Elmadam, the son of Er, the son of Jesus, the son of Eliezer, the son of Jorim, the son of Matthat, the son of Levi, the son of Symeon, the son of Judas, the son of Joseph, the son of Jonam, the son of Eliakim, the son of Melea, the son of Menna, the son of Mattatha, the son of Nathan, the son of David, the son of Jesse, the son of Obed, the son of Boaz, the son of Salmon, the son of Nashon, the son of Amminadab, the son of Arni, the son of Hezron, the son of Perez, the son of Judah, the son of Jacob, the son of Isaac, the son of Abraham, the son of Terah, the son of Nahor, the son of Serug, the son of Reu, the son of Pelag, the son of Eber, the son of Shelah, the son of Cainan, the son of Arphaxad, the son of Shem, the son of Noah, the son of Lamech, the son of Methuselah, the son of Enoch, the son of Jared, the son of Mahalaleel, the son of Cainan, the son of Enos, the son of Seth, the son of Adam, the son of God.

THIS passage begins with one most suggestive statement. It tells us that when Jesus began His ministry He was no less than about thirty years of age. Why did Jesus spend thirty years in Nazareth when He had come to be the Saviour of the world? It is commonly said that Joseph died fairly young and that Jesus had to take upon Himself the support of Mary and of His younger brothers and sisters, and that not until they were old enough to take the business on their own shoulders did He feel free to leave Nazareth and to go out into the wider world. Whether that be so or not three things are true. (i) It was essential that Jesus should carry out with the utmost fidelity the more limited tasks of family duty before He could be entrusted by God with the universal task of saving the world. It was by His fidelity, His conscientiousness, His performance of the narrow duties of home that Jesus fitted Himself for the great task He had to do. When Jesus Himself told the Parable of the Talents, the word of God to the faithful servants was, "Well done good and faithful servant; you have been faithful over a few things, I will make you ruler over many things" (Matthew 25: 21, 23). Beyond a doubt Jesus was putting His own experience into words when He said that. When Sir James Barrie's mother died, he said, "I can look back and I cannot see the smallest thing undone." It was because Jesus faithfully performed the smallest duties that the greatest task in all the world was given to Him. (ii) It gave Him the opportunity to live out His own teaching. Had He always been a homeless, wandering teacher with no human ties or obligations, men might have said to Him, "What right have you to talk about human duties and human relationships, you, who never fulfilled them?" But Jesus was able to say to others, not, "Do as I say," but, "Do as I have done." Tolstoi was the man who always talked about living the way of love; but his wife wrote poignantly of him, "There is so little genuine warmth about him; his kindness does not come from the heart, but merely from his principles. His biographies will tell of how he helped the labourers to carry buckets of water, but no one will ever know that he never gave his wife a rest and never—in all these thirty-two years—gave his child a drink of water or spent five minutes by his bedside to give me a chance to rest a little from all my labours." But no one could ever say that of Jesus. He lived at home what He preached abroad. (iii) If Jesus was to help men He had to know how men lived. And because He spent these thirty years in Nazareth, He knew the problems of making a living, the haunting insecurity of the life of the working

man, the ill-natured customer, the man who would not
pay his debts. It is the glory of the incarnation that there is
no problem in life and living which we face which Jesus
did not also face.

Here we have Luke's genealogy of Jesus. The Jews
were interested in genealogies. Genealogies,
especially of the priests, who had to prove unbroken
descent from Aaron, were kept amongst the public
records. In the time of Ezra and Nehemiah we
read of priests who lost their office because
they could not produce their genealogy (Ezra
2: 61-63; Nehemiah 7: 63-65). But the problem
of this genealogy is its relationship with that in
Matthew 1: 1-17. The facts are these—only
Luke gives the section from Adam to Abraham;
the section from Abraham to David is the same
in both; but the section from David to Joseph
is almost completely different. Ever since men
studied the New Testament they have tried to
explain the differences. (i) It is said that both
genealogies are symbolic and that Matthew gives
the *royal* descent of Jesus and Luke the *priestly*
descent. (ii) One of the earliest suggestions of
all was that Matthew in fact gives the genealogy
of *Joseph* and Luke of *Mary*. (iii) The most
ingenious explanation is as follows. In Matthew
1: 16 Joseph's father is *Jacob*; Luke 3: 23 it is
Heli. According to the Jewish law of levirate
marriage (Deuteronomy 25: 5f) if a man died
his brother must, if free to do so, marry the
widow and ensure the continuance of the line.
Now when that happened a son of such a marriage
could be called the son either of the first or the
second husband. It is suggested that Joseph's
mother married twice. Joseph was in actual
fact the son of Heli, the second husband, but he
was in the eyes of the law the son of Jacob, the
first husband who had died. It is then suggested
that while Heli and Jacob had the same mother
they had different fathers and that Jacob's
father was descended from David through
Solomon and Heli's father was descended from
David through Nathan. This ingenious theory
would mean that *both* genealogies are correct.
In fact, all that we can say is that we do not know.

Two things are to be noted about the genealogy of Jesus which Luke gives. (i) It stresses the real humanity of Jesus. It stresses the fact that He was a man amongst men. He was no phantom or demi-god. To save men He became in the most real sense a man. (ii) Matthew stops at Abraham; Luke goes right back to Adam. To Matthew, Jesus was the possession of the Jews; to Luke, He was the possession of all mankind, because His line is traced back not to the founder of the Jewish nation but to the founder of the human race. It is one of Luke's great thoughts that he removes the national and racial boundaries even from the ancestry of Jesus.

THE BATTLE WITH TEMPTATION

Luke 4: 1-13

Jesus came back from the Jordan full of the Holy Spirit. He was led by the Spirit into the wilderness, and for forty days He was tempted by the devil; and in those days He ate nothing, and when they were completed He was hungry. The devil said to Him, " If you really are the Son of God, tell these stones to become bread." Jesus answered him, " It stands written, ' Man shall not live by bread alone.' " He took Him up and showed Him in an instant of time all the kingdoms of the inhabited world. The devil said to Him, " I will give you all this power and the glory of them, because it has been handed over to me, and I can give it to whomsoever I wish. If then you worship me all of it will be yours." Jesus answered him, " It stands written, ' You must worship the Lord God and Him only must you serve.' " He brought Him to Jerusalem and set Him on a pinnacle of the Temple, and said to Him, " If you really are the Son of God throw yourself down from here, for it stands written, ' He has given His angels instructions concerning you, to take care of you, and they will bear you up in their hands lest you dash your foot against a stone.' " Jesus answered him, " It has been said, ' You must not try to test the Lord your God.' " So when He had gone through the whole gamut of temptation, the devil left Him for a time.

WE have already seen how there were certain great mile-
stones in the life of Jesus and here is one of the greatest of all.
In the Temple when He was twelve there had come the
dawning realization that God was His Father in the most
unique way. In the emergence of John, for Him the hour
had struck and in His baptism God's approval had come
to Him. So at this time Jesus was just about to begin
His campaign. Before a man begins a campaign he must
choose the methods he will use. The Temptation Story
shows us Jesus choosing once and for all the method by
which He proposed to seek to win men to God. It shows us
Jesus rejecting the way of power and glory and accepting
the way of suffering and the Cross.

Before we go on to think of this story in detail there are
two general points we must note. (i) This is the most
sacred of stories, for it can have come from no other source
than His own lips. At some time He must have Himself
told His disciples about this most intimate experience of
His soul. (ii) Even at this time Jesus must have been
conscious of quite exceptional powers. The whole point
of the Temptations is that they could only have come to a
man who could do astonishing things. It is no temptation
to us to turn stones into bread or leap from a Temple
pinnacle, for the simple reason that it is impossible. These
are temptations which could only have come to a man whose
powers were unique and who had to decide how to use them.

First of all let us think of the scene. It happened in the
wilderness. The inhabited part of Judaea stood on the
central plateau which was the backbone of Southern
Palestine. Between it and the Dead Sea there stretched a
terrible wilderness, thirty-five by fifteen miles. It was
called Jeshimmon, which means " The Devastation."
The hills were like dust heaps; the limestone looked
blistered and peeling; the rocks were bare and jagged;
the ground sounded hollow to the horses' hooves; it
glowed with heat like a vast furnace and it ran out to the
precipices, 1,200 feet high, which swooped down to the

Dead Sea. It was there in that awesome devastation that Jesus was tempted.

We must not think that the three temptations came and went like scenes in a play. We must think of Jesus deliberately retiring to this lonely place and for forty days wrestling with the problem of how He could win men. It was a long battle and a battle which never ended until the Cross, for the story ends by saying that the Tempter left Jesus—*for a season*.

(i) The first temptation was to turn stones into bread. This wilderness was not a wilderness of sand. It was covered by little bits of limestone exactly like loaves. The Tempter said to Jesus, " If you want people to follow you, use your wonderful powers to give them material things." The Tempter was suggesting that Jesus should *bribe people with material gifts* into following Him. Back came Jesus' answer which is a quotation of Deuteronomy 8: 3. " A man," He said, " will never find life in material things." The task of Christianity is not to produce new conditions, although the weight and voice of the Church must be behind all efforts to make life better for men. But the real task is to produce *new men*; and given the new men the new conditions will follow.

(ii) In the second temptation Jesus in imagination stood upon a mountain from which the whole civilized world could be seen. The Tempter said, " Worship me, and all will be yours." *That is the temptation to compromise.* The devil said, " I have got people in my grip. Don't set your standards so high. Strike a bargain with me. Just compromise a little with evil and men will follow you." Back comes Jesus' answer, " God is God, and right is right and wrong is wrong. There can be no compromise in the war with evil." Once again Jesus quotes scripture (Deuteronomy 6: 13; 10: 20). It is a constant temptation to seek to win men by compromising with the standards of the world. G. K. Chesterton said that the tendency of the world it to see things in terms of an indeterminate gray; but the duty of the Christian is to see things in terms of black and white. As Carlyle said, " The Christian must be consumed by the conviction of the infinite beauty of holiness and the infinite damnability of sin."

(iii) In the third temptation Jesus in imagination saw Himself on the pinnacle of the Temple where Solomon's Porch and the Royal Porch met. There was a sheer drop of 450 feet down into the Kedron Valley below. This temptation was the temptation *to give the people sensations*. " No," said Jesus, " you must not make senseless experiments with the power of God " (Deuteronomy 6: 16). Jesus saw quite clearly that if He produced sensations He could be a nine days' wonder. But the sensationalist never lasts. It is the hard way of service and of suffering which leads to the Cross, but after the Cross to the crown.

THE GALILAEAN SPRINGTIME

Luke 4: 14, 15

> So Jesus returned in the power of the Spirit to Galilee; and the story of Him spread throughout the whole countryside. He kept on teaching in their synagogues; and He was held in high reputation by all.

No sooner had Jesus left the wilderness but He was faced with another decision. He knew that for Him the hour had struck; He had settled once and for all the method which He was going to take. Now He had to decide, *Where would He start?*

(i) He began in *Galilee.* Galilee was an area in the north of Palestine about fifty miles from north to south and twenty-five miles from east to west. The name itself means a circle and comes from the Hebrew word *Galil.* It was so called because it was encircled by non-Jewish nations. Just because of that new influences had always played upon Galilee and it was the most forward-looking and the least conservative part of Palestine. It was an extraordinarily densely populated part of Palestine. Josephus, who was himself at one time governor of the area, says that it had 204 villages or towns, none with a population less than 15,000. It seems incredible that there could be about 3,000,000 people congregated in Galilee. It was a land of extraordinary fertility. There was a proverb which said that, "It is easier to raise a legion of olive trees in Galilee than to bring up one child in Judaea." The wonderful climate and the superb water supply made it the garden of Palestine. The very list of trees which grew there shows how amazingly fertile it was—the vine, the olive, the fig, the oak, the walnut, the terebinth, the palm, the cedar, the cypress, the balsam, the firtree, the pine, the sycomore, the baytree, the myrtle, the almond, the pomegranate, the citron and the oleander. The Galilaeans themselves were the Highlanders of Palestine. Josephus says of them, "They were ever fond of innovations and by nature disposed to changes, and delighted in seditions. They were ever ready to follow a leader who would begin an insurrection. They were quick in temper and given to quarrelling." "The Galilaeans," it was said, "have never been destitute of courage." "They were ever more anxious for honour than for gain." So that is the land in which Jesus began. It was His own land; and it would give Him, at least at the beginning, an audience who would listen and kindle at His message.

(ii) *He began in the Synagogue.* The Synagogue was the real centre of religious life in Palestine. There was only one Temple; but the law said that wherever there were ten Jewish families there must be a Synagogue; and so in every town and village it was in the Synagogue that the people met to worship. There were no sacrifices in the Synagogue. The Temple was designed for sacrifice; the Synagogue for teaching. But how could Jesus gain an entry into the Synagogue and how could he, a layman, the carpenter from Nazareth, deliver His message there?

41

In the Synagogue service there were three parts. (*a*) The worship part in prayer was offered. (*b*) The reading of the scriptures. Seven people from the congregation read. As they read the ancient Hebrew, which was no longer widely understood, was translated by the Targumist into Aramaic or Greek, in the case of the Law, one verse at a time, in the case of the prophets three verses at a time. (*c*) The teaching part of the service. In the Synagogue there was no professional ministry; there was no one person to give the address; the president would invite any distinguished person present to speak and then discussion and talk would follow. That is how Jesus got His chance. The Synagogue and its platform at this stage were open to Him.

(iii) The passage ends by saying that He was held in high reputation by all. This period of Jesus' ministry has been called the Galilaean springtime. He had come like a breath of the very wind of God. The opposition had not yet crystallised. Men's hearts were hungry for the word of life, and they had not yet realized what a blow He was to strike at the orthodoxy of His time. A man with a message will always command an audience.

WITHOUT HONOUR IN HIS OWN COUNTRY

Luke 4: 16-30

So Jesus came to Nazareth where He had been brought up; and, as was His habit, He went into the Synagogue on the Sabbath day, and He stood up to read the lesson. The roll of the prophet Isaiah was given to Him. He opened the roll and found the passage where it is written, " The Spirit of the Lord is upon me because He has anointed me to bring the Good News to the poor. He has sent me to announce release to the captives, and recovering of sight to the blind, to set at liberty those who have been bruised, to proclaim that the year which everyone is waiting for has come." And He folded up the roll and handed it back to the officer and sat down ; and the eyes of all in the

Synagogue were fixed intently on Him. He began to say to them, " To-day this scripture has been fulfilled in your ears." And all witnessed to Him and were amazed at the words of grace that came from His mouth. And they said, " Is this not the son of Joseph? " He said to them, " You are bound to quote the proverb to me, ' Physician, heal yourself; we have heard about all that happened in Capernaum; do the same kind of things in your own home country.' " He said, " This is the truth that I tell you. No prophet is accepted in his own home country. In truth I tell you there were many widows in Israel in the days of Elijah, when the heaven was shut up for three years and six months and when there was a great famine all over the earth. And to none of them was Elijah sent but he was sent to Sarepta, to a widow of Sidon. There were many lepers in Israel in the times of Elisha the prophet; and none of them was healed; but Naaman the Syrian was." And the people in the Synagogue were filled with anger as they listened to these things; and they rose up and hustled Him out of the town. They took Him to the brow of the hill on which their town is built, to throw Him down; but He passed through the midst of them and went upon His way.

ONE of Jesus' very early visits was to Nazareth, His home town. Nazareth was not a village. It is called a *polis* which means a town or city; and it may well have had as many as 20,000 inhabitants. It stood in a little hollow in the hills on the lower slopes of Galilee near the Plain of Jezreel. But a boy had only to climb to the hill-top above the town and he could see an amazing panorama for miles around. Sir George Adam Smith describes the scene from the hilltop. The history of Israel stretched out before the watcher's eye. There was the plain of Esdraleon where Deborah and Barak had fought; where Gideon had won his victories; where Saul had crashed to disaster and where Josiah had been killed in battle; there was Naboth's vineyard and the place where Jehu slaughtered Jezebel; there was Shunem where Elisha had lived; there was Carmel where Elijah had fought his epic battle with the prophets of Baal; and, blue in the distance, there was the Mediterranean and the isles of the sea. But not only the history of Israel was there; the world itself unfolded itself from the hilltop in Nazareth. Three great roads skirted it. There was the road from the south with the pilgrims to Jerusalem on it. There was the great Way of the Sea which led from Egypt to Damascus with the laden caravans moving along it. There was the great road to the east with the caravans from Arabia on it and the Roman legions marching out to the eastern frontiers of the Empire. It is quite wrong to think of Jesus as being brought up in a backwater; He was brought up in a town in sight of history and with the traffic of the world almost at its doors.

We have already described the Synagogue service and this passage gives us a vivid picture of it in action. It was not a book which Jesus took, for at this time everything was written on rolls. It was from Isaiah 61 that He read. In verse 20 the Authorised Version speaks misleadingly of *the minister*. The official in question was the *Chazzan*. He had many duties. He had to take out and put back the sacred rolls of scripture; he had to keep the Synagogue clean; he had to announce the coming of the Sabbath with three blasts of the silver trumpet from the Synagogue roof; and he was also the teacher in the village school. Verse 20 says that Jesus sat down. That gives us the impression that He was finished. In point of fact it means that He was about to start because the speaker gave the address seated and Rabbis taught sitting down. (cp. Our own phrase, a professor's *chair*).

What angered the people was the apparent compliment that Jesus paid to Gentiles. The Jews were so sure that they were God's people that they utterly despised all other peoples. They believed that " God had created the Gentiles to be fuel for the fires of hell." And here was this young Jesus, whom they all knew, preaching as if the *Gentiles* were specially favoured by God. It was beginning to dawn upon them that there were things in this new message the like of which they had never dreamed of.

We must note two other things before we leave this passage.

(i) It was Jesus' habit to go to the Synagogue on the Sabbath Day. There must have been many things with which He radically disagreed and which grated on Him— *yet He went.* The worship of the Synagogue might be far from perfect; yet Jesus never omitted to join Himself to God's worshipping people on God's day.

(ii) We have only to read the passage of Isaiah that Jesus read to see the difference between Jesus and John the Baptist. John was the preacher of doom and at his message men must have shuddered with terror. It was a *gospel*—Good News—which Jesus brought. Jesus too knew the wrath of God but it was always the wrath of love.

THE SPIRIT OF AN UNCLEAN DEVIL

Luke 4: 31-37

> Jesus came down to Capernaum, a town in Galilee, and He was teaching them on the Sabbath day; and they were astonished at His teaching because His speech was with authority. There was in the Synagogue a man who had a spirit of an unclean demon and he cried out with a loud voice, " What have we to do with you, Jesus of Nazareth? Have you come to destroy us? I know who you are—the Holy One of God." So Jesus rebuked it. " Be muzzled," He said, " and come out of him." And after the demon had thrown him into the midst of them, it came out of him and it did him no harm. Astonishment fell on them all and they kept saying to each other, " What word is this? because He gives orders to unclean spirits with authority and with power and they come out." And the story of Him went out to every place in the surrounding district.

WE would have liked to know as much about Capernaum as we do about Nazareth, but it is the strange fact that there is even doubt as to the site of this lake-side town where so much of Jesus' mighty work was done.

This passage is specially interesting because it is the first passage in Luke where we encounter demon possession. The ancient world believed that the air was thickly populated with evil spirits. These spirits, they believed, sought an entry into men. Often they did enter a man through either food or drink. All illness was caused by these evil spirits. The Egyptians believed that there were thirty-six different parts of the human body and any of them could be entered and controlled by one of these evil spirits. There could be a spirit of deafness, of dumbness, of fever; spirits which took a man's sanity and wits away; spirits of lying and of deceit and of uncleanness. It was such a spirit that Jesus, in this passage, exorcised from this man. To many people this is a problem. On the whole, modern thought regards this belief in spirits as primitive and superstitious and as something which men have outgrown. And yet Jesus seemed to believe in them. There are three possibilities. (i) Jesus actually did believe in them. If that is so, Jesus as far as scientific knowledge went was nothing in advance of His own age; He was under all the limitations of contemporary medical thought. There is no need to refuse such a conclusion for, if Jesus was really a man, in scientific things He must have had the knowledge then open to a man. (ii) Jesus Himself did not believe in them, but the sufferer did believe, and most intensely. Therefore Jesus could only cure people by assuming their beliefs about themselves to be true. If a person is ill and someone says to him, " There's nothing wrong with you," that is no help. The reality of the pain has to be admitted before a cure can follow. The people believed they were possessed of devils and Jesus, like a wise doctor, knew He could not heal them unless He assumed that their view of their own trouble was real. (iii) Modern thought has been swinging round to the admission that perhaps there is something in demons after all. There are certain troubles which have no bodily cause at all, as far as can be discovered. There is no reason why the man is ill, but he is ill. Since there is no physical explanation some now think that there must be a spiritual one and that demons are not so unreal after all.

The people were astonished at Jesus' power—and no wonder. The east was full of people who could exorcise demons. But their methods were weird and wonderful. An exorcist would put a ring under the afflicted person's nose. He would recite a long spell; and then all of a sudden there would be a splash in a basin of water which he had put near to hand—and the demon was out ! A magical root called Baaras was specially effective. When a man approached it, it shrank into the ground unless gripped, and to grip it was certain death. So the ground round it was dug away; a dog was tied to it; the struggles of the dog tore up the root; and when the root was torn up the dog died, as a substitute for a man. What a difference between all this hysterical paraphernalia and the calm single word of command of Jesus ! It was the sheer authority which staggered them.

Jesus' authority was something quite new. When the Rabbis taught they supported every statement with quotations. They always said, " There is a saying that . " Rabbi so and so said " that . . . " They always ealed to authority. When the prophets spoke, they saith the Lord." Theirs was a delegated When Jesus spoke, He said, " I say to you." no authorities to buttress Him; He did not egated authority; He was authority incarnate. something new; here was a man who spoke as one who knew.

In every sphere of life the expert bears an air of authority. A musician tells how when Toscanini mounts the rostrum authority flows from him and the orchestra feels it. When we need technical advice we call in the expert and we take his word for it. *Jesus is the expert in life.* He speaks and men know that this is beyond human argument—this is God.

A MIRACLE IN A COTTAGE

Luke 4: 38, 39

> Jesus left the Synagogue and came into Simon's
> house; and Simon's mother-in-law was in the grip of a
> major fever. They asked Him to do something for her.
> He stood over her and rebuked the fever and it left
> her. Immediately she got up and began to serve them.

HERE Luke, the doctor, writes. *In the grip of a major fever*—
every word is a medical word. *In the grip of* is the medical
Greek for someone who is very definitely laid up with
some illness. The Greek medical writers divided fevers
into two classes—major and minor. Luke knew just
how to describe this illness.

There are three great truths in this short incident.

(i) Jesus was always ready to serve. He had just left
the Synagogue. Every preacher knows what he feels like
after a service. Virtue is gone out of him; he has need of
rest. The last thing he wants is a crowd of people and a
fresh call upon him. But no sooner had Jesus left the Synagogue and entered Peter's house than the insistent cry
of human need was at him. He did not claim that He was
tired and must rest. He answered it without complaint.
The Salvation Army people tell of a Mrs. Berwick in t
days of the London blitzes. She had been in charge of
Army's social work in Liverpool and she h
London. People had queer ideas in the time
and they had the idea that somehow Mrs. Be
was safe; and so they gathered there. Thou
retired, the instinct to help was there. She got to
a simple first-aid box and then she put a notice in her
window, " If you need help knock here." Always Jesus was
ready to help; His followers must be the same.

(ii) Jesus did not need a crowd to work a miracle. Many
a man will put out an effort in a crowd that he will not
make among his own private circle. Many a man is at his
best in society and at his worst at home. All too commonly
we are gracious, courteous, obliging to strangers and the

very opposite when there is no one but our own folk to see. But Jesus was prepared to put out all His power in a village cottage in Capernaum when the crowds were gone.

(iii) Whenever Peter's mother-in-law was cured *immediately she began to serve them.* She realized that she had been given back her health to spend it in the service of others. She wanted no fussing and no petting; she wanted to get on with cooking and serving her own folk and Jesus. Mothers are always like that. We would do well to remember that if God gave us the priceless gift of health and strength, He gave us it that we might use it always in the service of others.

THE INSISTENT CROWDS

Luke 4: 40-44

> When the sun was setting all who had friends who were ill with all kinds of sicknesses brought them to Jesus; and He laid His hands upon each one of them and cured them. Out of many there came demons, shouting out and saying, " You are the Son of God." And He rebuked them and would not allow t~~hem to~~ speak, because they knew that He was the A~~nointed~~ One. When day came, He went out and went to ~~a~~ desert place; and the crowds kept looking for Him and they tried to restrain Him so that He would not go away from them; but He said to them, " I must tell the Good News of the Kingdom of God to other towns too, because that is what I was sent to do."

(i) Early in the morning Jesus went out to be alone. He was only able to meet the insistent needs of men because He first companied with God. Once, in the 1914-18 war, there was a staff conference due to begin. All were present except one—Marshal Foch, the commander-in-chief himself. At last an officer who knew him well said, " I think I know where we may find him." He led them round to a ruined chapel which was close beside General Headquarters and there, before the shattered altar, the great soldier was kneeling in prayer. He knew that before he met men he must first meet God.

(ii) And yet there is no word of complaint or resentment when Jesus' privacy was invaded by the crowds. Prayer is great but in the last analysis human need is greater. Florence Allshorn, the great missionary teacher, used to run a training college for missionaries. She knew human nature and she had no time for people who suddenly discovered that their quiet hour was due just when the dishes were to be washed ! Pray we must; but prayer must never be an escape from reality. Prayer cannot preserve a man from the insistent cry of human need. It must prepare him for it; and sometimes, too soon, and in a hurry, he will need to rise from his knees and get to work—even when he does not want to.

(iii) Jesus would not let the demons speak. Over and over again we will get on Jesus' lips this injunction to silence. Why? For this very good reason—the Jews had their own popular ideas of the Messiah. To them the Messiah was to be a conquering king who would set his foot upon the eagle's neck and sweep the Romans from Palestine. Palestine was in an inflammable condition. Rebellion was always just below the surface and often broke out. Jesus knew that if the report went out that He was the Messiah these revolutionaries would be ready to flare up. Before men could call Him Messiah, He had to teach them what being Messiah meant, that it meant not being the conquering king but the suffering servant. Jesus' injunctions to silence were given because people did not yet know what Messiahship meant, and if they started out with the wrong ideas death and destruction would surely follow.

(iv) Here is the first mention of the Kingdom of God in Luke's gospel. Jesus came preaching the Kingdom of God (Mark I: 15). That was the essence of His message. What did He mean by the Kingdom of God? When we look at this we find an amazing paradox. For Jesus the

Kingdom was three things at the same time. (*a*) It was *past*. Abraham, Isaac and Jacob were in the Kingdom and they had lived centuries ago (Luke 13: 28). (*b*) It was *present*. " The Kingdom," He said, " is within you, or among you " (Luke 17: 21). (*c*) It was *future*. It was something which God was still to give and for which men must ever pray. How can the Kingdom be all these things at the same time? Turn to the Lord's Prayer. There are two petitions in it side by side. Thy Kingdom come; Thy will be done in earth as it is in Heaven (Matthew 6: 10, 11). Now the Hebrews, as any verse of the psalms will show, had a way of saying things twice; and always the second way explained, or developed, or amplified the first way. Now put these two phrases together—Thy Kingdom come; Thy will be done in earth as it is in heaven. The second explains the first; and therefore, *The Kingdom of God is a society upon earth where God's will is as perfectly done as it is in heaven.* So then if any man in the past has perfectly done God's will, He is in the Kingdom; if any man does it now, He is in the Kingdom; but the day when all men will do that will is still far distant; therefore the consummation is still to come; and so the Kingdom is past and present and future all at the same time. Other men do that will spasmodically, sometimes obeying, sometimes disobeying. Only Jesus always and at all times did it perfectly. That is why He is the foundation and the incarnation of the Kingdom. He came to enable all men to do the same. To do God's will is to be a citizen of the Kingdom of God. We may well pray—" Lord, bring in Thy Kingdom, beginning with me."

THE CONDITIONS OF A MIRACLE

Luke 5: 1-11

Jesus was standing on the shore of the Lake of Gennesaret while the crowds pressed in upon Him to listen to the word of God. He saw two boats riding close to the shore. The fishermen had disembarked

from them and were washing their nets. He embarked
on one of the boats, which belonged to Simon, and
asked him to push out a little from the land. He sat
down and continued to teach the crowds from the
boat. When He stopped speaking, He said to Simon,
" Push out into the deep water and let down your
nets for a catch." Simon answered, " Master, we
have toiled all night long and we caught nothing;
but, if you say so, I will let down the nets." When
they had done so they enclosed a great crowd of
fishes; their nets were torn with the numbers; so
they signalled to their partners in the other boat to
come and help them. They came and they filled
both the boats so that they began to sink. When Simon
Peter saw this he fell at Jesus' knees. " Leave me,
Lord," he said, " because I am a sinful man." Wonder
gripped him and all who were with him at the number
of fishes they had caught. It was the same with James
and John, Zebedee's sons, who were partners with
Simon. Jesus said to Simon, " From now on you will
be catching men." So they brought the boats to land
and they left everything and followed Him.

THE famous sheet of water in Galilee is called by three
names—the Sea of Galilee, the Sea of Tiberias and the
Lake of Gennesaret. It was thirteen miles long by eight
miles wide. It lies in a dip in the earth's surface and is
680 feet below sea level. That fact gives it its almost tropical
climate. Nowadays it is almost deserted, but in the days
of Jesus it had nine townships clustered round its shores,
none of them with fewer than 15,000 people. Gennesaret is
really the name of the lovely plain on the west side of the
lake. It is a most fertile piece of land. The Jews loved
to play with derivations, and they had three derivations
for Gennesaret all of which show how beautiful it was.
(i) From *kinnor*, which means a harp because " its fruit
is as sweet as the sound of a harp." (ii) From *gan*, a garden,
and *sar*, a prince—hence " the prince of gardens." (iii) From
gan, a garden, and *asher*, riches—hence " the garden of
riches."

We have to note, first of all, that, without anything
being said, we are here confronted with a turning point

in the career of Jesus. Last time we heard Him preach He was in the Synagogue; now He is at the lakeside. True, He will be back in the Synagogue again; but the time is coming when the door of the Synagogue will be shut to Him and when His Church will be the lakeside and the open road, and His pulpit a boat. He would go anywhere where men would listen to Him. " Our societies," said John Wesley, " were formed from those who were wandering upon the dark mountains, that belonged to no Christian Church; but were awakened by the preaching of the Methodists, who had pursued them through the wilderness of this world to the High-ways and the Hedges— to the Markets and the Fairs—to the Hills and the Dales— who set up the Standard of the Cross in the Streets and Lanes of the Cities, in the Villages, in the Barns, and Farmers' Kitchens, etc.—and all this done in such a way, and to such an extent, as never had been done before since the Apostolic age." " I love a commodious room," said Wesley, " a soft cushion and a handsome pulpit, but field preaching saves souls." When the Synagogue was shut Jesus took to the open road.

There is in this story what we might call a list of the conditions of a miracle. (i) There is the eye that sees. There is no need to think that Jesus *created* a shoal of fishes for the occasion. In the Sea of Galilee there were phenomenal shoals which covered the sea as if it was solid for as much as an acre. Most likely Jesus' keen eye saw just such a shoal and His keen sight made it look like a miracle. We need the eye that really sees. Many people have seen the steam raise the lid of a kettle; only James Watt saw it and thought of a steam engine. Many people have seen an apple fall; only Isaac Newton saw it and went on to think out the law of gravity. The earth is full of miracles for the eye that sees. (ii) There is the spirit that will make an effort. If Jesus said it, tired as he was, Peter was prepared to try again. For most people the disaster of life is that they give up just one effort too soon. (iii) There is the spirit which will attempt what seems hopeless. The night was past and the night was the time for fishing. All the circumstances were unfavourable, but Peter says, " Let circumstances be what they may, if you say so, we will try again." Too often we wait because the time is not opportune. If we wait for a perfect set of circumstances we will never begin at all. If we want a miracle we must take Jesus at His word when He bids us attempt the impossible.

TOUCHING THE UNTOUCHABLE
Luke 5: 12-15

> While Jesus was in one of the towns—look you—a man who was a severe case of leprosy saw Him. He fell before Him and besought Him, " Lord, if you are willing to do so you are able to cleanse me." Jesus stretched out His hand and touched him. " I am willing," He said. " Be cleansed." Immediately the leprosy left him. Jesus enjoined him to tell no one. " But," He said, " go and show yourself to the priest, and bring the offering for cleansing, as Moses' law laid it down, to prove to them that you are cured." Talk about Him spread all the more; and many crowds assembled to listen to Him and to be cured of their illnesses.

IN Palestine there were two kinds of leprosy. There was one which was rather like a very bad skin disease, and it was the less serious of the two. There was one in which the disease, starting from a small spot, ate away the flesh until the wretched sufferer was left with only the stump of a hand or a leg. It was literally a living death. The regulations concerning leprosy are in Leviticus, chapters 13 and 14. The most terrible thing about leprosy was the isolation it brought. The leper was to cry " Unclean! Unclean!" wherever he went; he was to dwell alone; " without the camp shall be his habitation " (Leviticus 13: 45, 46). He was banished from the society of men and exiled from home. The result was, and still is, that the psychological consequences of leprosy were as serious as the physical. Dr. A. B. MacDonald, in an article on the leper colony in Itu, of which he is in charge, writes, " The leper is sick in mind as well as body. For some reason there is an attitude to leprosy different from the attitude to any other disfiguring disease. It is associated with shame and horror, and carries, in some mysterious way, a sense of guilt, although innocently acquired like most contagious troubles. Shunned and despised, frequently do lepers consider taking their own lives and some do." The leper was hated by others until he came to hate himself. That is the kind of man who came to Jesus; he was unclean; *and Jesus touched him.*

(i) Here is a tremendous truth—*Jesus touched the untouchable.* Jesus' hand went out to the man from whom everyone else would have shrunk away. Two things emerge. First, when we despise ourselves, when our hearts are filled with bitter shame, let us remember, that, in spite of the shame, Christ's hand is still stretched out. Mark Rutherford wished to add a new beatitude, " Blessed are those who heal us of our self-despisings." That is what Jesus did and does. Second, it is of the very essence of Christianity to touch the untouchable, to love the unlovable, to forgive the unforgivable. Jesus did so—and so must we.

(ii) Jesus sent the man to carry out the normal, prescribed routine for cleansing. The regulations are described in Leviticus 14. That is to say a miracle did not dispense with what medical science of the time could do. It did not absolve the man from carrying out the prescribed rules and regulations. We will never get miracles by neglecting the gifts and the sciences and the wisdom God has given us. It is when man's skill combines with God's grace that the wonder happened—and still happens.

(iii) Verse 15 tells us of the popularity Jesus enjoyed. But it was only because people wanted something out of Him. There are so many who desire the gifts of God but who repudiate the demands of God—and, than that, there could be nothing more dishonourable.

THE OPPOSITION INTENSIFIES

Luke 5: 16, 17

> Jesus withdrew into the desert places and He continued
> in prayer. On a certain day He was teaching and,
> sitting listening, there were Pharisees and experts
> in the law who had come from every village in Galilee
> and from Judaea and Jerusalem. And the power of
> the Lord was there to enable Him to heal.

THERE are only two verses here; but as we read them we
must pause, for this indeed is a milestone. The Scribes
and the Pharisees had arrived on the scene. The opposition
which would never be satisfied until it had killed Jesus had
emerged into the open.

If we are to understand what happened to Jesus we
must understand something about the Law, and the
relationship of the Scribes and the Pharisees to it. When
the Jews returned from Babylon about 440 B.C. they knew
well that, humanly speaking, their hopes of national
greatness were gone. They therefore deliberately decided
that they would find their greatness in being a people of
the law. They would bend all their energies to knowing
and keeping God's law. The basis of the law was the Ten
Commandments. These commandments are great wide
principles for life. They are not rules and regulations;
they do not legislate for each event and for every circumstance. For a certain section of the Jews that was not
enough. They desired not great principles; they sought
a rule to cover every conceivable situation in life. From
the Ten Commandments they proceeded to develop and
elaborate these rules. Let us take an example. The commandment says, " Remember the Sabbath day to keep
it holy "; and then goes on to lay it down that on the
Sabbath no work must be done (Exodus 20: 8-11). But
that was not enough for the Jews. They asked, " What is
work? " They went on to define work under thirty-nine
different heads which they called " Fathers of Work."
Even that was not enough. Each of these heads was

infinitely sub-divided. Literally thousands of rules and regulations began to emerge. These were called the Oral Law, and they began to be set not only at level with the Ten Commandments but even above them. Again, let us take an actual example. One of the works forbidden on the Sabbath was carrying a burden. Jeremiah 17: 21-24 says, " Take heed to yourselves and bear no burden on the Sabbath day." But, these legalists insisted, a burden must be defined. So the definition was given. A burden is " food equal in weight to a dried fig, enough wine for mixing in a goblet, milk enough for one swallow, oil enough to anoint a small member, water enough to moisten an eye-salve, paper enough to write a custom-house notice upon, ink enough to write two letters, reed enough to make a pen " . . . and so on endlessly. So for a tailor to leave a pin or needle in his robe on the Sabbath was to break the law and to sin; to pick up a stone big enough to fling at a bird on the Sabbath was to sin. Goodness became identified with these endless rules and regulations. Let us take another example. To heal on the Sabbath was to work. It was laid down that only if life was in actual danger could healing be done; and then steps could only be taken to keep the sufferer from getting worse, not to improve his condition. So a plain bandage could be put on a wound, but not any ointment; plain wadding could be put into a sore ear, but not medicated. It is easy to see that there is no limit to this. The Scribes were the experts in the law who knew all these rules and regulations, and who deduced them from the law. The name Pharisee means " The Separated One "; and the Pharisees were those who had separated themselves from ordinary people and ordinary life in order to keep these rules and regulations. Note two things. First, for the Scribes and Pharisees these rules were a matter of life and death; to break one of them was deadly sin. Second, only people desperately in earnest would ever have tried to keep them, for they must have made life supremely uncomfortable.

It was only the best people who would even make the attempt. Jesus had no use for rules and regulations like that. For Him, the cry of human need superseded all such things. But to the Scribes and Pharisees He was a law-breaker, a bad man who broke the law and taught others to do the same. That is why they hated Him, and in the end killed Him. It is the tragedy of the life of Jesus that those who were most in earnest about their religion drove Him to the Cross. It was the irony of things that the best people of the day ultimately crucified Him. From this time on there was to be no rest for Him. Always He was to be under the scrutiny of these hostile and critical eyes. The opposition had crystallised and there was but one end.

Jesus knew this and before He met the opposition He withdrew to pray. The love in the eyes of God comforted Him for the hate in the eyes of men. The approval of God nerved Him to meet the criticism of men. He drew strength for the battle of life from the peace of God—and it is enough for the disciple that he should be as his Lord.

FORGIVEN AND HEALED

Luke 5: 18-26

Now—look you—there came men bearing on a bed a man who was paralysed, and they were trying to carry him in and to lay him before Jesus. When they could find no way to carry him in because of the crowd they climbed up on to the roof and they let him down, bed and all, through the tiles right into the middle of them in front of Jesus. When Jesus saw their faith, He said, " Man, your sins are forgiven you." The Scribes and Pharisees began to raise questions. " Who," they said, " is this who insults God? Who can forgive sins but God alone?" Jesus was well aware of what they were thinking. He answered, " What are you thinking about in your hearts? Which is easier—to say, ' Your sins are forgiven you,' or to say, ' Rise and walk '? But that you may know that the Son of Man has authority on earth to forgive sins (He said to the paralysed man), I tell you, rise, take up your bed, and go to your own house." And immediately he stood up in front of them and lifted up the bedding on which he was lying and went away to his house, glorifying God. Astonishment gripped them all and they glorified God and were filled with awe. " To-day," they said, " we have seen amazing things."

HERE we have a vivid story. Jesus was in a house teaching. The Palestinian house was flat-roofed. The roof had only the slightest tilt, sufficient to make the rain water run off. It was composed of beams laid from wall to wall and quite a short distance apart. The space between the beams was filled with close packed twigs, compacted together with mortar and then marled over. It was the easiest thing in the world to take out the packing between two beams. In fact coffins were very often taken in and out of a house via the roof.

What does the passage about forgiving sins mean? To understand it we must remember that sin and suffering were in Palestine inextricably connected. It was implicitly believed that if a man was suffering he had sinned. And therefore the sufferer very often had an even morbid sense of sin. That is why Jesus began by telling the man that his sins were forgiven. Without that the man would never believe that he could be cured. This shows how in debate the Scribes and Pharisees were completely routed. They objected to Jesus claiming to extend forgiveness to the man. But on their own arguments and assumptions the man was ill because he had sinned; and if he was cured that was the final proof that his sins were forgiven. The complaint of the Pharisees had recoiled on them and left them speechless.

The wonderful thing about this story is that here is a man who was saved by the faith of his friends. When Jesus saw their faith—the eager faith of those who had stopped at nothing to bring their friend to Jesus won that cure. It still happens. (i) There are those who have been saved by the faith of their parents. Carlyle used to say, that still across the years there came his mother's voice to him, " Trust in God and do the right." When Augustine was living a reckless and immoral life his devout mother came to ask the help of a Christian bishop. " It is impossible," he said, " that the child of such prayers and tears should perish." Many of us would gladly witness that we owe all that we are and ever will be to the faith of godly parents. (ii) There are those who are daily saved by the faith of those who love them. When H. G. Wells was newly married, and when success was bringing new temptations to him, he said, " It was as well for me that behind the folding doors at 12 Mornington Road there slept one so sweet and clean that it was unthinkable that I should appear before her squalid or drunken or base." Many of us would do the shameful thing but for the fact that we could not meet the pain and sorrow in someone's eyes.

In the very structure of life and love—blessed be God— there are the precious influences which save men's souls.

THE GUEST OF AN OUTCAST

Luke 5: 27-32

After that Jesus went out, and He saw a tax-collector, called Levi, sitting at his tax-collector's table. He said to him, " Follow Me! " He left everything and rose and followed Him. And Levi made a great feast for Him in his house; and a great crowd of tax-collectors and others who were their friends sat down at table with them. The Pharisees and Scribes complained at this, and said to the disciples, " Why do you eat and drink with tax-collectors and sinners? " Jesus answered, " Those who are healthy have no need of a doctor but those who are ill have. I did not come to invite the righteous but sinners to repentance."

HERE we have the call of Matthew (cp. Matthew 9: 9-13). Of all people in Palestine the tax-collectors were the best hated. At this time Palestine was a country subject to the Romans. The tax-collectors had taken service under the Roman government; and therefore, they were regarded as quislings, and renegades and traitors. The taxation system lent itself to abuse. The Roman custom was to farm out the taxes. They assessed a district at a certain figure, and then they sold the right to collect the taxes within it to the highest bidder. So long as the buyer handed over the assessed figure at the end of the year he was entitled to retain whatever else he could extract from the people; and since there were no newspapers or wireless, and no ways of making public announcements which would reach everyone, the common people had no real idea of what they had to pay. There were two types of taxes. First, there were stated taxes. There was a poll tax which all men from 14 to 65, and all women from 12 to 65, had to pay simply for the privilege of existing. There was a ground tax which consisted of one-tenth of all grain grown, and one-fifth of wine and oil. This could be paid in kind or commuted into money. There was income tax, which was one per cent. of a man's income. In these taxes there was not a great deal of room for extortion. Second, there were all kinds of duties. A tax was payable for using the main roads, the harbours, the markets. A tax was payable on a cart, on each wheel of it, and on the animal which drew it. There was purchase tax on certain articles, and there were import and export duties. A tax-collector could bid a man stop on the road and unpack his bundles and could charge him well nigh what he liked. If a man could not pay sometimes the tax-collector would offer to lend him money at an exorbitant rate of interest and so get him further into his clutches. Robbers, murderers and tax-collectors were classed together. A tax-collector was barred from the Synagogue. A Roman writer tells us that he once saw a monument to an honest tax-collector.

An honest specimen of this renegade profession was so rare that when he occurred he received a monument. Matthew was like that, and Jesus chose him as an apostle.

(i) The first thing that Matthew did was to invite Jesus to a feast—he could well afford it—and to invite his fellow tax-collectors and their outcast friends to meet Jesus. Matthew's first instinct was to share the wonder he had found. John Wesley once said, " No man ever went to Heaven alone; he must either find friends or make them." It is a Christian duty to share the blessedness that we have found.

(ii) The Scribes and Pharisees objected. The Pharisees—the Separated Ones—would not even have let the skirt of their robe touch the like of Matthew. Jesus made the perfect answer. Once Epictetus called his teaching " the medicine of salvation." Jesus pointed out that it is only sick people who need doctors; and people like Matthew and his friends were the very people who needed Him most of all. It would be well if we were to regard the sinner not as a criminal but as a sick man; and if we were to look on the man who has made a mistake not as someone deserving contempt and condemnation but as needing love and help to find the right way.

THE HAPPY COMPANY

Luke 5: 33-35

> They said to Him, " John's disciples fast frequently and pray. So do the disciples of the Pharisees; but your disciples eat and drink." Jesus said to them, " You cannot make the children of the bridechamber fast while the bridegroom is with them. But the days will come—and when the bridegroom is taken away from them in those days they will fast."

WHAT amazed and shocked the Scribes and the Pharisees was the normality of the followers of Jesus. Collie Knox tells how once a well-loved chaplain said to him, " Young Knox, don't make an agony of your religion." It was said of Burns that he was haunted rather than helped by his religion. The orthodox Jews had an idea—not yet altogether dead—that a man was not being religious unless he was being uncomfortable. They had systematised their religious observances. They fasted on Mondays and Thursdays; and often they whitened their faces so that no one could fail to see that they were fasting. True, fasting was not so very serious because it lasted only from sunrise to sunset and after that ordinary food could be taken. The idea was to call God's attention to the faster. Sometimes they even thought of it in terms of sacrifice. By fasting a man was in essence offering nothing less than his own flesh to God. Even prayer was systematised. Prayer was to be offered at 12 midday, 3 p.m. and 6 p.m. Jesus was in any event opposed radically to religion by rule. He used a vivid picture. When two young people married in Palestine they did not go away for a honeymoon; they stayed at home; and for a week they kept open house. They dressed in their best; sometimes they even wore crowns; for the week they were king and queen and their word was law. They would never have a week in their hard-wrought lives like that again. And the favoured guests who shared this festive week were called the children of the bridechamber.

(i) It is extremely suggestive that more than once Jesus likens the Christian life to a wedding feast. Joy is a primary Christian characteristic. It was said of a famous American teacher by one of her students, " She made me feel as if I was bathed in sunshine." Far too many people think of Christianity as something which compels them to do all the things they do not want to do and hinders them from doing all the things they do want to do. Laughter has become a sin, instead of—as a famous philosopher called it—" a sudden glory." Robert Louis Stevenson was right, when he wrote in *The Celestial Surgeon*,

" If I have faltered more or less
    In my great task of happiness;
    If I have moved among my race.
    And shown no glorious morning face;
    If beams from happy human eyes
    Have moved me not; if morning skies,
    Books, and my food, and summer rain
    Knocked on my sullen heart in vain:
    Lord, thy most pointed pleasure take
    And stab my spirit broad awake;
    Or, Lord, if too obdurate I,
    Choose Thou, before that spirit die,
    A piercing pain, a killing sin,
    And to my dead heart run them in ! "

(ii) But at the same time Jesus knew that there would come a day when the bridegroom would be taken away. He was not caught unawares by death. Ahead He saw the Cross; but even on the way to the Cross He knew that joy that no man taketh from us, because it is the joy of the presence of God.

THE NEW IDEA

Luke 5: 36-39

He spoke a parable to them like this: " Nobody puts a patch from a new garment on an old garment. If he does the new will tear it and the patch from the new will not match the old. No one puts new wine into old skins. If he does the new wine will burst the skins and it will be spilled and the skins will be ruined. But new wine must be put into new skins, and no one who drinks old wine wishes for new for he says, 'The old is good.' "

THERE is in religious people a kind of passion for the old. Nothing moves more slowly than a Church. The trouble

64

with the Pharisees was that the whole religious outlook of
Jesus was so startling new that they simply could not adjust
themselves to it. The mind soon looses the quality of
elasticity and will not accept new ideas. Jesus used two
illustrations. "You cannot put a new patch on an old
garment," He said. The strong new cloth will only rip
the rent in the old cloth wider. Bottles in Palestine were
made of skin. When new wine was put into them it fermented and gave off gas. If the bottle was new there was a
certain elasticity in the skin and it gave with the pressure;
but if it was old the skin was dry and hard and it would
burst. "Don't," says Jesus, "let your mind become like
an old wineskin. People say of wine, 'The old is better.'
It may be at the moment, but they forget that it is a
mistake to despise the new wine, for the day will come
when it has matured and it will be best of all." The whole
passage is Jesus' condemnation of the shut mind and his
plea that men should not reject new ideas.

(i) We should never be afraid of adventurous thought.
If there is such a person as the Holy Spirit God must ever
be leading us into new truth. Fosdick somewhere asks,
"How would medicine fare if doctors were restricted to
drugs and methods and techniques three hundred years
old?" And yet our standards of orthodoxy are far older
than that. The man with something new has always
to fight. Galileo was branded a heretic when he held that
the sun moved round the earth. Lister had to fight for
antiseptic technique in surgical operations. Simpson
had to battle against opposition in the merciful use of chloroform. Let us have a care that when we resent new thought
we are not simply demonstrating that our minds are
grown old and inelastic and let us never shirk the adventure
of thought.

(ii) We should never be afraid of new methods. That a
thing has *always* been done may very well be the best
reason for stopping doing it. That a thing has *never* been
done may very well be the best reason for trying it. No

business could exist on outworn methods—and yet the Church tries to. Any business which had lost as many customers as the Church has would have tried new ways long ago—but the Church resents all that is new. Once on a world tour Rudyard Kipling saw General Booth come aboard the ship. He came aboard to the beating of tambourines which Kipling's orthodox soul resented. Kipling got to know the General and told him how he disliked tambourines and all their kindred. Booth looked at him. " Young man," he said, " if I thought I could win one more soul for Christ by standing on my head and beating a tambourine with my feet I would learn how to do it." There is a wise and an unwise conservatism. Let us have a care that in thought and in action we are not hidebound reactionaries when we ought, as Christians, to be gallant adventurers.

THE INCREASING OPPOSITION

Luke 6: 1-5

> One Sabbath day, Jesus happened to be going through the corn fields, and His disciples were plucking the ears of corn and rubbing them in their hands and eating them. Some of the Pharisees said, " Why are you doing what it is illegal to do on the Sabbath? " Jesus answered, " Have you not read what David did when he and his comrades were hungry?—how he went into the house of God and took the loaves of the presence and ate them and gave them to his comrades, although it is not legal for any but the priests to eat them. The Son of Man," He said to them, " is the Lord of the Sabbath."

THIS is the first of two incidents which show the opposition to Jesus rapidly coming out into the open and which make it clear that the immediate charge against Jesus was that He was a breaker of the Sabbath law. He and His disciples were passing along one of the paths which intersected the corn fields. The fact that the disciples plucked the ears of corn was in itself no crime. One of the merciful laws of the Old Testament laid it down that anyone passing through a corn field was free to pluck the corn so long as he did not put a sickle into it (Deuteronomy 23: 25). On any other day there would have been no complaint; but this was the Sabbath. Four of the forbidden kinds of work were reaping, threshing, winnowing, and preparing food; and technically the disciples had broken every one of them. By plucking the corn they were guilty of reaping; by rubbing it in their hands, of threshing; by flinging away the husks, of winnowing; and the very fact that they ate it showed that they had prepared food on the Sabbath. To us the whole thing seems fantastic; but we must remember that to a strict Pharisee this was a deadly sin; one of the little rules and regulations had been broken; this to them was a matter of life and death.

They made their accusation and Jesus quoted the Old Testament to them. He quoted the incident in I Samuel 21: 1-6 when David and his comrades, when they were very hungry, ate the shewbread of the Tabernacle. A better name for it is The Bread of the Presence. Every Sabbath morning there were laid before God twelve wheaten loaves baked of flour sieved no fewer than eleven times. There was one loaf for every tribe. In the time of Jesus these loaves were laid on a table of solid gold, three feet long, one and a half feet broad, and nine inches high. The table stood lengthwise along the northern side of the Holy Place. The bread stood for the very presence of God and none but the priests might eat of it (Leviticus 24: 5-9). But David's need had taken precedence over rules and regulations. The Rabbis themselves said, " The Sabbath is made for you and not you for the Sabbath." That is to say at their highest and their best the Rabbis admitted that human need abrogated ritual law. If that be so, how much more is the Son of Man, with His heart of love and mercy, Lord of the Sabbath? How much more can He use it for His purposes of love? But the Pharisees had forgotten the claims of mercy because they were immersed in their rules and regulations. It is a most suggestive thing that they were watching Jesus and His disciples as they passed through the corn fields. Clearly they were spying; from now on every act of Jesus' life was to be watched and scrutinised by these bleak and critical and hostile eyes.

In this passage there is one great general truth. Jesus said to the Pharisees, " Have you not read what David did? " The answer of course was, " Yes "—but they had never seen what it meant. It is possible to read scripture meticulously, to know the Bible inside out from cover to cover, to be able to quote it verbatim and to pass any examination on it—and yet completely to miss its real meaning. Why did the Pharisees miss the meaning—and why do we so often miss it? (i) They did not bring to scripture *an open mind*. They came to scripture not to learn God's will, but to find proof texts to buttress up their own ideas. Far too often men have taken a theology to the Bible instead of finding their theology in the Bible. When we read scripture we must come saying, not, " Listen, Lord, for Thy servant is speaking," but, " Speak, Lord, for Thy servant is listening." (ii) They did not bring *a needy heart*. The man who comes with no sense of need always misses the deepest meaning of scripture. When need awakens, the Bible is a new book. When Bishop Butler was dying he was troubled. " Have you forgotten, my lord," said his chaplain, " that Jesus Christ is a Saviour? " " But," said the dying bishop, " how can I know that He is a Saviour for me? " " It is written," said the chaplain, " him that cometh unto Me I will in nowise cast out." And Butler answered, " I have read these words a thousand times and I never saw their meaning until now. Now I die in peace." The sense of need unlocked for him the treasury of scripture.

When we read God's book we must bring to it the open mind and the needy heart—and then to us also it will be the greatest book in the world.

THE DEFIANCE OF JESUS

Luke 6: 6-12

On another Sabbath Jesus went into the Synagogue and was teaching, and there was a man there whose right hand was withered. The Scribes and the Pharisees watched Him to see if He would heal on the Sabbath day in order to find a charge against Him. He knew well what they were thinking. He said to the man with the withered hand, " Rise, and stand in the midst." He rose and stood. Jesus said to them, " Here is a question for you—is it legal to do good on the Sabbath day or to do evil? To save a life or to destroy it? " He looked round on them and said to him, " Stretch out your hand." He did so and his hand was restored. They were filled with insane anger, and they discussed with each other what they could do to Jesus.

By this time the opposition to Jesus was quite open. Jesus was teaching in the Synagogue on the Sabbath day and the Scribes and Pharisees were there with the set purpose of watching Him so that, if He healed, they could charge Him with breaking the Sabbath. There is one interesting touch in the story. If we compare the story in Matthew 12: 10-13 and Mark 3: 1-6 with Luke's version of it, we find that only Luke tells us that it was the man's *right* hand which was withered. There speaks the doctor, interested in the details of the case. In this incident Jesus quite openly broke the law. To heal was to work, and work was prohibited on the Sabbath day. True, if there was any danger to life steps might be taken to help a sufferer. For instance, it was always legal to treat diseases of the eye or throat. But this man was in no danger of his life; he might have waited until the next day without peril. But Jesus laid down the great principle that, whatever the rules and regulations may say, it is always right to do a good thing on the Sabbath day. Jesus asked the piercing questions, " Is it legal to save life or to destroy it on the Sabbath? " That must have struck home, for while He was seeking to help the life of the man, they were doing all they could to destroy him. It was He who was seeking to save and they who were seeking to destroy.

In this story there are three characters.

(i) There is *the man with the withered hand*. We can tell two things about him. (*a*) One of the apocryphal gospels, that is, one of the gospels which never gained admission into the New Testament, tells us that he was a stone mason, and he came to Jesus, beseeching His help and saying, " I was a stone mason earning my living with my hand; I beseech you, Jesus, give me back my health that I may not have to beg my bread with shame." *He was a man who wanted to work.* Gods always looks with approval on the man who wants to do an honest day's work. (*b*) *He was a man who was prepared to attempt the impossible.* He did not argue when Jesus told him to stretch out his useless hand; he tried and, in the strength Jesus gave him, he succeeded. *Impossible* is a word which should be banished from the vocabulary of the Christian. As a famous scientist said, " The difference between the difficult and the impossible is only that the impossible takes a little longer to do."

(ii) There is *Jesus*. There is in this story a glorious atmosphere of defiance. Jesus knew that He was being watched, but without hesitation He healed. He bade the man stand out in the midst. This thing was not going to be done in a corner. There is a story of one of Wesley's preachers who proposed to preach in a hostile town. He hired the town-crier to announce the meeting, and the town-crier announced it in a terrified whisper. The preacher took the bell from him and rang it and thundered out. " Mr. So and So will preach in such and such a place and at such and such a time to-night—*and I am the man.*" The real Christian displays with pride the banner of his faith and bids the opposition do its worst.

(iii) There were *the Pharisees*. Here were men who took the quite extraordinary course of hating a man who had just cured a sufferer. They are the outstanding example of men who loved their system more than they loved God. Their rules and regulations were dearer to them than God. We see this happen in Churches over and over again.

Disputes are not about the great matters of the faith but about matters of Church government and the like. Leighton once said, "The mode of Church government is unconstrained; but peace and concord, kindness and goodwill are indispensable." There is an ever-present danger of setting loyalty to a system above loyalty to God.

JESUS CHOOSES HIS MEN

Luke 6: 12-19

> In these days Jesus went away into a mountain to pray; and He spent the whole night in prayer to God. When day came He called His disciples. From them He chose twelve, whom He also called Apostles— Simon, whom He named Peter, and Andrew his brother, and James, and John, and Philip, and Bartholomew, and Matthew, and Thomas, and James the son of Alphaeus, and Simon who was called the Zealot, and Judas the son of James, and Judas Iscariot, who became a traitor. He came down with them and took His stand with them on a place in the plain; and there was a great crowd of His disciples there, and a great crowd of people from all Judaea and Jerusalem and from the coastal district of Tyre and Sidon, who had come to listen to Him and to be healed from their diseases; and those who were distressed by unclean spirits were healed and the whole crowd sought to touch Him because power went out from Him, and He healed all.

HERE we see Jesus choosing His men. It is interesting and salutary to see why He chose them, because it is for the same reasons and purposes that He still wants and needs men.

(i) Mark 3: 14 tells us that He chose them *that they might be with Him.* That means two things. (*a*) Jesus chose them to be His friends. It is the amazing thing that Jesus needed human friendship. It is of the very essence of the Christian faith that we can say in all reverence and in all humility that God cannot be happy without men.

Just because God is Father there is a blank in God's heart until the last man comes home. (b) Jesus knew that the end was coming. Had Jesus lived in a later age He might have written a book which would have carried His teaching all over the world. But, living when He did, Jesus chose these men that He might write His message upon them. They were to be His living books. They were to company with Him that they might some day take His message to all men.

(ii) Jesus chose them *from His disciples*. The word disciple means *a learner*. They were to be those who were always learning more and more about Him. A Christian is a man whose whole life is spent learning about that Lord whom He will some day meet face to face and will know even as He is known.

(iii) Jesus chose them to be *His apostles*. The Greek word *apostolos* means *someone who is sent out*. It can be used for an envoy or an ambassador. So they were to be His ambassadors to men. A little girl received in the Sunday School a lesson on the disciples. She did not get the word quite right, because she was very young; and she came home and told her parents that she had been learning about Jesus' *samples*. The ambassador is the man who in a foreign land stands for and speaks for and represents his country. He is supremely the sample of his country. The Christian is ever sent to be an ambassador for Christ, not by his words, but by his life and deeds.

About the Twelve themselves we may note two things.

(i) They were very *ordinary men*. There was not a wealthy, nor a famous, nor an influential man amongst them; they had no special education; they were men of the common folk. It is as if Jesus said, " Give me twelve ordinary men and I will change the world." The work of Jesus is not in the hands of men whom the world calls great, but in the hands of ordinary people like ourselves.

(ii) They were *a strange mixture*. To take but two of them—Matthew was a tax-collector, and, therefore, a traitor and a renegade to his own country. Simon was a Zealot, and the Zealots were fanatical nationalists, men who were sworn to assassinate every traitor and every Roman they could lay hands on. It is one of the miracles of the power of Christ that Matthew and Simon the Zealot could live at peace in the close company of the apostolic band. When men are really Christian the most diverse and divergent characters and types can live at peace together. It was said of Gilbert Chesterton and his brother Cecil, "They always argued, they never quarrelled." It is only in Christ that we can solve the problem of living together; and that is so because even the most opposite people are united because they both love Him. If we really love Him we will also love each other.

THE END OF THE WORLD'S VALUES

Luke 6: 20-26

> Jesus lifted up His eyes upon His disciples and said, "Happy are you poor, because yours is the Kingdom of God. Happy are you who are hungry now because you will be filled. Happy are you who weep now because you will laugh. Happy are you when men will hate you and shut you off from their company and insult you and cast out your name as an evil name, for the sake of the Son of Man; for—look you—your reward in heaven will be great. Their fathers used to treat the prophets in the same way. But woe to you who are rich because you have all the comfort you are going to get. Woe to you who are filled because you will be hungry. Woe to you who laugh now because you will grieve and weep. Woe to you when all men speak well of you, for that is what your fathers used to do to the false prophets."

LUKE'S Sermon on the Plain and Matthew's Sermon on the Mount (Matthew, chapters 5 to 7) closely correspond. Both start with a series of Beatitudes. There are differences between the versions of Matthew and Luke, but this one thing is clear—they are a series of bombshells. It may well

be that we have read them so often that we have forgotten
how revolutionary they are. They are quite unlike the
laws which a philosopher or a typical wise man might lay
down. Each one is a challenge. As Deissmann said, " They
are spoken in an electric atmosphere. They are not quiet
stars but flashes of lightning followed by a thunder of
surprise and amazement." Quite literally they take the
accepted standards and turn them upside down. The
people whom Jesus called happy the world would call
wretched; and the people Jesus called wretched the world
would call happy. Just imagine anyone say, " Happy are
the poor, and, Woe to the rich ! " To talk like that is to
put an end to the world's values altogether.

Where then is the key to this? The key comes in verse 24.
There Jesus says, " Woe to you who are rich because you
have all the comfort you are going to get." The word
Jesus uses there for *have* is the word which is used for
receiving payment in full of an account. It is a business
word, the word which a tradesman wrote on an account
when he had received payment in full. What Jesus is
saying is this, " If you set your heart and bend your whole
energies to obtain the things which the world values, you
will get them—but that is all you will ever get." In the
expressive modern phrase, literally, you have had it!
But if on the other hand you set your heart and bend all
your energies to be utterly loyal to God and true to Christ,
you will run into all kinds of trouble; you may by the
world's standards look unhappy, but your payment is
still to come; and when it comes it will be joy eternal.

We are here face to face with an eternal choice. It is a
choice which begins in childhood and never ends till life
ends. Will you take the easy way, and the way which
yields immediate pleasure and profit? or, Will you take the
hard way which yields immediate toil and sometimes
suffering? Will you seize on the pleasure and the profit
of the moment? or, Are you willing to look ahead and
sacrifice them for the greater good? Will you concentrate

on the world's rewards? or, Will you concentrate on Christ? If you take the world's way you must abandon the values of Christ. If you take Christ's way you must abandon the values of the world. Jesus had no doubt which way in the end brought happiness. F. R. Maltby said, " Jesus promised His disciples three things—that they would be completely fearless, absurdly happy and in constant trouble." G. K. Chesterton, whose principles constantly got him into trouble, once said, " I like getting into hot water. It keeps you clean! " It is Jesus' teaching that the joy of heaven will amply compensate for the trouble of earth. As Paul said, " Our light affliction is but for a moment and works for us a far more exceeding and eternal weight of glory " (2 Corinthians 4: 17). The challenge of the Beatitudes is, " Will you be happy in the world's way, or in Christ's way? "

THE GOLDEN RULE

Luke 6: 27-38

Jesus said, " But to you who are listening I say, Love your enemies, do good to those who hate you, bless those who curse you, pray for those who ill-use you. To him who strikes you on one cheek offer the other cheek also. If anyone takes away your cloak, do not stop him taking your tunic too. Give to everyone who asks you; if anyone takes away your belongings do not demand them back again. As you would like men to act towards you, so do you act towards them. If you love those who love you, what special grace is there in that? Even sinners love those who love them. If you are kind to those who are kind to you, what special grace is there in that? Even sinners do that. If you lend to those from whom you wish to get, what special grace is in that? Even sinners lend to sinners in order to get as much back again. But you must love your enemies; and do good to them; and lend with no hope of getting anything in return. Your reward will be great and you will be the sons of the Most High, because He is kind both to the thankless

75

and to the wicked. Be merciful as your Father in heaven is merciful; do not judge and you will not be judged; do not condemn and you will not be condemned; forgive and you will be forgiven. Give and it will be given to you. People will give into your bosom, good measure pressed together, shaken down, running over; for with what measure you measure it will be measured to you back again.''

THERE is no commandment of Jesus which has caused so much discussion and debate as the commandment to love our enemies. Before we can obey it we must discover what it means. In Greek there are three words for to love. There is *eran*, which describes passionate love, the love of a man for a maid. There is *philein*, which describes our love for our nearest and dearest, the warm affection of the heart. Now neither of these two words is used here. The word used here is *agapan*, which needs a whole paragraph to translate it. *Agapan* describes an active feeling of benevolence towards the other person; it means that no matter what that person does to us we will never allow ourselves to desire anything but his highest good; and we will deliberately and of set purpose go out of our way to be good and kind to him. This is most suggestive. We cannot love our enemies as we love our nearest and dearest. To do so would be unnatural, impossible and even wrong. But we can see to it that, no matter what a man does to us, even if he insults, ill-treats and injures us, we will seek nothing but his highest good. One thing emerges from this. The love we bear to our dear ones is something we cannot help. We speak of *falling* in love; it is something which happens to us. But this love towards our enemies is not only something of the heart; it is something of the will. It is something which by the grace of Christ we will ourselves to do.

This passage has in it two great facts about the Christian ethic.

(i) The Christian ethic is *positive*. It does not consist in *not doing* things but in *doing* them. Jesus gave us the

Golden Rule which bids us do to others as we would have them do to us. That rule exists in many writers of many creeds in its *negative* form. Hillel, one of the great Jewish Rabbis, was asked by a man to teach him the whole law while he stood on one leg. He answered, " What is hateful to thee, do not to another. That is the whole law and all else is explanation." Philo, the great Jew of Alexandria, said, " What you hate to suffer, do not do to anyone else." Isocrates, the Greek orator, said, " What things make you angry when you suffer them at the hands of others, do not you do to other people." The Stoics had as one of their basic rules, " What you do not wish to be done to yourself, do not you do to any other." When Confucius was asked, " Is there one word which may serve as a rule of practice for all one's life? " he answered, " Is not Reciprocity such a word? What you do not want done to yourself, do not do to others." *Everyone of these forms is negative.* It is not unduly difficult to keep oneself from such action; but it is a very different thing to go out of your way to do to others what you would want them to do to you. The very essence of Christian conduct is that it does not consist in not doing bad things, but in actively doing good things.

(ii) The Christian ethic is based on *the extra thing*. Jesus described the common ways of sensible conduct and then dismissed them with the question, " What special grace is in that? " So often people claim to be just as good as their neighbours. Very likely they are. But the question of Jesus is, " How much *better* are you than the ordinary person? " It is not our neighbour with whom we must compare ourselves; we may well stand that comparison very adequately; it is *God* with whom we must compare ourselves; and in that comparison we are all in default.

(iii) What is the reason for this Christian conduct? The reason is that it makes us like God, for that is the way in which God acts. God sends His rain on the just and the unjust. He is kind to the man who brings Him joy and equally kind to the man who grieves His heart. God's love embraces saint and sinner alike. It is that love that we must copy; if we, too, seek nothing but even our enemy's highest good we will in truth be the children of God.

Verse 38 has the strange phrase, " People will give into your bosom." The Jew wore a long loose robe down to the feet, and round the waist a girdle. The robe could be pulled up so that the bosom of the robe above the girdle formed a kind of outsize pocket in which things could be carried. So the modern equivalent of the phrase would be, " People will fill your pocket."

RULES FOR LIFE AND LIVING

Luke 6: 39-46

> Jesus spoke a parable to them: " Surely a blind man cannot lead a blind man? If he tries to do so will not both fall into the ditch? The disciple cannot advance beyond his teacher, but every disciple will be equipped as his teacher is. Why do you look at the speck of dust that is in your brother's eye and never notice the plank that is in your own eye? Or, how can you say to your brother, ' Brother, let me take out the speck of dust that is in your eye,' when you yourself do not notice the plank in your own eye? You hypocrite! First put the plank out of your own eye and then you will see clearly to put out the speck of dust that is in your brother's eye. There is no good tree which produces rotten fruit, nor again, is there a rotten tree which produces good fruit. Each tree is recognized by its own fruit. People do not gather figs from thistles nor do they gather grapes from a bramble bush. The good man produces good from the treasure of his heart. The evil man produces evil from the evil. The mouth speaks out of whatever abounds in the heart."

To us this reads like a disconnected series of separate sayings. Two things are possible. It may well be that Luke is collecting together here sayings of Jesus which were spoken on different occasions and is giving us a kind of compendium of rules for life and living. Or, this may be an instance of the Jewish method of preaching. The Jews called preaching *Charaz*, which means *stringing beads*. The Rabbis held that the preacher must never linger more than a few moments on any topic but, in order to maintain interest, must move quickly from one topic to another. Jewish preaching, therefore, often seems to us to be disconnected.

The passage falls into four sections.

(i) Verses 39 and 40. Jesus warned those who listen that no teacher can lead his scholars beyond that stage which he himself has reached. That is a double warning to us. In our learning we must seek only the best teacher of all for only He can lead us farthest on. In our teaching we must ever remember that we cannot teach what we do not know.

(ii) Verses 41 and 42. Here is an example of the humour of Jesus. It must have been with a smile that Jesus drew the picture of a man with a plank in his own eye trying to extract a speck of dust from someone else's eye. Jesus taught that we have no right to criticise unless we ourselves are free of faults. That simply means that we have no right to criticise at all, because " there is so much bad in the best of us and so much good in the worst of us that it ill becomes any of us to find fault with the rest of us."

(iii) Verses 43 and 44 remind us that a man cannot be judged in any other way than by his deeds. It was said to a teacher, " I cannot hear what you say for listening to what you are." Teaching and preaching are both " truth through personality." Fine words will never take the place of fine deeds. That is very relevant to-day. We fear the menace of Communism and of other secular movements. We will never defeat these movements by writing books and pamphlets and holding discussion groups. The only

79

way to prove the superiority of Christianity is to show by our lives that it produces better men and women.

(iv) Verse 45. In this verse Jesus reminded men that the words of their lips are in the last analysis the product of their hearts. No man can speak of God with his mouth unless the Spirit of God be in his heart. Nothing shows the state of a man's heart so well as the words he speaks when he is not being careful and considering his words, but when he is talking freely and saying, as we say, the first thing which comes into his head. If you ask a person to direct you to a certain place, one person may tell you it is near such and such a *church*; another, that it is near such and such a *cinema*; another, that it is near such and such a *football ground*; another, that it is near such and such a *public house*. The very words of the answer to a chance question show where a man's thoughts most naturally turn and where the interests of his heart lie. Always our speech betrays us.

THE ONLY SURE FOUNDATION

Luke 6: 47-49

> Jesus said, " Why do you call me, Lord, Lord, and do not what I say? I will show you what everyone who comes to me and listens to my words and does them is like. He is like a man building a house, who dug deep down into the earth and laid the foundation on a rock. When the flood rose the river dashed against that house but it could not shake it because it was well founded. But he who has listened to me and has not done what I say is like a man who built his house on the top of earth without any foundation. The river dashed against it and immediately it collapsed, and great was the fall of it."

To get the real picture behind this parable we have to read Matthew's version of it as well in Matthew 7: 24-27. In Luke's version the river does not seem to make sense;

that is because Luke was not a native of Palestine and had not a clear picture of the circumstances in his own mind; whereas Matthew did belong to Palestine and knew just what the picture was. In Palestine in summer many of the rivers dried up altogether and left a sandy river bed empty of water. But in winter, after the September rains had come, the empty river bed became a raging torrent. Now many a man, looking for a site for a house, found an inviting stretch of sand and built there, only to discover when the winter came that he had built his house in the middle of a raging river which swept the house away. But the wise man searched for rock, where it was much more difficult to build and where it was hard labour to cut out the foundations. But when the wild winter weather came his toil was amply repaid, for his house stood strong and firm and secure. In either form the parable teaches us the importance of laying the right foundation for life. The only true foundation for life is obedience to the teaching of Jesus.

What made the foolish builder choose so unwisely?

(i) The foolish builder wanted *to avoid toil*. He could not be bothered to dig into the rock. The sand was much easier, and much more attractive, and much less trouble. He wanted the easy way. It may be easier to take our way than it is to take Jesus' way but the end is ruin. It may seem hard to take Jesus' but it is the way to security here and hereafter.

(ii) The foolish builder was *short-sighted*. He never troubled to think what his chosen site would be like six months afterwards. In every decision in life there is a short view and a long view. Happy is the man who never barters future good for present pleasure. Happy is the man who sees things, not in the light of the moment, but in the light of eternity.

When we learn that the hard way is often the best way, and that the long view is always the right view, then we will found our lives upon the teaching of Jesus and no storms will ever shake them.

A SOLDIER'S FAITH

Luke 7: I-IO

When Jesus had completed all His words in the hearing of the people, He went into Capernaum. The servant of a certain centurion was so ill that he was going to die, and he was very dear to him. When he heard about Jesus he sent some Jewish elders to Him and asked Him to come and save his servant's life. They came to Jesus and strenuously urged Him to come. " He is," they said, " a man who deserves that you should do this for him, for he loves our nation and has himself built us our Synagogue." So Jesus went with them. When He was now quite near the house the centurion sent friends to Him. " Sir," he said, " do not trouble yourself. I am not worthy that you should come under my roof; nor do I count myself fit to come to you; but just speak a word and my servant will be cured. For I myself am a man under orders, and I have soldiers under me, and I say to one, ' Go,' and he goes; and to another, ' Come,' and he comes; and I say to my servant, ' Do this,' and he does it." When Jesus heard this He was amazed at him. He turned to the crowd who were following Him and said, " I tell you I have not found such great faith not even in Israel." And those who had been sent returned to the house and found the servant completely cured.

THE central character in this story is a Roman centurion. This centurion was no ordinary man.

(i) First and foremost, *he was a centurion*, and no centurion was an ordinary man. A centurion was the equivalent of a company sergeant-major; and the centurions were the backbone of the Roman army. Wherever centurions are spoken of in the New Testament they are spoken of well (cp. Luke 23: 47; Acts IO: 22; 22: 26; 23: 17, 23, 24; 24: 23; 27: 43). Polybius, the historian, describes the qualifications of centurions. They must be not so much " seekers after danger as men who can command, steady in action, and reliable; they ought not to be over anxious to rush into the fight; but when hard pressed they must be ready to hold their ground and die at their posts."

The centurion must have been a man amongst men or he would never have held the post which was his.

(ii) *He had a completely unusual attitude to his slave.* He loved this slave and would go to any trouble to save him. In the eyes of Roman law, a slave was defined as a living tool; he had no rights; a master could ill-treat him and even kill him if he chose. A Roman writer on estate management recommends the farmer to examine his implements every year and to throw out those which are old and broken, and to do the same with his slaves. Normally when a slave was past his work he would have been thrown out to die. The attitude of this centurion to his slave was quite unusual.

(iii) *He was clearly a deeply religious man.* A man needs to be more than superficially interested before he will go the length of building a Synagogue. It is true that the Romans encouraged religion from the cynical motive that it kept people in order. They regarded it as the opiate of the people. Augustus recommended the building of Synagogues for that very reason. As Gibbon said in a famous sentence, " The various modes of religion which prevailed in the Roman world were all considered by the people as equally true; by the philosopher as equally false; *and by the magistrate as equally useful.*" But this centurion was no administrative cynic; he was a sincerely religious man.

(iv) *He had an extremely unusual attitude to the Jews.* If the Jews despised the Gentiles, the Gentiles hated the Jews. Anti-semitism is not a new thing. The Romans called the Jews a filthy race; they spoke of Judaism as a barbarous superstition; they spoke of the Jewish hatred of mankind; they accused the Jews of worshipping an ass's head and annually sacrificing a Gentile stranger to their God. True, many of the Gentiles, weary of the many gods and the loose morals of paganism, had accepted the Jewish doctrine of the one God and the austere Jewish ethic. But the whole atmosphere of this story implies a close bond of friendship between this centurion and the Jews.

(v) *He was a humble man.* He knew quite well that a strict Jew was forbidden by the law to enter the house of a Gentile (Acts 10: 28). He knew that a strict Jew would not allow a Gentile into his house, nor have any communication with him. He would not even come to Jesus himself. He persuaded his Jewish friends to approach the Master. This man who was accustomed to command had an amazing humility in the presence of true greatness.

(vi) *He was a man of faith.* His faith is based on the soundest argument. He argued from the here and now to reach the there and then. He argued from his own experience to God. If his authority produced the results it did, how much more must that of Jesus? He came with that perfect confidence which looks up and says, " Lord, I *know* you can do this." If we only had a faith like that for us too the miracle would happen and life would become new.

THE COMPASSION OF CHRIST

Luke 7: 11-17

Next, after that, Jesus was on His way to a town called Nain; and His disciples and a great crowd accompanied Him on the journey. When He came near the gate of the town—look you—a man who had died was being carried out to burial. He was his mother's only son, and she was a widow. There was a great crowd of townspeople with her. When the Lord saw her He was moved to the depths of His heart for her and said to her, " Don't go on weeping! " He went up and touched the bier. Those who were carrying it stood still. " Young man," He said, " I tell you, rise! " And the dead man sat up and began to speak. And He gave him back to his mother. And awe gripped them all. They glorified God saying, " A great prophet has been raised up amongst us," and, " God has graciously visited His people." This story about Him went out in all Judaea and all the surrounding countryside.

In this passage, and in the one immediately preceding it, once again Luke, the doctor, speaks. In verse 10 the word which we translated *completely cured* is the technical medical term for *sound in wind and limb*. In verse 15 the word which is used for *sitting up* is the technical term for a patient *sitting up in bed*.

This incident happened at Nain, which was a day's journey from Capernaum. Nain lies between Endor and Shunem, where Elisha, as the old story runs, raised another widow's son (2 Kings 4: 18-37). To this day, ten minutes' walk from Nain out on the road to Endor, there is a cemetery of rock tombs in which the dead are laid.

In many ways this is the loveliest story in all the gospels.

(i) It tells us of *the pathos and the poignancy of human life*. The funeral procession would be headed by the band of professional mourners with their flutes and their cymbals, uttering in a kind of frenzy their shrill cries of grief. There is all the ageless sorrow of the world in the austere and simple sentence, " He was his mother's only son and she was a widow."

" Never morning wore to evening
But some heart did break."

In Shelley's *Adonais*, his lament for Keats, he writes,

" As long as skies are blue, and fields are green,
Evening must usher night, night urge the morrow,
Month follow month with woe, and year wake year
to sorrow."

Virgil, the Roman poet, in an immortal phrase spoke about " The tears of things "—*sunt lacrimae rerum*. It is in the nature of things that we live in a world of broken hearts.

(ii) But to the pathos of human life, *Luke adds the compassion of Christ*. Jesus was moved to the depths of His heart. There is no stronger word in the Greek language for pity and sympathy and feeling, and it is a word which, again and again in the gospel story, is used of Jesus (Matthew 14: 14; 15: 32; 20: 34; Mark 1: 41; 8: 2). Here to the ancient world must have been a staggering thing. The noblest faith in antiquity was that of Stoicism. The Stoics believed that the primary characteristic of God was *apathy*. By *apathy* they meant *incapability of feeling*. If someone can make another sad or sorry, glad or joyful, it means that, at least for the moment, he can influence the other person. If he can influence him that means that, at least for the moment, he is greater than he and superior to him. Now, no one can be greater than God; therefore, no one must influence God; therefore, in the nature of things, God must be incapable of feeling. And here men were presented with the amazing conception of one who was the Son of God and who was moved to the depths of His being.

" In ev'ry pang that rends the heart,
      The Man of sorrows has a part."

For many that is the most precious thing about the God who was the God and Father of our Lord Jesus Christ.

(iii) But to the compassion of Jesus, Luke adds *the power of Jesus*. Jesus went up and touched the bier. It was not a coffin, for coffins were not used in the east. Very often long wicker work baskets were used for carrying the body to the grave. It was a dramatic moment. As one great commentator says, " Jesus claimed as His own what death had seized as his prey." It may well be that here we have a miracle of diagnosis; that Jesus with these keen eyes of His saw that the lad was in a cataleptic trance and saved him from being buried alive, as so many were in Palestine. It does not matter; the fact remains that Jesus claimed for life a lad who had been marked for death. Jesus is not only the Lord of life; He is the Lord of death who Himself triumphed over the grave and who has promised that, because He lives, we shall live also (John 14: 19).

THE FINAL PROOF

Luke 7: 18-29

John's disciples told him about all these things; so John called two of his disciples and sent them to the Lord saying, " Are you He who is to come, or, are we to look for another? " When they arrived, the men said to Him, " John, the Baptiser, has sent us to you. Are you the One who is to come," he asks, " or are we to look for another? " At that time He cured many of their diseases and afflictions and of evil spirits, and to many blind people He gave the gift of sight. " Go," He answered them, " and tell John what you have seen and heard. The blind recover their sight; the lame walk; the lepers are cleansed; the deaf hear; the dead are raised up; the poor have the Good News told to them; and blessed is he who does not find a stumbling-block in me."

When John's messengers had gone away, Jesus began to say to the crowds concerning John, " What did you go out into the desert to see? A reed shaken by the wind? But what did you go out to see? A man dressed in soft clothes? Look you—those who wear expensive clothes and live in luxury are in royal palaces. But what did you go out to see? A prophet? Yes, I say to you, and something more than a prophet. This is he of whom it stands written—' Look you, I send my messenger before you to prepare your way before you.' I tell you there is no one greater amongst those born of women than John. But he who is least in the Kingdom of God is greater than he." When the people and the tax-collectors heard this they called God righteous for they had been baptized with John's baptism.

THERE was a day when John sent emissaries to Jesus to ask if He really was the Messiah, God's Anointed King, or if they must look for someone else.

(i) This incident has worried many thinkers because they have been surprised at the apparent doubt in the

mind of John. Various explanations have been advanced.
(*a*) It is suggested that John took this step, not for his
own sake, but *for the sake of his disciples*. He was sure
enough; but they had their qualms and he desired that
they should be confronted with proof unanswerable.
(*b*) It is suggested that John wished to hurry Jesus on,
that he thought that it was time that Jesus moved towards
decisive action. (*c*) The simplest explanation is the best.
Think what was happening to John. John, the child of the
desert and of the wide-open spaces, was confined in a
dungeon cell in the castle of Machaerus. Once one of the
Macdonalds, a Highland chieftain, was confined in a little
cell in Carlisle Castle. In his cell there was one little
window. To this day you may see the marks in the sand-
stone of the feet and the hands of the Highlander as he
lifted himself up and clung to the window ledge, as day
by day he gazed with infinite longing out upon the border
hills and valleys that he would never walk again. Shut in
his cell, choked by the narrow walls, John asked this
question because his cruel captivity had put tremors in
his heart.

(ii) Note the proof that Jesus offered. He pointed at
the facts. The sick and the suffering and the humble
poor were experiencing the power and hearing the word
of the Good News. Here is a point which is seldom realized—
this is not the answer John expected. If Jesus was God's
Anointed One, John would have expected Jesus to say,
"My armies are massing. Caesarea, the headquarters of
the Roman government, is about to fall. The sinners are
being obliterated. And judgment has begun." John would
have expected Jesus to say, "The wrath of God is on the
march." Jesus said, "The mercy of God is here." Let us
remember that where pain is soothed and sorrow turned
to joy, where sorrow and suffering and death are vanquished,
there is the Kingdom of God. Jesus answer was, "Go back
and tell John that the love of God is here."

(iii) After John's emissaries had gone, Jesus paid His own tribute to John. People had crowded out into the desert to see and hear John. They had not gone out to see a reed shaken in the wind. That may mean one of two things. (*a*) Nothing was commoner by Jordan's banks than a reed shaken in the wind. It was in fact a proverbial phrase for the commonest of sights. It may then mean that the crowds went out to see no ordinary sight. (*b*) It may stand for fickleness. It was no vacillating, swaying character men went out to see, not a man like a swaying reed, but a man immovable as a mighty tree. They had not gone out to see some soft effeminate soul, like the silk-clad courtiers of the royal palace. What then had they gone out to see? (*a*) First, Jesus pays John a great tribute. All men expected that before God's Anointed King arrived upon the earth, Elijah would return to prepare the way and to act as His herald (Malachi 4: 5). John was the herald of the Highest. (*b*) Second, Jesus states quite clearly the limitations of John. The least in the Kingdom of Heaven was greater than he. Why? Some have said that it was because John had wavered, if but for a moment, in his faith. It was not that. It was because John marked a dividing line in history. Since John's proclamation had been made Jesus had come; eternity had invaded time; heaven had invaded earth; God had arrived in Jesus; and therefore life could never be the same again. We date all time as before Christ and after Christ—B.C. and A.D. Jesus is the dividing line. And, therefore, all who come after Him and who receive Him are of necessity granted a greater blessing than all who went before. The entry of Jesus into the world divided all time into two; and the entry of Jesus into our lives divided all life in two. If any man be in Christ he is a new creature (2 Corinthians 5: 17). He is created all over again.

As Bilney, the martyr said, " When I read that Christ Jesus came into the world to save sinners, it was as if day suddenly broke on a dark night."

THE PERVERSITY OF MEN

Luke 7: 30-35

> But the Pharisees and the Scribes frustrated God's purpose for themselves because they were not baptized by Him. "To whom," asked Jesus, "will I compare the men of this generation? And to whom are they like? They are like children seated in the market place and called to one another. 'We have piped to you,' they say, 'and you did not dance. We have sung you a dirge and you did not weep.' John the Baptiser came neither eating bread nor drinking wine, and you say, 'He has a demon.' The Son of Man came eating and drinking and you say, 'Look! a gluttonous man and a wine-drinker, the friend of tax-collectors and sinners.' But wisdom is justified by her children."

THIS is a passage which has two great warnings in it.

(i) It tells us of the perils of free-will. The Scribes and the Pharisees had succeeded in frustrating God's purpose for themselves. The tremendous truth of Christianity is that the coercion of God is not the coercion of force but the coercion of love. It is precisely there that we can glimpse the sorrow of God. It is always love's greatest tragedy to look upon some loved one who has taken the wrong way and to see what might have been, what could have been and what was meant to have been. That is life's greatest heartbreak. Sir William Watson has a poem called *Lux Perdita*, the "Lost Light."

> "These were the weak, slight hands
> That might have taken this strong soul, and bent
> Its stubborn substance to thy soft intent,
> And bound it unresisting with such bands
> As not the arm of envious heaven had rent.
>
> These were the calming eyes
> That round my pinnace could have stilled the sea,
> And drawn thy voyager home, and bid him be
> Pure with their pureness, with their wisdom wise,
> Merged in their light, and greatly lost in thee.

But thou—thou passedst on,
With whiteness clothed of dedicated days,
Cold, like a star; and me in alien ways
Thou leftest, following life's chance lure, where shone
The wandering gleam that beckons and betrays."

It is true that,

" Of all sad words of tongue and pen
The saddest are those, ' It might have been.' "

God's tragedy, too, is the might have been of life. As
G. K. Chesterton said, " God had written not so much a
poem, but rather a play; a play He had planned as perfect,
but which had necessarily been left to human actors and
stage managers, who had since made a great mess of it."
God save us from making shipwreck of life and bringing
heartbreak to God by using our freewill to frustrate His
purposes.

(ii) It tells of the sheer perversity of men. John had
come, living with a hermit's austerity, and the Scribes
and Pharisees had said that he was a mad eccentric, that
some demon had taken his wits away. Jesus had come,
living the life of men and entering into all their activities,
and they had taunted Him with loving earth's pleasures
far too much. We all know the days when a child will girn
at anything; we all know the moods when nothing will
please us. The human heart can be lost in a perversity
in which any appeal that God may make will be met with
wilful and wayward and childish discontent.

(iii) But there are the few who answer; and God's
wisdom is in the end justified by those who are God's
children. Man may misuse their freewill to frustrate
God's purposes; men in their perversity may be blind
and deaf to all God's appeal. Had God used the force
of coercion and laid on man the iron bonds of a will that
could not be denied then there would have been a world of
automata and a world without trouble. But God chose
the dangerous way of love, and love in the end will triumph.

A SINNER'S LOVE

Luke 7: 36-50

> One of the Pharisees invited Jesus to eat with him.
> He went into the Pharisee's house and reclined at
> table; and—look you—there was a woman in the
> town, a bad woman. She knew that He was at table
> in the Pharisee's house, so she took an alabaster phial
> of perfume and stood behind Him, beside His feet,
> weeping. She began to wash His feet with tears,
> and she wiped them with the hairs of her head; and
> she kept kissing His feet and anointing them with the
> perfume. When the Pharisee, who had invited Him,
> saw this, he said to himself, " If this fellow was a
> prophet, He would have known who and what kind
> of a person this woman is who keeps touching Him,
> for she is a bad woman." Jesus answered him, " Simon,
> I have something to say to you." He said, " Master,
> say it." Jesus said, " There were two men who were
> in debt to a certain lender. The one owed him £20,
> the other £2. Since they were unable to pay he can-
> celled the debt to both. Who then will love him the
> more? " Simon answered, " I presume, he to whom
> the greater favour was shown." He said to him,
> " Your judgment is correct." He turned to the woman
> and said to Simon, " Do you see this woman? I
> came into your house—you gave me no water for
> my feet. She has washed my feet with her tears, and
> wiped them with the hairs of her head. You did not
> give me any kiss. But she, from the time I came in,
> has not ceased to kiss my feet. You did not anoint my
> head with oil. She has anointed my feet with perfume.
> Wherefore, I tell you, her sins—her many sins—are
> forgiven for she loved much. He to whom little is
> forgiven loves little." He said to her, " Your sins are
> forgiven." Those who were at table with Him began
> to say to themselves, " Who is this who forgives even
> sins? " He said to the woman, " Your faith has
> saved you. Go in peace."

THIS is one of the stories which is so vivid that it makes
one believe that Luke may well have been an artist.

(i) The scene is in the courtyard of the house of Simon
the Pharisee. The houses of well-to-do people were built

round an open courtyard in the form of a hollow square. Often in the courtyard there was a garden and a fountain; and there in the warm weather meals were eaten. It was the custom in the east that when a Rabbi was at a meal in such a house, all kinds of people came in—they were quite free to do so—to listen to the pearls of wisdom which fell from his lips. That explains the presence of the woman. When a guest entered such a house three things were always done. The host placed his hand on the guest's shoulder and gave him the kiss of peace. That would be a mark of respect which was never omitted in the case of a distinguished Rabbi. The roads were only dust tracks, and shoes were only soles held in place by straps across the foot. So always cool water was poured over the guest's feet to cleanse and comfort them. Either a pinch of sweet-smelling incense was burned or a drop of attar of roses was placed on the guest's head. These things good manners demanded, and in this case not one of them was done. In the east the guests did not sit, but reclined, at table. They lay on low couches, resting on the left elbow, leaving the right arm free, with the feet stretched out behind; and during the meal the sandals were taken off. That explains how the woman could be standing at Jesus' feet.

(ii) Simon was a Pharisee, one of The Separated Ones. Why should such a man invite Jesus to his house at all? There are three possible reasons. (*a*) It is just possible that he was an admirer and a sympathiser with Jesus, for not all the Pharisees were His enemies (cp. Luke 13 : 31). But the whole atmosphere of discourtesy makes that unlikely. (*b*) It could be that Simon had invited Jesus to His house with the deliberate intention of enticing Him into some word or action which might have been made the basis of a charge against Him. Simon may have been an *agent provocateur*. Again, it is not likely, because in verse 40 Simon gives Jesus the title, Rabbi. (*c*) Most likely, Simon was a collector of celebrities; and with a half-

patronising contempt had invited this startling young
Galilaean to have a meal with him. That would best
explain the strange combination of a certain respect with
the omission of the courtesies of the occasion. Simon was
a man who tried to patronise Jesus.

(iii) The woman was a bad woman, and a notoriously
bad woman. She was a prostitute. No doubt she had
listened to Jesus speak from the edge of the crowd, and
had glimpsed in Him the hand which would lift her from
the mire of her ways. Round her neck she wore, like all
Jewish women, a little phial of concentrated perfume;
they were called alabasters; and they were very costly.
She wished to pour it on His feet, for it was all she had to
offer. But as she saw Him the tears came and fell upon
His feet. For a Jewish woman to appear with hair unbound
was an act of the gravest immodesty. On her wedding day
a girl bound up her hair and never would she appear with
it unbound again. The fact that this woman loosed her
long hair in public showed how she had forgotten everyone
except Jesus.

The whole story demonstrates a contrast between two
attitudes of mind and heart. (i) Simon was conscious of
no need and therefore felt no love, and therefore received
no forgiveness. Simon's impression of himself was that he
was a good man in the sight of men and of God. (ii) The
woman was conscious of nothing else than a clamant need,
and therefore was overwhelmed with love for Him who
could supply it, and therefore received forgiveness.

The one thing which shuts a man off from God is self-
sufficiency. And the strange thing is that the better a man
is the more he feels his sin. Paul could speak of sinners
" of whom I am chief " (2 Timothy I: 15). Francis of
Assisi could say, " There is nowhere a more wretched and
a more miserable sinner than I." It is true to say that the
greatest of sins is to be conscious of no sin; but a sense
of need will open the door to the forgiveness of God, because
God is love, and love's greatest glory is to be needed.

ON THE ROAD

Luke 8: 1-3

> After that, Jesus travelled through the country, town by town, and village by village, preaching the Good News of the Kingdom of God. The Twelve were with Him, as were certain women, who had been cured from evil spirits and from illnesses. There was Mary, who is called Mary Magdalene, out of whom there went seven devils, and Joanna, the wife of Chuza, who was Herod's agent, and Susanna and many others. It was their habit to minister to their needs out of their resources.

THE time which we saw coming has now come. Jesus is on the road. The Synagogues were not now open to Him, as once they had been. He had begun, as it were, in the Church, where any man with a message from God might justly expect to find a responsive and receptive audience. Instead of a welcome He had found opposition; instead of eager listeners He had found the Scribes and Pharisees bleakly waiting to catch Him out in His words and deeds; so now He took to the open road, and the hillside and the lake shore.

(i) Once more we are confronted with a fact which we have already noted. This passage lists a little group of women who served Him out of their resources. It was always considered to be a pious act to support a Rabbi, and the fact that the devoted followers of Jesus helped Him in this way was in direct line with ordinary custom and practice. But, as with the disciples, so with these women, we cannot fail to see how mixed a company they were. There was Mary Magdalene, that is Mary from the town of Magdala, out of whom He had cast seven devils. Clearly she had a past that was a dark and terrible thing. There was Joanna. She was the wife of Chuza, Herod's *epitropos*. A king had many perquisites and much private property; his *epitropos* was the official who looked after the king's financial interests. In the Roman Empire, even in provinces

which were governed by proconsuls appointed by the
senate, the Emperor still had his *epitropos* to safeguard
his interests. So then there could be no more trusted and
important official. It is an amazing thing to find Mary
Magdalene, with the dark past, and Joanna, the lady of
the court, in the one company. It is one of the supreme
achievements of Jesus that He can enable the most diverse
people to live together without in the least losing their
own personalities or qualities. G. K. Chesterton writes
about the text which says that the lion will lie down with
the lamb. " But remember that this text is too lightly
interpreted. It is constantly assumed . . . that when the
lion lies down with the lamb the lion becomes lamb-like.
But that is brutal annexation and imperialism on the part
of the lamb. That is simply the lamb absorbing the lion
instead of the lion eating the lamb. The real problem is—
Can the lion lie down with the lamb and still retain his
royal ferocity? *That* is the problem the Church attempted;
that is the miracle she achieved." There is nothing which
the Church needs more than to learn how to yoke in common
harness the diverse temperaments and qualities of different
people. If we are failing it is our own fault, for, in Christ,
it can be done—it has been done.

(ii) In this list of women we have a group whose help
was practical. Being women, they would not in Palestine
be allowed to preach; but they gave the gifts they
had. There was an old shoemaker who once had wished
to become a minister, but the way had never opened up.
He was the friend of a young divinity student; and when
the lad one day was called to his first charge the old man
asked him for one favour. He asked to be allowed always
to make the lad's shoes, as long as life remained to him,
so that he might feel that the preacher was wearing his
shoes in the pulpit into which he could never come himself.
It is not always the person in the foreground who is doing
the greatest work. How many a man who occupies a
public position could not sustain it for one week without

the privacy of the home behind him! There is no gift which cannot be used in the service of Christ. Many of His greatest servants are in the background, unseen but essential to His cause.

THE SOWER AND THE SEED

Luke 8: 4-15

When a great crowd had gathered, and when they came to Him from every city, Jesus spoke to them by means of a parable. The sower went out to sow his seed. As he sowed some seed fell by the wayside. It was trampled upon and the birds of the heaven devoured it. Other seed fell on rocky ground where it grew up and withered because there was no moisture. Other seed fell in the middle of thorns and the thorns grew up along with it and choked the life out of it. Other seed fell into good ground and it produced a crop a hundredfold. As He told the story He said, " He that has an ear to hear let him hear."

The disciples asked Him what the parable meant. He said, " It is given to you to know the secrets of the Kingdom of God. To the others it is presented in parables, so that they may see, and yet not see, and so that they may hear and yet not understand."

The meaning of the parable is this. The seed is the word of God. Those by the wayside stand for those who have heard, and then the devil comes and takes the word from their hearts so that they may not believe and be saved. Those on the rocky ground stand for those, who, whenever they hear the word, gladly receive it; but they have no root; they believe for a time; but when a time of trial comes they fall away. The seed that fell among thorns stands for those, who, when they have heard, go their way and are suffocated by the cares, the wealth and the pleasures of this life, and so never complete their crop. The seed that is in the good ground stands for those who have heard the word and keep hold of it in a heart that is fine and good and bear fruit with fortitude.

IN this parable Jesus used a picture that all His hearers would recognize. It is in fact quite likely that He was looking at some sower sowing his seed as He spoke.

The parable speaks of four kinds of ground. (i) The common ground in Palestine was split into long narrow strips; between the strips there were paths which were rights of way; when the seed fell on these paths which were as hard as the road it had no chance of getting it. (ii) There was the rocky ground. This does not mean ground that was full of stones. It means ground which was only a thin skin of earth over a shelf of limestone rock. In such ground there was no moisture and no nourishment, and the growing plant was bound to wither and die. (iii) The ground which was full of thorns was ground which at the moment looked clean enough. It is possible to make any bit of ground *look* clean simply by turning it over. But the seeds of the weeds and the fibrous roots of the wild grasses had been left in it. The good seed and the weeds grew together, and weeds always grow more strongly than good plants; and so the life was choked out of the good seed. (iv) The good ground was ground that was deep and clean and well-prepared.

Verses 9 and 10 have always been puzzling verses. It sounds as if Jesus was saying that He spoke in parables so that people would not be able to understand; and we cannot believe that Jesus would deliberately cloak His meaning to hide it from His listeners. Various explanations have been suggested. (i) Matthew (13: 13) puts it slightly different. He says that Jesus spoke in parables *because* people could not rightly see and understand. Matthew seems to say that it was not to hinder people from seeing and understanding but to help them that Jesus so spoke. (ii) Matthew quotes immediately after this a saying of Isaiah 6: 9, 10. Isaiah in effect says, " I have spoken to them the word of God and the only effect in fact is that they have not understood a word of it." So then the saying of Jesus may indicate not the object of His teaching in parables but the result of it. The net result was that people just did not understand. (iii) What Jesus really meant is this—people can become so dull and heavy and blunted in mind that when God's truth comes to them they cannot see it. It is not God's fault. They have become so mentally lazy, so blinded by prejudice, so unwilling to see anything they do not want to see, that the result is that they have become incapable of assimilating God's truth.

There are two interpretations of this parable.

(i) It is suggested that the parable means that the fate of the word of God depends on the heart into which it is sown. (*a*) The hard path represents the shut mind, the mind which, as we put it, will not take it in. (*b*) The shallow ground represents those who accept the word but who never think it out and who never realize its consequences and who therefore collapse when the strain comes. (c) The thorny ground stands for those whose lives are so busy that the things of God get crowded out. We must ever remember that the things which crowd out the highest need not necessarily be bad things. They may in themselves be good things. The worst enemy of the best is the second best. (c) The good ground stands for the good heart. The good hearer does three things. First, he listens attentively. Second, he keeps what he hears in his mind and heart and thinks over it until he discovers its meaning for himself. Third, he acts upon it. He translates what he has heard into terms of action.

(ii) It is suggested that the real interpretation of the parable is this. Think of the situation. Jesus has been banished from the Synagogues. The Scribes and the Pharisees and the religious leaders are up against Him. Inevitably the disciples would be disheartened. It is to them Jesus speaks this parable and in it He is saying, "Every farmer knows that some of his seed will be lost; it cannot all grow. But that does not discourage him or make him stop sowing because he knows that in spite of that the harvest is sure." It is Jesus saying to His disciples, "I know we have our setbacks and our discouragements; I know we have our enemies and our opponents; but, never despair; in the end the harvest is sure."

So this parable can be both a warning to us as to how we hear and receive the word of God and an encouragement to banish all despair in the certainty that not all the setbacks can defeat the ultimate harvest of God.

LAWS FOR LIFE

Luke 8: 16-18

> No one lights a lamp and then hides it under a vessel or puts it under a bed. No! he puts it on a lamp-stand so that those who come in may see the light. There is nothing hidden which will not be made manifest; there is nothing secret which will not be known and brought into the open. Take care, then, how you listen; for to him who has it will be given; and from him who has not there shall be taken away even what he thinks he has.

HERE we have three sayings, each with its own warning for life.

(i) Verse 16 stresses the essential conspicuousness of the Christian life. Christianity is in its very nature something which must be seen. It is easy to find prudential reasons why we should not flaunt our Christianity in the world's face. In almost every person there is an instinctive fear of being different. The world is always likely to persecute those who do not conform to pattern. A writer tells how he kept hens. In the hen-run all the hens were precisely the same in marking except one. The one different hen was pecked to death by the other occupants of the hen-run. Even in the animal world to be different is a crime. Hard as it may be, the duty is laid upon us of never being ashamed to show whose we are and whom we serve; and if we regard the matter in the right way it will be, not a duty, but a privilege. A short time before the Coronation most houses and shops were displaying their flags. I was out on a country road at that time; and in a little copse by the roadside I came upon a tinker's camp. It consisted of only one little tent, and beside the tent there fluttered on a pole a Union Jack nearly as big as the tent itself. It was as if that vagrant tinker said, " I haven't got much in this world; but I am going to attach my colours to what I have." The Christian, however humble his position and his sphere, must never be ashamed to show his colours.

(ii) Verse 17 stresses the impossibility of secrecy. There are three people from whom we try to hide things. (*a*) Sometimes we try to hide things from ourselves. We shut our eyes to the consequences of certain actions and habits, the consequences of which we are well aware. It is like a man deliberately shutting his eyes to symptoms of an illness which he knows he has. We have only to state that to see the incredible folly of it. (*b*) Sometimes we try to hide things from our fellow men. Things have a way of coming out. The man with a secret is an unhappy man. The happy man is the man with nothing to hide. It is told that once an architect offered to build for Plato a house in which every room would be hidden from the public eye. " I will give you twice the money," said Plato, " if you build me a house into every room of which all men's eyes can see." Happy is the man who can speak like that. (c) Sometimes we try to hide things from God. No man ever attempted a more impossible task. We would do well to have before our eyes forever the text which says, " Thou, God, seest me."

(iii) Verse 18 lays down the universal law that the man who has will get more; and that the man who has not will lose what he has. If a man is physically fit and keeps himself so his body will be ready for ever greater efforts ; if he lets himself go flabby he will lose even the abilities he has. The more a student learns the more he can learn; but if he refuses to go on learning then he will lose the knowledge he has. This is just another way of saying that there is no standing still in life. All the time we are either going forward or going back. The seeker will always find; but the man who stops seeking will lose even what he has.

TRUE KINSHIP

Luke 8: 19-21

> Jesus' mother and brothers came to Him, and they could not get at Him because of the crowd. He was given a message, "Your mother and your brothers are standing outside and they want to see you." "My mother and my brothers," He answered them, "are those who hear the word of God and do it."

IT is not difficult to see that, at least during His lifetime, Jesus' family were not in sympathy with Him. Mark 3: 21 tells us how His kinsmen came and tried to restrain Him because they believed Him to be mad. In Matthew 10: 36 Jesus warns His followers that a man's foes may well be those of his own household—and He was speaking out of hard and bitter experience.

There is in this passage a great and a practical truth. It may very well be that a man finds himself closer to people who are not related to him than he does to his own kith and kin. The deepest relationship of life is not merely a blood relationship; it is the relationship of mind to mind and heart to heart. It is when people have common aims, common principles, common interests, a common goal in life that they become really and truly kin. Now let us remember the definition of the Kingdom which we have already worked out. The Kingdom of God is a society upon earth where God's will is as perfectly done as it is in heaven. It was Jesus' supreme quality that He, of all people, alone succeeded in fully achieving that identity of His will and the will of God. Therefore, all whose one aim in life is to make God's will their will are the true kindred of Jesus. We speak of all men being the sons of

God; and in one very real and very precious sense that is true, because God loves saint and sinner; but the deepest kind of sonship is ethically conditioned. It is when a man puts his will in line with God's will, by the help of the Holy Spirit, that real kinship begins. The Stoics declared that that was the only way to happiness in this life. They had the conviction that everything that happens—joy and sorrow, triumph and disaster, gain and loss, sunshine and shadow—is the will of God. When a man refuses to accept it he batters his head against the walls of the universe and can bring himself nothing but pain and trouble of heart. When he looks up to God and says, " Do with me as you wish," then there is the way to joy.

If all that be so two things emerge.

(i) There is a loyalty which surpasses all earthly loyalties; there is something which takes precedence of the dearest things on earth. In that sense Jesus Christ is a demanding master, for He will share a man's heart with nothing and with no one. Love is necessarily exclusive. We can only love one person at a time and serve one master at a time. (ii) That is hard; but there is this great wonder—that when a man gives himself thus absolutely to Christ he becomes one of a family whose boundaries are the earth. Whatever loss he may experience is counterbalanced by his gain. As John Oxenham wrote:

> " In Christ there is no East or West,
> In Him no South or North,
> But one great fellowship of love
> Throughout the whole wide earth.
>
> In Him shall true hearts everywhere
> Their high communion find,
> His service is the golden cord
> Close-binding all mankind.
>
> Join hands, then, brother of the faith,
> Whate'er your race may be!
> Who serves My Father as a son
> Is surely kin to Me.

In Christ now meet both East and West,
In Him meet South and North,
All Christly souls are one in Him,
Throughout the whole wide earth."

The man who, through Jesus Christ, seeks the will of God has entered into a family which includes all the saints in earth and in heaven.

CALM AMIDST THE STORM

Luke 8: 22-25

One day Jesus and His disciples embarked upon a ship. " Let us go over," He said to them, " to the other side of the lake." So they set sail. As they sailed He fell asleep. A violent squall of wind came down upon the lake; and the boat began to fill with water; and they were in peril. They came to Him and woke Him. " Master, Master," they said, " we are perishing." When He awoke, He rebuked the wind and the surf of the water. They ceased their raging, and there was a calm. " Where is your faith? " He said to them. But they were awe-stricken and amazed. " Who can this be," they said to each other, " because He gives His orders even to the winds and the water, and they obey Him? "

LUKE tells this story with an extraordinary economy of words, and yet with an extraordinary vividness. It was no doubt for much needed rest and quiet that Jesus decided to cross the lake. As they sailed He fell asleep. It was a lovely thing to think of the sleeping Jesus. He was tired just as we become tired. He, too, could reach the point of exhaustion when the claim of sleep is imperative. He trusted His men. They were the fishermen of the lake; He was content to leave things to their skill and seamanship and to relax. He trusted God; He knew that He was as near to God by sea as ever He was by land.

And then the storm came down. The Sea of Galilee is famous for its sudden squalls. A traveller says, " The sun had scarcely set when the wind began to rush down towards the lake, and it continued all night long with increasing violence, so that when we reached the shore next morning the face of the lake was like a huge boiling caldron." The reason of these storms is this. The Sea of Galilee is more than six hundred feet below sea level. It is surrounded by table lands beyond which the great mountains rise. The rivers have cut deep ravines through the table lands down into the sea. These ravines act like great funnels to draw down the cold winds from the mountains; and thus the storms arise. The same traveller tells how they tried to pitch their tents in such a gale. " We had to double-pin all the tent-ropes, and frequently were obliged to hang on with our whole weight upon them to keep the quivering tabernacle from being carried up bodily into the air." It was just such a sudden storm that struck the boat that day, and Jesus and His disciples were in peril of their lives. The disciples woke Jesus and with a word He calmed the storm.

Everything that Jesus did had more than a merely temporal significance. And the real meaning of this incident is that, *wherever Jesus is, the storm becomes a calm.*

(i) When Jesus comes, He calms *the storms of temptation.* Sometimes temptation comes to us with an almost over-mastering force. As Stevenson once said, " You know the Caledonian Railway Station in Edinburgh? One cold bleak morning I met Satan there." It comes to us all to meet Satan. If we meet that tempest of temptation alone we perish; but with Christ there comes the calm in which temptations lose their power.

(ii) When Jesus comes, He calms *the storms of passion.* Life is doubly difficult for the man with the hot heart and the blazing temper. A friend met such a man. " I see," he said, " that you have succeeded in conquering your temper." " No," said the man, " I didn't conquer it. Jesus conquered it for me."

> " When deep within our swelling hearts
>   The thoughts of pride and anger rise,
> When bitter words are on our tongues
>   And tears of passion in our eyes,
> Then we may stay the angry blow,
>   Then we may check the hasty word,
> Give gentle answers back again,
>   And fight a battle for our Lord."

But it is a losing battle unless Jesus be with us to give us the calm of victory.

(iii) When Jesus comes, *He calms the storms of sorrow.* Into every life some day the tempest of sorrow must come, for sorrow is ever the penalty of love and if a man loves he will sorrow. When Pusey's wife died, he said, " It was as if there was a hand beneath my chin to hold me up." In that day, in the presence of Jesus, the tears are wiped away and the wounded heart is soothed.

THE DEFEAT OF THE DEMONS

Luke 8: 26-40

They came in their voyage to the district of the Gerasenes, which is across the lake from Galilee. When Jesus had disembarked on the land there met Him a man from the town who had demons. For a long time he had gone unclothed, and he did not stay in a house but amongst the tombs. When he saw Jesus he uttered a great cry and fell down before Him and shouted, " What have you and I to do with each other, Jesus, you Son of the Most High God? I beseech you—don't torture me! "—for Jesus had commanded the unclean spirit to come out of the man. For many a time it had snatched at him, and he was kept bound with chains and fetters, but when he was driven into the deserted places by the demons, he would burst the fetters. Jesus answered, " What is your name? " He said, " A regiment "—because many demons had entered into him, and they begged Him not to order them to depart to the abyss. There was a herd of many pigs there, feeding on the mountain-side. The demons asked Him to allow them to go into them. He did so. So the demons came out of the man and into the pigs, and the herd rushed down the precipice into the lake and were drowned. When those who were in charge of them saw what had happened, they fled and brought the story to the town and to the countryside round about. They came out to see what had happened. They came to Jesus and found the man from whom the demons had gone out sitting there at Jesus' feet, clothed and in his senses— and they were afraid. Those who had seen what had happened told them how the demon-possessed man had been cured; and the whole crowd from the Gerasene countryside asked Him to go away from them, because they were in the grip of a great fear. So He embarked on the ship and went away. The man from whom the demons had gone out begged to be allowed to go with Him; but He sent him away. " Go back," He said, " to your home and tell the story of all that God did for you." So he went away and proclaimed throughout the whole town all that God had done for him.

WE will never even begin to understand this story unless we realize that whatever we think about the demons, they were intensely real to the people of Gerasa and to the man whose mind was deranged. This man was a case of violent insanity. He was too dangerous to live amongst men and he lived amidst the tombs, which were believed to be the home and the haunt of demons. We may well note the sheer courage of Jesus in dealing with this man. The man had a maniacal strength which enabled him to snap his fetters. His fellow-men were very certainly so terrified of him that they would never try to do anything for him; but Jesus faced him calm and unafraid. When Jesus asked the man his name, he answered, " Legion." A Roman legion was a regiment of 6,000 soldiers. Doubtless this man had seen a Roman legion on the march, and his poor, afflicted mind felt that there was not one demon, but a whole regiment of demons inside him. It may well be that the very word haunted him, because very possibly he may have seen atrocities carried out by a Roman legion when he was a child. It is perfectly possible that it was these very atrocities which left a scar upon his mind and which ultimately sent him mad.

Far too much difficulty has been made out of the demons and the pigs. Jesus has been condemned for sending the demons into the innocent swine. That has been characterised as a cruel and immoral action. Again we must remember the intensity of the belief of these people in demons. The man, thinking the demons were speaking through him, besought Jesus not to send the demons into the abyss of hell to which they would be consigned in the final judgment. Let us see if we can form a picture of what happened. The man—and this is the essence of this part of the story—would never have believed that he was cured unless he had ocular and visible demonstration. Nothing less than the visible departure of the demons would have convinced him. Surely what happened was this. The herd of swine was feeding there on the mountain side. Jesus was exerting His power to cure what was a very stubborn case. Suddenly the man's wild cries and shouts and screams disturbed the swine and they went dashing down the steep place into the sea in blind terror. " Look! " said Jesus, " Look! There your demons are gone! " Jesus *had* to find a way to get into the mind of this poor man; and in that way He found it. In any event, can we compare the value of a herd of swine with the value of a man's immortal soul? If it cost the lives of these swine to save this man's soul, are we to complain? Is it not the case of a perverse fastidiousness which complains that swine were killed in order to heal a man? Surely we ought to preserve a sense of proportion. If the only way to convince this man of his cure was that the swine should perish, it seems a quite extraordinarily blind objection that the swine perished.

We must look at the reaction of two sets of people.

(i) There were *the Gerasenes*. They besought Jesus to

go away. (*a*) They hated having the routine of life disturbed. Life went peacefully on and then there arrived this disturbing Jesus and they hated Him. More people hate Jesus because He disturbs them than for any other reason. If Jesus says to a man, " You must give up this habit, you must change your life "; if Jesus says to an employer, " You can't be a Christian and make people work under conditions like that "; if Jesus says to a landlord, " You can't take money for slums like that "—one and all are liable to say to Him, " Go away and let me be in peace." That is an answer we are all liable to give. (*b*) They loved their swine more than they valued the soul of a man. One of life's supreme dangers is to value things above persons. That very tendency created the slums and created vicious working conditions. Much nearer home, that very tendency makes us selfishly demand our ease and comfort even if it means that someone who is tired has to slave and toil for us. No thing in this world can ever be as important as a person.

(ii) There was *the man who was cured*. Very naturally he wanted to come with Jesus, and Jesus sent him home. Christian witness, like Christian charity, begins at home. It would be so much easier to live and speak for Christ among people who do not know us. It is our duty, where Christ has set us, there to witness for Him. And if it should happen that we are the only Christian in the shop, the office, the school, the factory, the circle in which we live or work, that is not matter for lamentation. It is a challenge to us in which God says, " Go and tell the people you meet every day what I have done for you."

AN ONLY CHILD IS HEALED

Luke 8: 40-42 and 49-56

> When Jesus came back the crowd welcomed Him for they were all waiting for Him. A man called Jairus came to Him. He was the president of the Synagogue.

He threw himself at Jesus' feet and asked Him to come to his house, because he had an only daughter who was about twelve years of age and she was dying. As He went the crowd pressed round about Him . . . While He was still speaking someone came from the president's house. " Your daughter is dead," he said. " Don't bother the Master any more." Jesus heard this. " Don't be afraid," He said. " Just have faith and she will be cured." When He had come to the house He allowed no one to come in with Him, except Peter and John and James, and the girl's father and mother. They were all weeping and wailing for her. " Stop weeping," He said, " for she is not dead but sleeping." They laughed Him down because they were sure she was dead. He took hold of her hand and said to her, " Child, rise! " Her breath came back to her and immediately she rose. He told them to give her something to eat. Her parents were out of themselves with amazement; but He enjoined them to tell no one what had happened.

HERE is all the pathos of life suddenly turned to gladness. Very keenly Luke felt the tragedy of this girl's death. There were three things which made it so poignant. (a) She was an only child. Only Luke tells us that. The light of her parents' life had gone out. (b) She was about twelve years of age. That is to say she was just at the dawn of womanhood because children in the East develop much more quickly than in the West. She could even have been contemplating marriage at that age. What should have been the morning of life had become the night. (c) Jairus was the president of the Synagogue. That is to say, he was the man who was responsible for the administration of the Synagogue and the ordering of public worship. He had reached the highest post that life could give him in the respect of his fellow men. No doubt he was well to do; no doubt he had climbed the ladder of earthly ambition and prestige. It seemed as if life—as it sometimes does—had given lavishly of many things but was about to take the most precious thing away. All the pathos of life—which we know so well—is in the background of this story.

The wailing women had already come. To us it sounds almost repulsively artificial. But to hire these wailing women was in Palestine a token of respect to the dead that would never have been omitted. They were sure she was dead, but Jesus said that she was asleep. It is perfectly possible that Jesus meant this quite literally. It may well be that here we have a real miracle of diagnosis; that Jesus saw that the girl was in a deep trance, and that she was just on the point of being buried alive. From the evidence of the tombs in Palestine it is clear that many were buried alive. It could happen the more easily because climatic conditions in Palestine make burial within a matter of hours a sheer necessity. However that may be Jesus by His power gave her back her life.

We must note one very practical touch. Jesus ordered that the girl should be given something to eat. Is it possible that He was thinking just as much of the mother as of the girl? The mother, with the pain of grief and the sudden shock of joy, must have been almost on the point of collapse. At such a time to do some practical thing with one's hands is a life-saver. And it may well be that Jesus, in His kindly wisdom which knew human nature so well, was giving the overwrought mother a job to do to calm her nerves.

But by far the most interesting character in this story is Jairus.

(i) Jairus was clearly *a man who could pocket his pride.* He was the president of the Synagogue. By this time the Synagogue doors were rapidly closing on Jesus, if they had not already closed. He could have had no love for Jesus, and he, too, must have regarded Jesus as a breaker of the law. But in his hour of need, he pocketed his pride and asked for help. There is a famous story of Roland, the paladin of Charlemagne. He was in charge of the rearguard of the army and he was suddenly caught by the Saracens at Roncesvalles. The battle raged fiercely against terrible odds. Now Roland had a horn called Olivant which he had taken from the giant Jatmund and

its blast could be heard thirty miles away. So mighty was
it that, as they said, the birds fell dead when its blast tore
through the air. Oliver, his friend, besought him to blow
the horn so that Charlemagne would hear and come back
to help. But Roland was too proud to ask for help. One
by one his men fell fighting till only he was left. Then at
last with his dying breath he blew the horn, and when
Charlemagne heard he came hasting back. But it was too
late, for Roland, too, was dead. He was too proud to ask
for help. It is easy to be like that, to think that we can
handle life ourselves. But the way to find the miracles
of the grace of God is to pocket our pride and humbly to
confess our need and to ask. Ask and ye shall receive—
but there is no receiving without asking.

(ii) Jairus was clearly *a man of a stubborn faith.* Whatever
he felt, he did not wholly accept the verdict of the wailing
women; for with his wife he went into the room where
the girl lay. He hoped against hope. No doubt in his heart
there was the unvoiced feeling, " You never know what this
Jesus can do." And none of us knows all that Jesus can
do. In the darkest day we can still hope in the unsearchable
riches and the all-sufficient grace and the unconquerable
power of God.

NOT LOST IN THE CROWD

Luke 8: 43-48

There was a woman who had had a flow of blood for
twelve years. She had spent all her living on doctors
and she could not be cured by any of them. She came
up behind Jesus and she touched the tassel of His
robe; and immediately her flow of blood was stayed.
Jesus said, " Who touched me? " When they were
all denying that they had done so, Peter and his
companions said, " Master, the crowds are all round
you and press in upon you." Jesus said, " Someone
has touched me, for I know that power has gone out
of me." The woman saw that she could not hide.
She came all trembling; she threw herself at His feet;

and in front of everyone she told Him why she had touched Him, and that she had been cured there and then. " Daughter," He said to her, " your faith has cured you. Go in peace."

THIS story laid hold on the heart and the imagination of the early Church. It was believed that the woman was a Gentile from Caesarea Philippi. Eusebius, the great Church historian (A.D. 300), relates how it was said that the woman had at her own cost erected a statue commemorating her cure in her native city. It was said that that statue remained there until Julian, the Roman Emperor who tried to bring back the pagan gods, destroyed it, and erected his own in place of it, only to see his own statue blasted by a thunderbolt from God.

The shame of the woman was that ceremonially she was unclean (Leviticus 15: 19-33). Her issue of blood had cut her off from life. That was why she did not come openly to Jesus but crept up in the crowd; and that was why at first she was so embarrassed when Jesus asked who touched Him.

All devout Jews wore robes with fringes on them (Numbers 15: 37-41; Deuteronomy 22: 12). The fringes ended in four tassels of white thread with a blue thread woven through them. They were to remind the Jew every time he dressed and every time he saw them that he was a man of God and committed to the keeping of the laws of God. Later, when it was dangerous to be a Jew, these tassels were worn on the undergarments. Nowadays they still exist on the *talith* or shawl that the Jew wears round his head and shoulders when he is at prayer. But in the time of Jesus they were worn on the outer garment, and it was one of these the woman touched.

Luke, the doctor, here speaks again. Mark says of the woman that she had spent her all on the doctors and was no better, *but rather grew worse* (Mark 5: 26). But Luke misses out the final phrase because he did not like this gibe against the doctors!

The lovely thing about this story is that from the moment Jesus was face to face with the woman, there seems to be nobody there but He and she. It happened in the middle of the crowd; but the crowd was forgotten and Jesus spoke to that woman and treated her as if she was the only person in the world. She was a poor, unimportant sufferer, with a trouble that made her unclean, and yet to that one unimportant person, Jesus gave all of Himself.

We are very apt to attach labels to people and to treat them according to their relative importance. To Jesus a person had none of these man-made labels. He or she was simply a human soul in need. Love never thinks of people in terms of human importances. A distinguished visitor once came to call on Thomas Carlyle. He was working and could not be disturbed, but Jane, his wife, agreed to take this visitor up and open the door just a chink that he might at least see the sage. She did so, and as they looked in at Carlyle, immersed in his work and oblivious of all else, penning the books that made him famous all over the world, she said, " That's Tammas Carlyle about whom all the world is talking—*and he's my man.*" It was not in terms of the world's labels Jane thought, but in terms of love. A traveller tells how she was travelling in Georgia in the days before the Second World War. She was taken to see a very humble, poor, old woman in a little cottage. The old peasant woman asked her if she was going to Moscow. The traveller said she was. " Then," asked the woman, " would you mind delivering a parcel of home-made toffee to my son?" He could not get anything like it in Moscow. The son's name was Josef Stalin. We do not normally think of the late dictator of all the Russias as a man who liked toffee—but his mother did! For her the man-made labels did not matter.

Almost everybody would have regarded the woman in the crowd as totally unimportant. For Jesus she was someone in need, and therefore He, as it were, withdrew from the crowd, and gave Himself to her. " God loves each one of us as if there was only one of us to love."

EMISSARIES OF THE KING

Luke 9: 1-9

Jesus called The Twelve together and gave them power and authority over all demons, and to cure diseases. He sent them out to proclaim the Kingdom of God, and to cure those who were ill. He said to them, " Take nothing for the road, neither a staff nor a wallet, nor bread nor money, nor two tunics. Whatever house you go into, stay there, and leave from there. As for whoever do not receive you— when you leave that town shake off the dust from your feet as evidence against them." So they went out, and they went through the villages, preaching and healing everywhere.

Herod, the tetrarch, heard about the things which were going on. He did not know what to make of them, because it was said by some, " John is risen from the dead "; and by some, " Elijah has appeared "; and by others, " One of the prophets of the ancient days has risen again." But Herod said, " John I myself beheaded. Who is this about whom I hear such reports? " And he tried to see Him.

IN the ancient days there was in effect only one way of spreading a message abroad, and that was by word of mouth. Newspapers did not exist; books had to be hand-written, and a book the size of the New Testament would have cost £40 per copy to produce. Wireless, that great disseminator of news, had not even been dreamed of. That is why Jesus sent out The Twelve on this mission. He Himself was under the limitations of time and space. His helpers had to be mouths to speak for Him.

They were to travel light. That was simply because the man who travels light travels far and fast. The more a man is cluttered up with material things the more he is shackled to one place. God needs a settled ministry; but God also needs those who will abandon earthly things to adventure for Him.

If they were not received they were to shake off the dust off their feet when they left the town. When Rabbis entered Palestine after some journey in a Gentile land, they shook off the last particle of heathen dust from their feet. A village or town which would not receive them was to be treated as a strict Jew would treat a heathen country. It had refused its opportunity and had condemned itself.

That this ministry was mightily effective is plain from Herod's reaction. Things were happening. Perhaps Elijah, the forerunner, had at last come. Perhaps even the great promised prophet had arrived (Deuteronomy 18: 15). But " Conscience doth make cowards of us all," and there was a lingering fear in Herod's mind that John, the Baptiser, whom he thought he had eliminated, had come back to haunt him.

The one thing which stands out about the ministry which Jesus laid upon The Twelve is this—over and over again in this short passage *it joins preaching and healing*. It joins concern for men's bodies and men's souls. It was something which did not deal only in words, however comforting; it dealt in deeds. It was a message which was not confined to news of eternity; it proposed to change conditions on earth. It was the reverse of a religion of " pie in the sky." It insisted that health to men's bodies was as integral a part of God's purpose as health to their souls. Nothing has done the Church more harm than the repeated statement that the things of this world do not matter. In the middle thirties of our own times there was unemployment, and unemployment which invaded respectable and decent homes. The father's skill was rusting in idleness; the mother was trying to make a shilling do what a pound ought to do; children could not understand what was going on except that they went hungry. Men grew bitter or grew dully broken. To go and tell such people that material things makes no difference was an unforgiveable thing, especially if the teller was in reasonable comfort himself. General Booth was once blamed for offering food and meals to poor people instead of the simple gospel. The old warrior flashed back, " It is impossible to comfort men's hearts with the love of God when their feet are perishing with cold." Of course, it is possible to overstress material things. But it is equally possible to neglect them. The Church will forget only at her peril that Jesus first sent out His men *to preach the Kingdom and to heal*, to save men in body and in soul.

FOOD FOR THE HUNGRY

Luke 9: 10-17

> When the apostles returned they told Jesus all that they had done. So He took them and withdrew privately to a place called Bethsaida. When the crowds found out where He was they followed Him; and He welcomed them, and talked to them about the Kingdom of God, and healed those who had need of healing. The day began to draw to a close. The Twelve came to Him. "Send the crowd away," they said, "that they may go to the surrounding villages and countryside and find some place to stay and get food because here we are in a desert place." He said to them, "Do you give them food to eat." They said, "All we have is five loaves and two fishes—unless we go and buy food for all this people." For there were about five thousand men. He said to His disciples "Make them sit down in companies of fifty." They did so, and they got them all seated. He took the five loaves and the two fishes and looked up into heaven and blessed them and broke them and gave them to His disciples to set before the crowd. And all of them ate and were satisfied; and what they had left over was taken up and there were twelve baskets of the fragments.

THIS is the only miracle of Jesus which is related in all the four gospels (cp. Matthew 14: 13; Mark 6: 30; John 6: 1). It begins with a lovely thing. The Twelve had come back from their tour. Never was a time when Jesus needed more to be alone with them, so He took them to the neighbourhood of Bethsaida, which was a village on the far side of the Jordan to the north of the Sea of Galilee. When the people discovered where He had gone they followed Him out in their hordes—*and He welcomed them.* There is all the divine compassion here. Most people would have resented the invasion of their hard-won privacy. How would we feel if we had sought out some lonely place to be with our most intimate friends and suddenly a clamorous mob of people turned up with their insistent demands? Sometimes we are too busy to be disturbed. But, to Jesus, human need took precedence over everything.

The evening came; home was far away; and the people were tired and hungry. Jesus, astonishingly, ordered His disciples to give the people a meal. There are two ways in which a man can quite honestly look at this miracle. First, he can see in it simply a miracle in which Jesus created food for this vast multitude. Second, some people think that this is what happened. The people were hungry— *and they were utterly selfish.* They all had something with them, but they would not even produce it for themselves in case they had to share it with others. The Twelve laid before the multitude their little store, and thereupon others were moved to produce their little store, and in the end there was more than enough for everyone. So it may be regarded as a miracle which turned selfish, suspicious folk into generous people, a miracle of what happens, when moved by Christ, people are moved to share.

Before Jesus distributed the food He blessed it; He said grace. There was a Jewish saying that " he who enjoys anything without thanksgiving is as though he robbed God." The blessing which was said in every home in Palestine before every meal ran like this, " Blessed art Thou, Jehovah, our God, King of the world, who causest bread to come forth from the earth." Jesus would not eat without giving thanks to the Giver of all good gifts.

This is a story which tells us many things.

(i) *Jesus was concerned that men were hungry.* It would be a most interesting thing to try to work out how much time Jesus spent, not talking, but easing men's pain and satisfying men's hunger. Jesus still needs the service of men's hands. The mother who has spent a lifetime cooking meals for a hungry family; the nurse, the doctor, the friend, relation or parent, who has sacrificed life and time to ease another's pain; the social reformer who has burned himself out to seek better conditions for men and women— they have all preached a far more effective sermon than the man who talks, even if he is an orator.

(ii) *The help which Jesus gives is generous.* There was enough, and more than enough. In love there is no nice calculation of the less and more. God is like that. When we sow a packet of seeds we usually have to thin the plants out, and we often have to throw away far more than we can keep. God has created a world where there is more than enough for all if men will share it.

(iii) As always there is a permanent truth in an action in time. *In Jesus all men's needs are supplied.* There is a hunger of the soul; there is in every man, sometimes at least, a longing to find something in which he may invest his life. Our hearts are restless until they rest in Him. " My God shall supply all your need," said Paul (Philippians 4: 19)—even in the desert places of this life.

THE GREAT DISCOVERY

Luke 9: 18-22

> It happened that when Jesus was praying alone His disciples were with Him. He asked them, " Who do the crowds say that I am? " They answered, " Some say that you are John the Baptiser; others that you are Elijah; others that one of the prophets of the ancient days has risen again." He said to them, " But *you*—who do you say that I am? " Peter answered, " The Anointed One of God." Jesus warned and enjoined them to tell this to no one. " The Son of Man," He said, " must suffer many things, and must be rejected by the elders and chief priests and scribes, and must be killed, and must be raised again on the third day."

THIS is one of the most crucial moments in the whole life of Jesus. He asked this question when He was already turning His face to go to Jerusalem (Luke 9: 51). He well knew what awaited Him there, and the answer to this question was of supreme importance. What Jesus *knew* was that He Himself was going to a Cross to die. What He *wanted to know* before He went was, " Was there anyone who had really discovered who He was?" The answer would make all the difference. If there was no answer, but dull incomprehension, it meant that all His work had gone for nothing. If there was an answer of realization, however incomplete, it meant that He had lit such a torch in the hearts of men as time would never put out. How Jesus' heart must have lifted when Peter's sudden discovery rushed to his lips—" You are the Anointed One of God!" When Jesus heard that He knew He had not failed.

But not only had The Twelve to discover that fact; they had also to discover what that fact meant. They had grown up against a background of thought in which they had been taught to expect from God a conquering King who would lead them to world dominion. Peter's eyes would blaze with flaming excitement when he said this. But Jesus had to teach them that God's Anointed One had come to die upon a Cross. He had to take their ideas of God and of God's purposes and turn them upside down; and from this time that is what He set Himself to do. They had discovered who He was; now they had to discover what that discovery meant.

There are two great general truths in this passage.

(i) Jesus began by asking what men were saying about Him; and then, suddenly, He flashes the question at The Twelve, " Who do *you* say that I am?" It is never enough to know what other people have said about Jesus. A man might be able to pass any examination on what has been said and thought about Jesus; he might have read every book about Christology which has been written in every language upon earth and still not be a Christian. Jesus must always be our own personal discovery. Our religion can never be a carried tale. To every man Jesus comes asking, not, "Can you tell me what others have said and written about me?" but, "Who do *you* say that I am?" Paul did not say, "I know *what* I have believed"; he said, "I know *whom* I have believed" (2 Timothy 1: 12). Christianity does not mean reciting a creed; it means knowing a person.

(ii) In this passage we listen to the word *must* on the lips of Jesus. "I must," He said, "go to Jerusalem and die." It is of the greatest interest to look at the times in Luke's gospel when Jesus said *must*. "I *must* be in my Father's house," He said (2: 49). "I *must preach* the Kingdom," He said (4: 43). "I *must* walk to-day and to-morrow," He said (13: 33). Over and over again He told His disciples how He *must* go to His Cross (9: 22; 17: 25; 24: 7). Jesus was one who knew that He had a destiny to fulfil. God's will was His will. He had no other object but to do upon earth what God had sent Him to do. The Christian, like His Lord, is a man under orders.

THE CONDITIONS OF SERVICE

Luke 9: 23-27

> Jesus said to them all, "If any man wishes to come after me, let him deny himself, and day by day let him take up his cross and follow me. Whoever wishes to save his life will lose it. Whoever loses his life for my sake will save it. What profit is it to a man if he gains the whole world and loses himself or has himself confiscated? Whoever is ashamed of me and of my words, of him shall the Son of Man be ashamed when He shall come in His own glory, and in the glory of His Father and of the holy angels. I tell you truly that there are some of these who are standing here who will not taste death until they see the Kingdom of God."

HERE Jesus lays down the conditions of service for those who would follow Him.

(i) A man must deny himself. What does that mean? A great scholar comes at the meaning in this way. Peter once *denied* his Lord. That is to say, he said of Jesus, " I do not know the man." To deny ourselves is to say, " I do not know myself." It is to ignore the very existence of oneself. It is to treat the self as if it did not exist. Usually we treat ourselves as if our self was far and away the most important thing in the world. If we are to follow Jesus we must obliterate self and forget that self exists.

(ii) A man must take up his cross. What does that mean? Jesus well knew what crucifixion meant. When He was a lad of about eleven years of age Judas the Galilaean had led a rebellion against Rome. He had raided the royal armoury at Sepphoris, which was only four miles from Nazareth. The Roman vengeance was swift and sudden. Sepphoris was burned to the ground; its inhabitants were sold into slavery; and two thousand of the rebels were crucified on crosses which were set in lines along the roadside that they might be a dreadful warning to others tempted to rebel. To take up our cross means to be prepared to face things like that for loyalty to God; it means to be ready to endure the worst that man can do to us for the sake of being true to God.

(iii) A man must spend his life, not hoard it. The whole gamut of the world's standards must be changed. The questions are not, " How much can I *get*? " but, " How much can I *give*? " Not, " What is the *safe* thing to do? " but, " What is the *right* thing to do? " Not, " What is the minimum permissible in the way of work? " but, " What is the maximum possible? " The Christian must realize that he is given life, not to keep it for himself, but to spend it for others; not to husband its flame, but to burn himself out for Christ and for men.

(iv) Loyalty to Jesus will have its reward, and disloyalty its punishment. If we are true to Him in time, He will be true to us in eternity. If we seek to follow Him in this world, in the next world He will point to us as one of His people. But if by our lives we disown Him, even though with our lips we confess Him, the day must come when He cannot do other than disown us.

(v) In the last verse of this passage, Jesus says that some of those standing there will see the Kingdom of God before they die. Some people wish to maintain that when Jesus said this He was looking forward to His return in glory, that He declared that that would happen within the lifetime of some of those standing there, and that therefore He was completely mistaken. That is not so. What Jesus was saying is this, " Before this generation has passed away you will see signs that the Kingdom of God is on the way." Beyond a doubt that was true. Something came into the world which, like leaven in dough, began to change the world. It would be well if, sometimes, we turned from our pessimism and thought rather of the light that has been slowly breaking on the world.

As A. H. Clough wrote,

" Say not the struggle naught availeth,
    The labour and the wounds are vain,
The enemy faints not, nor faileth,
    And as things have been they remain.

If hopes were dupes, fears may be liars;
    It may be, in yon smoke conceal'd,
Your comrades chase e'en now the fliers,
    And, but for you, possess the field.

For while the tired waves, vainly breaking,
    Seem here no painful inch to gain,
Far back, through creeks and inlets making,
    Comes silent, flooding in, the main.

And not by eastern windows only,
    When daylight comes, comes in the light;
In front the sun climbs slow, how slowly!
    But westward, look, the land is bright! "

Be of good cheer—The Kingdom is on the way—and we do well to thank God for every sign of its dawning.

THE MOUNTAIN TOP OF GLORY

Luke 9: 28-36

About eight days after these words, Jesus took Peter and John and James and went up into a mountain to pray. While He was praying the appearance of His face became different and His clothing became white as the lightning's flash. And—look you— two men were talking with Him, who were Moses and Elijah. They appeared in glory, and they talked about the departure which He was going to accomplish in Jerusalem. Peter and his friends were heavy with sleep. When they were fully awake they saw His glory, and the two men standing with Him. And when they were going to leave Him, Peter said, " Master, it is good for us to be here. So let us make three booths, one for you and one for Moses and one for Elijah," for he did not know what he was saying. As he was saying this a cloud came and overshadowed them and they feared as they entered into the cloud. A voice came from the cloud saying, " This is My Beloved Son, My Chosen One! Hear Him! " And when the voice had passed, Jesus was found alone. They kept silent in those days and did not tell anyone anything about what they had seen.

HERE we have another of the great hinges in Jesus' life upon earth. We must remember that He was just about to set out to Jerusalem and to the Cross. We have already looked at one great moment when He asked His disciples who they believed Him to be in order that He might discover if anyone had realized who He was. But there was one thing which Jesus would never do—He would never take any step without the approval of God. In this scene that is what we see Him seeking and receiving. What happened on the Mount of Transfiguration we can never know, but we do know that something tremendous did happen. Jesus had gone there to seek the approval of God for the decisive step that He was about to take. There Moses and Elijah appeared to Him. Moses was the great law-giver of the people of Israel; Elijah was the greatest of the prophets. It was as if the princes of Israel's life and thought and religion told Jesus to go on. Jesus could set out to Jerusalem now, certain that at least one little group of men knew who He was, certain that what He was doing was the consummation of all the life and thought and work of His nation, and certain that God approved of the step that He was taking.

There is one vivid sentence here. It says of the three apostles, " When they were fully awake they saw His glory."

(i) In life we miss so much because our minds are asleep. There are certain things which are very liable to keep our minds asleep. (*a*) There is *prejudice*. We may be so set in our ideas that our minds are shut. A new idea knocks at the door of them but we are like sleepers who will not awake. (*b*) There is mental *lethargy*. There are so many who refuse the strenuous struggle of thought. " The unexamined life," said Plato, " is the life not worth living." But how many of us have really thought things out and thought them through? It was said of someone that he had skirted the howling deserts of infidelity, whereat a wiser man said that he would have been better to have fought his way through them. Sometimes we are so lethargic that we will not even face our questions and our doubts. (*c*) There is *the love of ease*. There is a kind of defence mechanism in us that makes us automatically shut the door against any disturbing thought. A man can drug himself mentally until his mind is sound asleep.

(ii) But life is full of things which are designed to waken us. (*a*) There is *sorrow*. Once Elgar said of a young singer, who was technically perfect, but quite without feeling and expression, " She will be great when something breaks her heart." Often sorrow can rudely awaken a man, but in that moment, through the tears he will see the glory. (*b*) There is *love*. Somewhere Browning tells of two people who fell in love. She looked at him. He looked at her as a lover can—" and suddenly life awoke." Real love is an awakening to horizons which we never dreamed were there.

(c) There is *the sense of need*. For long enough a man may live the routine of life, half asleep; and then all of a sudden into life there comes some completely insoluble problem, some quite unanswerable question, some overmastering temptation, some summons to an effort which he feels is beyond his strength. In that day there is nothing left for him to do but to " cry, clinging heaven by the hems." And that sense of need awakens him to God.

We would do well to pray, " Lord, keep me always awake to Thee."

COMING DOWN FROM THE MOUNT

Luke 9: 37-45

> On the next day, when they had come down from the mountain, a great crowd of people met Him. And—look you—a man shouted from the crowd, " Teacher, I beg you to look with pity upon my son, because he is my only child. And—look you—a spirit seizes him and he suddenly shouts out; he convulses him until he foams at the mouth; he shatters him and will hardly leave him. I begged your disciples to cast out the spirit but they could not do it." Jesus answered, " O faithless and twisted generation! How long will I be with you? How long will I bear you? Bring your son here." While he was coming the demon dashed him down and convulsed him. Jesus rebuked the unclean spirit and healed the boy, and gave him back to his father; and everyone was astonished at the majesty of God.
>
> While they were all wondering at the things which He kept doing, He said to His disciples, " Let these words sink into your ears—the Son of Man is going to be delivered into the hands of men." They did not know what this word meant; and its meaning was concealed from them so that they did not perceive it; and they were afraid to ask Him about this word.

No sooner had Jesus descended from the mountain top than the demands and the disappointments of life were upon Him. A man had come to the disciples seeking their help, for his only son was an epileptic. Of course his epilepsy was attributed to the malign activity of a demon. The word used in verse 42 is very vivid. As he was coming to Jesus, the demon *dashed him down*. It is the word which is used of a boxer dealing a knock-out blow to his opponent or of a wrestler throwing someone. It must have been a pitiful sight to see the lad convulsed; and the disciples were quite helpless to cure him. But when Jesus came He dealt with the situation with calm mastery and gave the boy back to his father, cured and healed.

In this passage two things stand out.

(i) The moment on the mount is absolutely necessary, but it cannot be prolonged beyond its own time. If the ascent to the mountain is essential the descent from the mountain is just as imperative. Peter, not really knowing what he was saying, would have liked to linger on the mountain top. He wished to build three tabernacles there that they might stay there in all the glory. Often there comes to us moments that we would like to prolong indefinitely. But after the time on the mountain top we must come back to the battle and the routine of life. We are not meant to live withdrawn upon the mountain top; that time is meant to give us strength for life's everyday. After the great struggle at Mount Carmel with the prophets of Baal, Elijah, in reaction, ran away. Out into the desert he went, and there as the old story runs, as he lay under a juniper tree asleep, an angel twice prepared a meal for him. And then there comes the sentence, " And he arose and did eat and drink and went in the strength of that meat forty days and forty nights " (I Kings 19: 1-8). To the mountain top of the presence of God we must go, but not to remain there, but to go in the strength of that time for many days. It was said of Captain Scott, the great explorer, that he was " a strange mixture of the dreamy and the practical, and never more practical than immediately after he had been dreamy." We cannot live forever in the moment on the mountain but we cannot live at all without it.

(ii) In no incident is the sheer competence of Jesus so clearly shown. When He came down from the mountain the whole situation was quite out of hand. The whole impression is that of people running about not knowing what to do. The disciples were helplessly baffled; the boy's father was bitterly disappointed and upset. Into this scene of disorder came Jesus. He gripped the whole situation in a flash, and in His mastery the disorder became a calm. So often we feel that life is out of control; that we have lost our grip on things. Only the Master of life can deal with life with this calm competence which brings everything under control.

(iii) But once again the incident finished with Jesus pointing at the Cross. Here was triumph; here Jesus had mastered the demons and astonished the people. And in that very moment when they were ready to acclaim Him, Jesus told them that He was on the way to die. It would have been so easy for Jesus to take the way of popular success; it was His greatness that He rejected it and chose the Cross. He would not Himself shirk that Cross to which He called others.

TRUE GREATNESS

Luke 9: 46-48

> There arose an argument amongst them as to which of them should be the greatest. But when Jesus knew the thoughts of their hearts He took a child and set him beside Him. "Whoever," He said to them, "receives this child in my name, receives me; and whoever receives me, receives Him that sent me. He who is least among you, he it is who is the greatest."

So long as The Twelve thought of Jesus' Kingdom as an earthly kingdom it was quite inevitable that they should be in competition for the highest places in it. Long ago the Venerable Bede suggested that this particular quarrel arose because Jesus had taken Peter, John and James up into the mountain top with Him, and because the others were jealous.

Jesus knew what was going on in their hearts. He took a child and placed him beside Himself; that seat would be the seat of highest honour. He went on to say that whoever received a little child, received Him; and whoever received Him, received God. What did He mean? The child was quite unimportant. The Twelve were the chosen lieutenants of Jesus; but this child occupied no place of honour and held no official position. So Jesus said, " If you are prepared to spend your lives serving people, helping people, loving people who, in the eyes of the world, do not matter at all, you are serving me and you are serving God." Jesus said, " If you are prepared to spend your life doing the apparently unimportant things and never trying to be what the world calls great, then you will be great in the eyes of God." There are so many wrong motives for service.

(i) There is the desire for *prestige*. A. J. Cronin tells of a district nurse he knew when he was in practice as a doctor. For twenty years, single-handed, she had served a ten-mile district. " I marvelled," he says, " at her patience, her fortitude and her cheerfulness. She was never too tired at night to rise for an urgent call. Her salary was most inadequate, and late one night, after a particularly strenuous day, I ventured to protest to her, ' Nurse, why don't you make them pay you more? God knows you are worth it.' ' If God knows I'm worth it,' she answered, ' that's all that matters to me.' " She was working, not for men, but for God. And when we work for God prestige will be the last thing that enters into our mind for we will know that our best is not good enough for God.

(ii) There is the desire for *place*. If ever a man is given a task or a position or an office in the Church, he should regard it not as an honour but as a responsibility. There are those who serve within the Church, not thinking really of those they serve, but thinking of themselves. A certain English Prime Minister was offered congratulations on attaining to that office. " I do not want your congratulations," he said, " but I do want your prayers." To be chosen for office is to be set apart for service, not elevated to honour in the eyes of men.

(iii) There is the desire for *prominence*. Many a person will serve or give so long as his service and his generosity are known, so long as he is thanked and praised. It is Jesus' own instruction that we should not let our left hand know what our right hand is doing. If we give, only to gain something out of the giving for ourselves, we have undone all the good we might have done.

TWO LESSONS IN TOLERANCE

Luke 9: 49-56

> John said to Jesus, " Master, we saw a man casting out demons in your name; and we stopped him because he does not follow with us." Jesus said to him, " Don't try to stop him, for he who is not against us is for us."
>
> When the days that He should be received up were on their way to being completed He fixed His face firmly to go to Jerusalem. He sent messengers on ahead. When they had gone on they went into a village of the Samaritans to make ready for Him; and they refused to receive them because His face was set in the direction of Jerusalem. When His disciples, James and John, learned of this they said, " Lord, would you like us to order fire to come down from heaven and destroy them? " He turned to them and rebuked them; and they went on to another village.

HERE we have two lessons in tolerance.

There were many exorcists in Palestine, all claiming to be able to cast out demons; and no doubt John regarded this man as a competitor and wished to eliminate him.

The direct way from Galilee to Jerusalem led through Samaria; but most Jews avoided it. There was a centuries' old quarrel between the Jews and the Samaritans (John 4: 9). The Samaritans in fact did everything they could to hinder and even to injure any bands of pilgrims who attempted to pass through their territory. For Jesus to take that way to Jerusalem was unusual; and to attempt to find hospitality in a Samaritan village was still more unusual. When Jesus did this He was extending a hand of friendship to a people who were enemies. In this case not only was hospitality refused, but the offer of friendship was spurned. No doubt James and John believed they were doing a most praiseworthy thing when they offered to call in divine aid to blot out the village.

There is no passage in which Jesus so directly teaches the duty of tolerance as in this. In many ways tolerance is a lost virtue, and, where it does exist, it exists from the wrong cause. Of all the greatest religious leaders none was such a pattern of tolerance as John Wesley. " I have no more right," he said, " to object to a man for holding a different opinion from mine that I have to differ with a man because he wears a wig and I wear my own hair; but if he takes his wig off and shakes the powder in my face, I shall consider it my duty to get quit of him as soon as possible." " The thing," he said, " which I resolved to use every possible method of preventing was a narrowness of spirit, a party zeal, a being straitened in our own bowels— that miserable bigotry which makes many so unready to believe that there is any work of God but among themselves." " We think," he said, " and let think." When his nephew, Samuel, the son of his brother Charles, entered the Roman Catholic Church, John Wesley wrote to him, " Whether in this Church or that I care not. You may be saved in either or damned in either; but I fear you are not born again." The Methodist invitation to the sacrament is simply, " Let all who love the Lord come here." The conviction that our beliefs and our methods alone are correct has been the cause of more tragedy and distress in the Church than almost any other thing. Oliver Cromwell wrote once to the intransigent Scots, " I beseech you by the bowels of Christ, think it possible that you may be mistaken." T. R. Glover somewhere quotes a saying, " Remember that whatever your hand finds to do, some- one thinks differently! "

There are many ways to God. God has His own secret stairway into every heart. God fulfils Himself in many ways; and no man and no Church has a monopoly of the truth of God.

But—and this is intensely important—our tolerance must be based not on indifference but on love. We are not tolerant because—as the modern phrase has it—we could not care less; but because we look at the other person, not with the eyes of criticism, but with the eyes of love. When Abraham Lincoln was criticized for being too cour- teous to his enemies and when he was reminded that it was his duty to destroy them, he gave the great answer, " Do I not destroy my enemies when I make them my friends? " Even if a man be utterly mistaken we must never regard him as an enemy to be destroyed, but as a strayed friend to be recovered by love.

THE HONESTY OF JESUS

Luke 9: 57-62

> As they were journeying along the road, a man said to Jesus, " I will follow you wherever you go." Jesus said to him, " The foxes have dens; the birds of the air have places to roost; but the Son of Man has nowhere to lay His head."
>
> He said to another man, " Follow Me! " " Lord," he said, " let me go first and bury my father." He said to him, " Let the dead bury their dead; but do you go and tell abroad the news of the Kingdom of God."
>
> Another man said to Him, " Lord, I will follow you; but let me first say good-bye to the folk at home." Jesus said to him, " No man who puts his hand to the plough and looks back is the right kind of man for the Kingdom of God."

HERE we have the words of Jesus to three would-be followers.

(i) To the first man, Jesus' advice was, " Before you follow me, count the cost." No one can ever say that he was induced to follow Jesus under false pretences. Jesus paid men the compliment of pitching His demands so high that they cannot be higher. It may well be that we have hurt the Church very seriously by trying to tell people that Church membership need not make so very much difference; we would be better to tell them that it must make all the difference in the world. We might have fewer people; but those we had would be totally pledged to Christ.

(ii) Jesus' words to the second man sound harsh, but they need not be so. In all probability the man's father was not dead, and not even nearly dead. His saying most likely meant, " I will follow you after my father has died." An English official in the East tells of a very brilliant Arab young man. So brilliant was he that it would have been perfectly possible for him to come to Oxford or Cambridge on a scholarship. Such a scholarship was offered to him. His answer was, " I will take it after I have buried my father." At the time his father was not much more than forty years of age. The point that Jesus was making is that in everything there is a crucial moment; if that moment is missed the thing most likely will never be done at all. This man in the story had stirrings in his heart to get out of his spiritually dead surroundings. If he missed the moment he would never get out. The psychologists tell us that every time we have a fine feeling, if we do not act on that feeling at once, the less likely we are to act on it each time. The emotion becomes a substitute for the action. Take one example—sometimes we feel that we would like to write a letter, perhaps of sympathy, perhaps of thanks, perhaps of congratulations, to someone. Unless we do it on the moment, if we put it off until to-morrow, it will in all likelihood never be written at all. It is Jesus' insistence that we must act at once when our hearts are stirred within us.

(iii) Jesus' words to the third man state a truth which no one can deny. No ploughman ever ploughed a straight furrow looking back over his shoulder. There are some whose hearts are in the past. They walk forever looking backwards and thinking wistfully of the good old days. Watkinson, the great preacher, tells how once at the seaside, when he was with his little grandson, they met an old minister. The old man was very disgruntled and, to add to all his troubles, he had a slight touch of sunstroke. The little boy had been listening, but had not picked it up quite correctly; and when they left the grumbling complaints of the old man, he turned to Watkinson and said, " Granddad, I hope *you* never suffer from a *sunset*! " The Christian marches on, not to the sunset, but to the dawn. The watchword of the Kingdom is not, " Backwards!" but, " Forwards!" To this man Jesus did not say either, " Follow!" or, " Return! " He said, " I accept no lukewarm service," and left the man to make his own decision.

LABOURERS FOR THE HARVEST

Luke 10: 1-16

After these things the Lord appointed other seventy men and sent them out in twos ahead of Him into every town and place where He intended to go. " The harvest is great," He said to them, " but the workers are few. Pray then the Lord of the harvest to send out workers for the harvest. Go! Look you—I am sending you out as sheep in the midst of wolves, Do not take a purse or a wallet or sandals. Greet no one on the road. Into whatever house you go. say first of all, ' Peace to this house! ' If it is a son of peace who lives there your peace will remain upon it; but if not it will return to you. Remain in the same house eating and drinking whatever they give you; for the workman deserves his pay. Do not go from house to house. If you go into any town and

they receive you, eat what is put before you. Heal
those in it who are ill, and keep saying to them, ' The
Kingdom of God has come near you!' If you go into
any town and they do not receive you, go out into
its streets and say, ' The very dust which clings to
our feet from this town, we wipe off against you.
But realize this—the Kingdom of God has come near
you!' I tell you, things will be easier for Sodom in
that day than for that town. Woe to you Chorazin!
Woe to you Bethsaida! For if the mighty works which
have been done in you had been done in Tyre and
Sidon, they would long ago have sat in dust and ashes
and repented. But at the judgment things will be
easier for Tyre and Sidon than for you. And you
Capernaum—will you be exalted to Heaven? You will
be cast down to Hell. He who listens to you, listens
to me; and he who sets no value on you, sets no value
on me; and he who sets no value on me, sets no value
on Him that sent me.''

THIS passage describes a wider mission than the first mission
of The Twelve. The number seventy was to the Jews a
symbolic number. (*a*) It was the number of the elders
who were chosen to help Moses with the task of leading
and directing the people in the wilderness (Numbers 11:
16, 17, 24, 25). (*b*) It was the number of the Sanhedrin,
the supreme council of the Jews. If we relate The Seventy to
either of these bodies they will be the helpers of Jesus.
(*c*) It was held to be the number of nations in the world.
Luke was the man with the universalist view, and it may
well be that he was thinking of the day when every nation
in the world would know and love his Lord.

There is one interesting sidelight here. One of the towns
on which woe is pronounced is Chorazin. It is implied
that Jesus did many mighty works there. In the gospel
history as we have it Chorazin is never even mentioned,
and we do not know one thing that Jesus did or one word
that Jesus spoke there. Nothing could show so vividly
how much we do not know about the life of Jesus. The
gospels are not biographies; they are only sketches of the
life of Jesus (cp. John 21: 25).

This passage tells us certain supremely important things about both the preacher and the hearer.

(i) The preacher is not to be cluttered up with material things; he is to travel light. It is easy to get entangled and enmeshed in the things of this life. Once Dr. Johnson, after seeing through a great castle and its policies, remarked grimly, " These are the things which make it difficult to die." Earth must never blot out heaven.

(ii) The preacher is to concentrate on his task. He is to greet no man on the way. This goes back to Elisha's instruction to Gehazi in 2 Kings 4: 19. It is not an instruction to discourtesy; but it does mean that the man of God must not turn aside or linger on the lesser things while the great things call him.

(iii) The preacher must not be in the work for what he can get out of it. He is to eat what is put before him; he must not move from house to house seeking better and more comfortable quarters. It was not long before the Church has its spongers. There is a work called *The Teaching of the Twelve Apostles*. It was written about A.D. 100, and it is the Church's first book of order. In those days there were prophets who wandered from town to town. It is laid down that if a prophet wishes to stay in a place for more than three days without working he is a false prophet; and if a prophet in the Spirit asks for money or a meal he is a false prophet! The labourer is worthy of his hire, but the servant of a crucified Master cannot be a seeker for luxury.

(iv) Of the hearer, this passage tells us that to have heard God's word is a great responsibility. A man will be judged according to what he had the chance to know. We allow things in a child we condemn in an adult; we forgive things in a savage we would punish in a civilized man. Responsibility is the other side of privilege.

(v) It is a terrible thing to reject God's invitation. There is a sense in which every promise of God that a man has ever heard can become his condemnation. If he receives these promises they are his greatest glory, but each one that he has heard and rejected will some day be a witness against him.

A MAN'S TRUE GLORY

Luke 10: 17-20

> The Seventy returned with joy. "Lord," they said, "at your name the demons are subject to us." He said to them, "I saw Satan fall like lightning from Heaven. Look you—I have given you authority to walk upon snakes and scorpions and over all the power of the Enemy. Nothing will hurt you. But do not rejoice in this—that the spirits are subject to you; but rejoice that your names are written in Heaven."

WHEN The Seventy returned they were radiant with the triumphs which they had wrought in the name of Jesus. Jesus said to them, "I saw Satan fall like lightning from Heaven." That is a difficult phrase to understand. It can have two meanings.

(i) It may mean, "I saw the forces of darkness and evil defeated; the citadel of Satan is stormed and the Kingdom of God is on the way." It may mean that Jesus knew that the deathblow to Satan and all his powers had been struck, however long his final conquest might be delayed; that, as a great scholar put it, D day has been accomplished and sooner or later V day is bound to follow.

(ii) But equally well it may be a warning against pride. The legend was that it was for a pride which rebelled against God that Satan was cast out of Heaven where once he had been the chief of the angels. It may be that Jesus was saying to The Seventy, "You have had your triumphs; keep yourselves from pride, for once the chief of all the angels fell to pride and was cast from heaven."

Certainly Jesus went on to warn His disciples against pride and over-confidence. It was true that they were given all power, but their greatest glory was that their names were written in heaven.

It will always remain true that a man's greatest glory is not what he has done but what God has done for him. It might well be claimed that the discovery of the use of chloroform saved the world more pain than any other single medical discovery. Once someone asked Sir James Simpson, its discoverer, "What do you regard as your greatest discovery?" The questioner naturally expected the answer, "The discovery of chloroform." But Simpson answered, "My greatest discovery was when I discovered that Jesus Christ is my Saviour." Even the greatest man can only say in the presence of God,

> "Nothing in my hand I bring,
> Simply to Thy Cross I cling;
> Naked, come to Thee for dress;
> Helpless, look to Thee for grace;
> Foul, I to the fountain fly;
> Wash me, Saviour, or I die."

It is pride which bars from heaven; it is humility which is the passport to the presence of God.

THE UNSURPASSABLE CLAIM

Luke 10: 21-24

At that time Jesus rejoiced in the Holy Spirit. "I thank you, O Father, Lord of Heaven and earth," He said, "that you have hidden these things from the wise and clever and that you have revealed them to babes. Yes, O Father, for so it was your good pleasure in your sight. All things have been handed over to me by my Father. No one knows who the Son is except the Father; and no one knows who the Father is except the Son, and he to whom the Son wishes to reveal Him." He turned to His disciples when they were in private and said, "Happy are the eyes which see the things which you are seeing for I tell you that many prophets and kings desired to see the things that you are seeing and did not see them, and to hear the things that you are hearing and did not hear them."

THERE are three great thoughts in this passage.

(i) Verse 21 tells us of the wisdom of simplicity. The simple mind could receive the truths that the learned mind could not take in. Once Arnold Bennet said that, " The only way to write a great book was to write it with the eyes of a child who sees things for the first time." It is possible to be too clever. It is quite possible to be so clever and so learned that in the end we cannot see the wood for the trees. Someone has said that the test of a really great scholar is how much he is able to forget. After all, we must always remember this—that Christianity does not mean knowing all the theories about the New Testament; still less does it mean knowing all the theologies and the Christologies; because Christianity does not mean *knowing about Christ*; it means *knowing Christ*; and to do that requires not earthly wisdom but heavenly grace.

(ii) Verse 22 tells of the unique relationship between Jesus and God. This is what the Fourth Gospel means when it says, " The Word became flesh " (John 1: 14), or when it makes Jesus say, " I and my Father are one," or, " He who hath seen me hath seen the Father " (John 10: 30; 14: 9). To the Greeks God was unknowable. There was a great gulf fixed between matter and spirit, man and God. " It is very difficult," they said, " to know God, and when you do know Him it is impossible to tell anyone else about Him." But when Jesus came He said, " If you want to know what God is like, look at me." Jesus did not so much tell men about God; He showed men God, because in Him were the mind and the heart of God towards men.

(iii) Verses 23 and 24 tell us that Jesus is the consummation of all history. In these verses Jesus said, " I am the One to whom all the prophets and the saints and the kings looked forward and for whom they longed." This is what Matthew means when over and over again in his gospel he wrote, " This was done that it might be fulfilled which was spoken by the prophet saying . . . "

cp. Matthew 2: 15, 17, 23). Jesus was the peak to which history had been climbing, the goal to which it had been marching, the dream which had ever haunted men of God. If we desire to express this in terms of modern thought we might dare to put it this way. We believe in evolution, the slow climb upwards of man from the level of the beasts Jesus is the end and climax of the evolutionary process because in Him, man met God, and He is at once the perfection of manhood and the fulness of godhead.

WHO IS MY NEIGHBOUR?

Luke 10: 25-37

Look you—an expert in the law stood up and asked Jesus a test question. " Teacher," he said, " What is it that, if I do it, I will become the possessor of eternal life? " He said to him, " What stands written in the law? How do you read? " He answered, " You must love the Lord your God with your whole heart, and with your whole soul, and with your whole strength, and with your whole mind, and your neighbour as yourself." " Your answer is correct," said Jesus. But he, wishing to put himself in the right, said to Jesus, " And who is my neighbour? " Jesus answered, " There was a man who went down from Jerusalem to Jericho. He fell amongst brigands who stripped him and laid blows upon him, and went away and left him half-dead. Now, by chance, a priest came down by that road. He looked at him and passed by on the other side. In the same way when a Levite came to the place he looked at him and passed by on the other side. A Samaritan who was on the road came to where he was. He looked at him and was moved to the depths of his being with pity. So he came up to him and bound up his wounds, pouring in wine and oil; and he put him on his own beast and brought him to an inn and cared for him. On the next day he put down two shillings and gave them to the inn-keeper. ' Look after him,' he said, ' and whatever more you are out of pocket, when I come back this way, I'll square up with you in full.' Which of these three, do you think, was neighbour to the man who fell into the hands of brigands?" He said, "He who showed mercy on him." "Go," said Jesus to him, "and do likewise."

FIRST, let us look at *the scene* of this story. The road from Jerusalem to Jericho was a notoriously dangerous road. Jerusalem is 2,300 feet above sea-level; the Dead Sea near which Jericho stood, is 1,300 feet below sea-level. So then, in little more than 20 miles, this road dropped 3,600 feet. It was a road of narrow, rocky defiles, and of sudden turnings which made it the happy hunting-ground of brigands. In the fifth century Jerome tells us that it was still called "The Red, or Bloody Way." In the 19th century it was still necessary to pay safety money to the local Sheiks before one could travel on it. As late as the early 1930's H. V. Morton tells us that he was warned to get home before dark, if he intended to use the road, because a certain Abu Jildah was an adept at holding up cars and robbing travellers and tourists, and escaping to the hills before the police could arrive. When Jesus told this story, He was telling about the kind of thing that was constantly happening on this Jerusalem to Jericho road.

Second, let us look at the *characters*. (*a*) There was *the traveller*. He was obviously a reckless and foolhardy character. People seldom attempted the Jerusalem to Jericho road alone if they were carrying goods or valuables. Seeking safety in numbers, they always travelled in convoys or caravans. This man had no one but himself to blame for the plight in which he found himself. (*b*) There was *the priest*. The priest hastened past the man. No doubt he was remembering that he who touched a dead man was unclean for seven days (Numbers 19: 11). He could not be sure, but he feared that the man was dead; and if he touched him, he would lose his turn of duty in the Temple; and he refused to risk that. He was a man who set the claims of ceremonial above those of charity. The Temple and its liturgy meant more to him than the pain

141

of man. (c) There was *the Levite*. He seems to have gone
nearer to the man before he passed on. The bandits were
in the habit of using decoys. One of their number would
act the part of a wounded man; and when some unsuspecting
traveller stopped over him, the others would rush upon
him and overpower him. The Levite was a man whose
motto was, " Safety first." He would take no risks to
help anyone else. (d) There was *the Samaritan*. The listeners
would obviously expect that with his arrival the villain
had arrived. He may not have been *racially* a Samaritan
at all. The Jews had no dealings with the Samaritans,
and yet this man seems to have been a kind of commercial
traveller who was a regular visitor to the inn. In John 8: 48
the Jews call Jesus a Samaritan. The name was sometimes
used to describe a man who was a heretic and a breaker
of the ceremonial law. Perhaps this man was a Samaritan
in the sense of being a man whom all orthodox good people
despised. We note two things about him. (i) His credit
was good! Clearly the innkeeper was prepared to trust
him. He may have been theologically unsound, but he
was an honest man. (ii) He alone was prepared to help.
A heretic he may have been, but the charity of God was
in his heart. It is no new experience to find the orthodox
more interested in dogmas than in help and to find the
man the orthodox despise to be the man who loves his
fellow men. In the end we will be judged not by the creed
we hold but by the life we live.

Third, let us look at *the teaching* of the parable. The
Scribe who asked this question was in earnest. Jesus asked
him what was written in the law, and then said, " How
do you read? " Strict orthodox Jews wore round their
wrists little leather boxes called phylacteries, which
contained certain passages of scripture—Exodus 13: 1-10;
11-16; Deuteronomy 6: 4-9; 11: 13-20. "Thou shalt
love the Lord thy God " is from Deuteronomy 6: 3 and 11:
13. So Jesus said to the Scribe, " Look at the phylactery
on your own wrist and it will answer your question."

To that the Scribes added Leviticus 18: 19, which bids a man love his neighbour as himself; but with their passion for definition the Rabbis sought to define who a man's neighbour was; and at their worst and their narrowest they confined the word *neighbour* to their *fellow Jews*. For instance, some of them said that it was illegal to help a Gentile woman in her sorest time, the time of childbirth, for that would only have been to bring another Gentile into the world. So then the Scribe's question, " Who is my neighbour? " was a genuine question. Jesus' answer involves three things. (i) We must help a man even when he has brought his trouble on himself, as the traveller by his recklessness had done. (ii) Any man of any nation who is in need is our neighbour. Our help must be as wide as the love of God. (iii) The help must be practical, and must not consist merely in *feeling* sorry. No doubt the priest and the Levite felt a pang of pity for the wounded man, but they *did* nothing. Compassion, to be real compassion, must issue in deeds.

What Jesus said to the Scribe, He says to us—" Go *you* and do the same."

THE CLASH OF TEMPERAMENTS

Luke 10: 38-42

> As they journeyed, Jesus entered into a village. A woman called Martha received Him into her house. She had a sister called Mary, and she sat at Jesus' feet and kept listening to His word. Martha was worried about much serving. She stood over them and said, " Lord, don't you care that my sister has left me alone to do the serving? Tell her to give me a hand." " Martha, Martha," the Lord answered her, " you are worried and troubled about many things. Only one thing is necessary. Mary has chosen the better part, and it is not going to be taken away from her."

IT would be hard to find more vivid character drawing in greater economy of words than we find in these verses.

(i) They show us *the clash of temperaments*. We have never allowed enough for the place of temperament in religion. Some people are naturally dynamos of activity; others are naturally quiet. It is hard for the active person to understand the person who sits and thinks and contemplates. And the person who is devoted to quiet times and to meditation is very apt to look down on the person who would rather be doing something. There is no right or wrong in this. God did not make everyone alike. One person may pray,

> " Lord of all pots and pans and things,
>   Since I've no time to be
> A saint by doing lovely things,
>   Or watching late with Thee,
> Or dreaming in the dawnlight,
>   or storming heaven's gates,
> Make me a saint by getting meals
>   And washing up the plates."

Another person may sit with folded hands but mind intense and think and pray, and both are serving God. God needs His Marys and His Marthas too.

(ii) But these verses show us something more—they show us *the wrong kind of kindness*. Think where Jesus was going when this happened. He was on His way to Jerusalem —to die. His whole being was taken up with the intensity of that inner battle to bend His will to the will of God. When Jesus came to that home in Bethany it was a great day; and Martha was eager to celebrate it by—as we say— laying on the best the house could give. So she rushed and fussed and cooked; *and that was precisely what Jesus did not want*. All He wanted was quiet. With the Cross before Him, and with the inner tension in His heart, He had turned aside to Bethany to find an oasis of calm away from the demanding crowds if only for an hour or two; and that is what Mary gave Him, and that is what Martha, in her kindness, did her best to destroy. " One thing is necessary " —quite possibly this means, " I don't want a big spread; one course, the simplest meal is all I want." It was simply that Mary understood and that Martha did not. Here is one of the great difficulties in life. So often we want to be kind to people—but we want to be kind to them *in our way*; and should it happen that our way is not the necessary way, we sometimes take offence and think that we are not appreciated. If we are trying to be kind the first necessity is to try to see into the heart of the person we desire to help—and then to forget all our own plans and to think only of what he or she needs. Jesus loved Martha, and Martha loved Him, but when Martha set out to be kind, it had to be her way of being kind, and she was really being unkind to Him whose heart cried for quiet. Jesus loved Mary and Mary loved Him, and Mary understood.

TEACH US TO PRAY

Luke II: I-4

> Jesus was praying in a certain place, and when He stopped, one of His disciples said to Him, " Lord, teach us to pray, as John taught his disciples." He said to them, " When you pray, say,
>
> > O Father, let your name be held in reverence.
> > Let your Kingdom come.
> > Give to us each day our bread for the day.
> > And forgive us our sins as we too forgive everyone who is in debt to us.
> > And lead us not into temptation."

IT was the regular custom for a Rabbi to teach his disciples a simple prayer which they might habitually use. John had done that for his disciples, and now Jesus' disciples came to Him asking Him to do the same for them. This is Luke's version of The Lord's Prayer. It is shorter than Matthew's, but it will teach us all we need to know about how to pray and what to pray for.

(i) It begins by calling God *Father*. That was the characteristic Christian address to God. (cp. Galatians 4: 6; Romans 8: 15; 1 Peter 1: 17). The very first word tells us that in prayer we are not coming to someone out of whom gifts have to be unwillingly extracted, but to a Father who delights to supply His children's needs.

(ii) In Hebrew *the name* meant much more than merely the name by which a person is called. *The name* means the whole character of the person as it is revealed and known to us. Psalm 9: 10 says, " They that know *Thy name* will put their trust in Thee." That means far more than knowing that God's name is Jehovah. It means those who know the whole character and mind and heart of God will gladly put their trust in Him.

(iii) We must note particularly the order of the Lord's Prayer. Before anything is asked for ourselves, God and His glory, and the reverence due to Him, come first. Only when we give God His place will all other things take their proper place.

(iv) The prayer covers all life. (*a*) It covers *present need*. It tells us to pray for our daily bread; but note it is bread *for the day* for which we pray. This goes back to the old story of the manna in the wilderness (Exodus 16: 11-21). Only enough for the needs of the day might be gathered. We are not to worry about the unknown future, but to live a day at a time.

> " I do not ask to see
> The distant scene—one step enough for me."

(*b*) It covers *past sin*. When we pray we cannot do other than pray for forgiveness for the best of us is a sinful man coming before the purity of God. (*c*) It covers *future trials*. *Temptation* in the New Testament means any testing situation. It includes far more than the mere seduction to sin; it covers every situation which is a challenge to and a test of a person's manhood and integrity and fidelity. We cannot escape it, but we can meet it with God.

Someone has said that the Lord's Prayer has two great uses in our own private prayers. If we use it at the beginning of our devotions it awakens all kinds of holy desires which will lead us on into the right pathways of prayer. If we use it at the end of our devotions it sums up all that we ought to pray for in the presence of God.

ASK AND YOU WILL RECEIVE

Luke 11: 5-13

> Jesus said to them, " Suppose one of you has a friend and goes to him towards midnight and says to him, ' Friend, lend me three loaves because a friend of mine has arrived at my house from a journey and I have nothing to set before him '; and suppose his friend answers from within, ' Don't bother me; the door has already been shut and my children are in bed with me; I can't get up and supply you ' I tell you, if he will not rise and supply him because he is his friend, he will rise and give him as much as he needs because of his shameless persistence. For I say to you, ' Ask and it will be given to you; seek and you will find; knock and it will be opened to you. For everyone who asks receives; and he who seeks finds; and to him who knocks it will be opened. If a son asks any father among you for bread, will he give him a stone? Or, if he asks a fish, will he, instead of a fish, give him a serpent? Or if he asks an egg, will he give him a scorpion? If you then, who are evil, know to give good gifts to your children, how much more will your Father who is in Heaven give the Holy Spirit to those who ask Him? ' "

In Palestine travellers often travelled late in the evening to avoid the heat of the midday sun. In Jesus' story just such a traveller had arrived towards midnight at his friend's house. In the east hospitality is a sacred duty; it was not enough to set before a man a bare sufficiency; the guest had to be confronted with an ample abundance. In the villages bread was baked at home. Only enough for the day's needs was baked, because, if it was kept and

147

became stale, no one would wish to eat it. So the late arrival of the traveller confronted the householder with an embarrassing situation, because his larder was empty and he could not fulfil the sacred obligations of hospitality. Late as it was, he went out to borrow from a friend. The friend's door was shut. In the east no one would knock on a shut door unless the need was imperative. In the morning the door was opened and remained open all day, for there was little privacy; but if the door was shut, that was a definite sign that the householder did not wish to be disturbed. But the seeking householder was not deterred. He knocked, and kept on knocking. The poorer Palestinian house consisted of one room with only one little window. The floor was simply of beaten earth covered with dried reeds and rushes. The room was divided into two parts, not by a partition, but by a low platform. Two-thirds of it were on ground level. The other third was slightly raised. On the raised part the charcoal stove burned all night, and round it the whole family slept, not on raised beds, but on sleeping mats. Families were large, and they slept close together for warmth. For one to rise was inevitably to disturb the whole family. Further, in the villages it was the custom to bring the livestock, the hens and the cocks and the goats, into the house at night. Is there any wonder that the man who was in bed did not want to rise? But the determined borrower knocked on with shameless persistence—that is what the Greek word means—until at last the householder, knowing that by this time the whole family was disturbed anyway, arose and gave him what he needed.

" That story," said Jesus, " will tell you about prayer." The lesson of this parable is not that we must persist in prayer; it is not that we must batter at God's door until we finally compel God for very weariness to give us what we want; until we coerce an unwilling God to answer. A parable literally means *something laid alongside*. If we lay something beside another thing to teach a lesson, that lesson may be drawn from the fact that the things are like each other or from the fact that the things are a contrast to each other. The point here is based, not on likeness, but on *contrast*. What Jesus said is, " If a churlish and unwilling householder can in the end be coerced by a friend's shameless persistence into giving him what he needs, *how much more* will God who is a loving Father supply all His children's needs? " " If you," said Jesus, " who are evil, know that you are bound to supply your children's needs, *how much more* will God? "

This does not absolve us from intensity in prayer. After all, we can only guarantee the reality and sincerity of our desire by the passion with which we pray; but it does mean this, that we are not wringing gifts from an unwilling God, but that we are going to one who knows our needs better than we know them ourselves, and whose heart towards us is the heart of generous love. If we do not receive what we pray for, it is not because God grudgingly refuses to give it to us, but because He has some better thing for us. There is no such thing as unanswered prayer. The answer given may not be the answer we desired or expected. Even when it is a refusal of our wishes it is the answer of the love and the wisdom of God.

A MALICIOUS SLANDER

Luke 11: 14-23

Jesus was casting out a dumb demon. When the demon came out the dumb man spoke and the crowds were amazed. Some of them said, " He casts out demons by the help of Beelzebul, who is the prince of demons." Others, trying to put Him to the test, sought a sign from heaven from Him. He knew what they were thinking. " Every kingdom," He said, " that is divided against itself is devastated; and every house that is divided against itself falls; so if Satan is divided against himself how will his kingdom stand? You must answer that question because you say that I cast out demons by the help of Beelzebul. If I cast out demons by the power of Beelzebul, by whose power do your sons cast them out? You have become your own judges. But if it is by the finger of God that I cast out the demons, then the Kingdom of God has come upon you. When a strong man in full panoply guards his own homestead, his goods are in peace. But when a stronger man than he comes and conquers him, he will take away the armour in which he trusted, and will divide his spoil. He who is not with me is against me; and he who does not gather with me scatters."

WHEN Jesus' enemies were helpless to oppose Him by fair means they resorted to slander. They declared that His power over the demons was due to the fact that He was in league with the prince of demons. They attributed His power not to God but to the devil. Jesus gave them a double and a crushing answer. First, He struck them a shrewd blow. There were many exorcists in Jesus' time in Palestine. Josephus, the Jewish historian, traces this power back to Solomon. Part of Solomon's wisdom was that he was skilful with herbs, and that he had invented incantations which drove out demons in such a way that they never came back again; and Josephus states that he had seen Solomon's methods used with success even in his own day. (Josephus, *Antiquities of the Jews* ; 8 : 5 : 2) So Jesus delivers a home-thrust. " If I," He said, " cast out devils because I am in league with the prince of devils, what of your own people who do the same thing? " " If you condemn me," He said, " you are only condemning yourselves." Second, He used a really unanswerable argument. No kingdom in which there is a civil war can survive. If the prince of devils is lending his power to defeat his own emissaries he is finished. There is only one way for a strong man to be defeated and that is for a still stronger man to master him. " Therefore," said Jesus, " if I cast out devils, so far from that proving that I am in league with the prince of devils, it proves that the devil's citadel is breached, the strong man of evil is mastered, and the Kingdom of God is here."

Out of this passage there emerge certain permanent truths.

(i) It is by no means uncommon for people to resort to slander when honest opposition is helpless. Gladstone, the great prime minister, was interested in the reformation of the fallen women of the streets of London. His enemies suggested that he was interested in them for very different and very inferior reasons. There is nothing so cruel as slander, for slander is apt to stick because the human mind is such that it always tends to think the worst, and very often the human ear would prefer to hear the derogatory rather than the complimentary tale. We need not think that we are altogether free of that particular sin. How often do we tend to think the worst of other people? How often do we deliberately impute low motives to someone whom we dislike? How often do we repeat the slanderous and the malicious tale and murder reputations over the tea-cups? To think of this will not cause complacency but calls for self-examination.

(ii) Once again we must note that Jesus' proof that the Kingdom had come was the fact that sufferers were healed and that health walked where disease had been. In the modern phrase, Jesus' aim was not only *soul* salvation; it was also *whole* salvation.

(iii) Luke finishes this section with the saying of Jesus that he who was not with Him was against Him, and that he who did not help to gather the flock helped to scatter it abroad. There is no place for neutrality in the Christian life. The man who stands aloof from the good cause automatically helps the evil cause. A man is either on the way or in the way.

THE PERIL OF THE EMPTY SOUL

Luke 11: 24-28

When the unclean spirit goes out of a man, it goes through waterless places seeking for rest. And when

it does not find it, it says, " I will go back to my house
from which I came out." So it comes and finds the
house swept and in order. Then it goes and gets in
addition seven spirits worse than itself, and they enter
in and settle there; and the last state of that man is
worse than the first.

When He was speaking a woman lifted up her
voice from the crowd and said, " Happy is the womb
that bore you and the breasts at which you sucked."
" But," He said, " rather, happy are those who hear
the word of God and keep it."

HERE is a grim and terrible story. There was a man from
whom an unclean spirit was expelled. The unclean spirit
wandered seeking rest and found none. It determined
to return to the man. It found the man's soul swept and
garnished—but empty. So the spirit went and collected
seven spirits worse than itself and came back and entered
in; and the man's last state was worse than his first.

(i) Here is the fundamental truth that you cannot
leave a man's soul empty. It is not enough to banish the
evil thoughts and the evil habits and the old ways and leave
the soul clean but empty. The empty soul is the soul in
peril. Adam C. Welch liked to preach on the text, " Be
not ye filled with new wine wherein is excess, but be filled
with the Spirit " (Ephesians 5: 18). When he did so his
opening sentence was, " You've got to fill a man with
something." It is not enough to drive out the evil; the
good must come in.

(ii) That means that we can never erect a real religion
on negatives. We can never found a religion on a series of
Thou shalt not's. Take a very clear example—one of
the great problems of the modern world is the problem of
Sunday observance. Too often the problem is approached
with a tirade against the things which people allow themselves to do on the Sunday, and with a catalogue of prohibitions and of forbidden things. But the man to whom
we speak has a perfect right to ask, " Well, what *may* I
do?" And unless we tell him, his last state is worse than

his first, for we have simply condemned him to idleness, and Satan is an adept at finding mischief for idle hands to do. It is always the peril of religion that it should present itself in a series of negatives. True, the cleansing is necessary; but after the rooting out of the evil there must come the filling with the good.

(iii) Herein is the great practical truth that the best way to avoid the evil is to do the good. The loveliest garden I ever saw was so full of flowers that there was scarcely room for a weed to grow. In no garden is it enough to uproot weeds; flowers must be sown and planted until the space which the weeds would have usurped is filled. Nowhere is this truer than in the world of thought and thoughts. Often we are troubled with wrong thoughts. If we go no further than to say to ourselves, " I must not think about that; I will not think about that," all that we do is to fix our thoughts upon it more and more. The cure is to think of something else, to banish the evil thought by thinking a good thought. We never become good by *not* doing things, but by filling life with lovely things.

Verses 27 and 28 show Jesus speaking sternly but truly. The woman who spoke was carried away by a moment of emotion. Jesus pulled her back to reality. The moment of emotion is a fine thing; but the greatest thing is a life of obedience in the routine things of everyday. No amount of fine feeling can take the place of faithful doing.

THE RESPONSIBILITY OF PRIVILEGE

Luke 11: 29-32

> When the crowds were thronging upon Him, He began to say, " This generation is a wicked generation. It seeks a sign, and no sign will be given to it except the sign of Jonah; for just as Jonah was a sign to the people of Nineveh so the Son of Man will be to this generation. The queen of the south will rise up in judgment with the men of this generation and will

condemn them, because she came from the ends of
the earth to hear the wisdom of Solomon, and—look
you—something greater than Solomon is here. The
men of Nineveh will rise up in judgment with this
generation and will condemn it, because they repented
at the preaching of Jonah, and—look you—something
greater than Jonah is here."

THE Jews wanted Jesus to do something sensational to
prove that He really was the Anointed One of God. Later
than this, about the year A.D. 45, a man called Theudas
arose claiming to be the Messiah. He persuaded the people
to follow him out to the Jordan with the promise that he
would cleave the river in two and give them a pathway
through it to the other side. Needless to say he failed, and
the Romans dealt summarily with his rising; but that is
the kind of thing that the people wanted Jesus to do to
prove His claims. They could not see that the greatest
sign that God could ever send was Jesus Himself. Just
as once long ago Jonah had been God's sign to Nineveh,
so now Jesus was God's sign to them—and they failed to
recognize Him. When Solomon was king the Queen of
Sheba recognized his wisdom and came from far to benefit
from it; when Jonah preached the men of Nineveh recognized the authentic voice of God and responded to it.
In the day of judgment these people would rise up and
condemn the Jews of Jesus' time, because these Jews had
had an opportunity and a privilege far beyond anything
they had ever had and had refused to accept it. The
condemnation of the Jews would be all the more complete
because their privileges were so great. Privilege and
responsibility go ever hand in hand. Think of two of our
greatest privileges and think how we use them.

(i) We have available to everyone the Bible, the word
of God. That did not cost nothing. There was a time
when it was death to teach the English Bible. When Wycliff
wrote to a certain scholar, about the year A.D. 1350, asking
him to teach the common people the gospel stories in the
English tongue, he answered, " I know well that I am

holden by Christ's law to perform thy asking, but, natheless, we are now so far fallen away from Christ's law, that if I would answer to thy askings *I must in case undergo the death*; and thou wottest well that a man is beholden to keep his life as long as he may." Later on, Foxe was to tell us that in those days men sat up all night to read and hear the word of God in English. " Some gave five marks (equal to £40 of our money), some more, some less for a book; some gave a load of hay for a few chapters of St. James or St. Paul in English." It was Tyndale who gave England its first printed Bible. To do so, as he said himself, he suffered, " poverty, exile, bitter absence from friends, hunger and thirst and cold, great dangers and innumerable other hard and sharp fightings." In 1536 he was martyred. When, some years before, the authorities had burned the book, he said, " They did none other thing than I looked for; no more shall they do if they burn me also." There is no book which cost so much as the Bible. To-day it is in serious danger of deserving the cynical definition of a classic—a book of which everyone has heard and which no one reads. We have the privilege of possessing the Bible, and that privilege is a responsibility for which we shall answer.

(ii) We have freedom to worship as we think right; and that, too, is a privilege which cost the lives of men; and the tragic thing is that so many people have used that freedom in order not to worship at all. That privilege, too, is a responsibility for which we shall answer.

If a man possesses Christ, and Christ's Book, and Christ's Church, he is the heir of all the privileges of God; and if he neglects them or refuses them he, like the Jews in the time of Jesus, is a man under condemnation.

THE DARKENED HEART

Luke 11: 33-36

No one lights a lamp and puts it in a cellar or under a bushel, but upon a lamp-stand, so that those who come in may see the light. The lamp of the body is your eye. When your eye is sound your whole body is full of light; but if the eye is diseased the whole body is full of darkness. Take care, then, lest the light that is in you is darkness. If, then, your whole body is full of light, without any part of darkness, it will be altogether bright as when the lamp with its ray gives you light.

THIS is a passage the meaning of which it is not easy to grasp. Very probably the meaning is this—the light of the body depends on the eye. If the eye is healthy the body receives all the light it needs; if the eye is diseased then the light turns to darkness. Just so, *the light of life depends on the heart.* If the heart is right the whole life is irradiated with light; if the heart is wrong all life is darkened. Jesus urges us to see that the inner lamp is always burning.

What then is it that darkens the inner light? What is it that can go wrong with our hearts?

(i) Our hearts may become *hard.* Sometimes, if we have to do something unaccustomed with our hands, the skin is irritated and ruffled, and we have pain; but if we repeat the action often enough the skin becomes hardened and we can do what once hurt us without any trouble or pain. It is so with our hearts. The first time we do a wrong thing we do it with a tremor and sometimes with a sore heart. Each time we repeat it the tremor grows less, until in the end we can do it without a qualm. There is a terrible hardening power in sin. No man ever took the first step to sin without the warnings sounding in his heart; but if he sins often enough the time comes when he ceases to care. That which we were once afraid and hesitant and reluctant to do becomes a habit. We have nobody but ourselves to blame if we allow ourselves to reach that stage.

(ii) Our hearts may become *dull.* It is the experience of life that it is tragically easy to accept things. In the beginning our hearts may be sore at the sight of the world's suffering and pain; but in the end most people become

so used to it that they accept it and feel nothing about it
at all. It is all too true that for most people the feelings
of youth are far more intense than those of age. That is
specially true of the Cross of Jesus Christ. Florence
Barclay tells how when she was a little girl she was taken
to church for the first time. It was Good Friday, and
the long story of the crucifixion was read and beautifully
read. She heard Peter deny and Judas betray; she heard
Pilate's bullying cross-examination; she saw the crown
of thorns, the buffetting of the soldiers; she heard of
Jesus being delivered to be crucified, and then there came
the words with their terrible finality, " and there they
crucified Him." No one in the church seemed to care;
but suddenly the little girl's face was buried in her mother's
coat, and she was sobbing her heart out, and her little
voice rang through the silent church, " Why did they do
it? Why did they do it? " That is how we all ought to
feel about the Cross, but we have heard the story so often
that we can listen to it with no reaction at all. God keep
us from the heart which has lost the power to feel the agony
of the Cross—borne for us.

(iii) Our hearts may be actively *rebellious*. It is quite
possible for a man to know the right way and deliberately
to take the wrong way. A man may actually feel God's
hand upon his shoulder and twitch that shoulder away.
With open eyes a man may take his way to the far country
when God is calling him home.

God save us from the darkened heart.

THE WORSHIP OF DETAILS AND THE NEGLECT
OF THE THINGS THAT MATTER

Luke 11: 37-44

After Jesus had spoken a Pharisee asked Him to
dine with Him. He came in and reclined at the table.
The Pharisee was surprised when he saw that He did
not dip His hands in water before He ate. The Lord

said to him, " You Pharisees cleanse the outside of the cup and the dish, but inside you are full of grasping and wickedness. Fools! Did He who made the outside not make the inside also? But cleanse the things that are within—and look you—all things will be pure for you.

But woe to you Pharisees! because you give tithes of mint and rue and every herb and pass by justice and the love of God. These you ought to have done without omitting the others. Woe to you Pharisees! because you love the chief seats in the Synagogues and greetings in the market places. Woe to you! because you are like tombs which are not seen, and the men who walk over them do not know that they are doing it."

THE Pharisee was surprised that Jesus did not wash His hands before eating. This was not a matter of cleanliness but of the ceremonial law. The law laid it down that before a man ate he must wash his hands in a certain way, and that he must also wash them between the courses. As usual every littlest detail was worked out. Large stone vessels of water were specially kept for the purpose because ordinary water might be unclean; the amount of water used must be at least a quarter of a log, that is enough to fill one and a half egg-shells. First the water must be poured over the hands beginning at the tips of the fingers and running right up to the wrist. Then the palm of each hand must be cleansed by rubbing the fist of the other into it. Finally, water must again be poured over the hand, this time beginning at the wrist and running down to the fingertips. To the Pharisee to omit the slightest detail of this was to sin. Jesus' comment was that if they were as particular about cleansing their hearts as they were about washing their hands they would be better men.

There were certain dues which the meticulously orthodox would never omit to pay. (a) *The first fruits of the soil.* The first fruits of the seven kinds—wheat, barley, vines, fig-trees, pomegranates, olives and honey—were offered in the Temple. (b) *There was the Terumah.* The first fruits were given to God, but the Terumah was a contribution to the upkeep of the priests. It was the presentation of the first fruits of every growing thing. The amount to be given was one-fiftieth of the total yield. (c) *There was the tithe.* The tithe was paid directly to the Levites, who, in turn, paid a tithe of what they received to the priests. It was one-tenth of " everything that can be used as food and is cultivated and grows out of the earth." The meticulousness of the Pharisees in tithing is shown by the fact that even the law said it was not necessary to tithe rue. No matter what their inner hearts and feelings were like, however much they neglected justice and forgot love, they never omitted the tithe.

The chief seats at the Synagogue were the seats out in front facing the audience. In the congregation itself the best seats were the front seats, and the seats decreased in honour the further back they got. The advantage of these seats was that they could be seen by all! The more exaggerated the respect of the greetings the Pharisees received in the streets the better they were pleased.

The point of verse 44 is this. Numbers 19: 16 lays it down that, whosoever in the open fields touches a grave shall be unclean for seven days. To be unclean was to be debarred from all religious worship. Now, it might be that a man might touch a grave without knowing that he was doing it. That did not matter; its touch made him unclean. Jesus said that the Pharisees were exactly like that. Although men might not know it their influence could do nothing but harm. All unawares, the man who came in contact with them, was being touched for evil. Men might not suspect the corruption but it was there; all the time they were being infected with wrong ideas of God and of the demands of God.

Two things stand out about the Pharisees and for these two things Jesus condemned them.

(i) They concentrated on *externals*. So long as the externals of religion were carried out that was all that mattered. Their hearts might be as black as hell; they might be utterly lacking in charity and even justice; so long as they went through the correct motions at the correct time they considered that they were good in the eyes of God. A man may be regular in his church attendance; he may be a diligent student of his Bible; he may be a generous giver to the Church; but if in his heart there are thoughts of pride and of contempt, if he has no charity in his dealings with his fellow men in the life of the everyday, if he is unjust to his subordinates or dishonest to his employer, he is not a Christian man. No man is a Christian when he meticulously observes the conventions of religion and forgets the realities.

(ii) They concentrated on *details*. Compared with love and kindness, justice and generosity, the washings of hands and the giving of tithes with mathematical accuracy were mere unimportant details. Once a man came to Dr. Johnson with a tale of woe. He worked in a paper factory; he had taken for his own purposes a very little piece of paper and a very little bit of string, and he had convinced himself that he had committed a deadly sin and would not stop talking about it. At last Johnson broke out on him, " Sir, stop bothering about paper and packthread when we are all living together in a world that is bursting with sin and sorrow." How often church courts and church people get lost in totally unimportant details of church government and administration, and even argue and fight about them, and forget the great realities of the Christian life!

THE SINS OF THE LEGALISTS

Luke II: 45-54

A Scribe answered, " Teacher, when you talk like that you are insulting us." Jesus said, " Woe to you Scribes too! because you bind burdens upon men that are hard to bear and you yourselves do not lay a finger on the burdens. Woe to you! because you build the tombs of the prophets whom your fathers killed! So you are witnesses that you agree with the deeds of your fathers, because they killed them and you build them tombs. Because of this God in His wisdom said, ' I will send prophets and apostles to them, some of whom they will slay and persecute, so that the blood of all the prophets, shed from the foundation of the world, will be required from this generation, from the blood of Abel to the blood of Zacharias who perished between the altar and the Temple.' Yes, I tell you, it will be required from this generation. Woe to you Scribes! You did not enter in yourselves and you hindered those who were trying to enter."

As Jesus went away from them, the Scribes and Pharisees began to watch Him intensely, and to try to provoke Him to discuss on many subjects, for they were laying traps for Him, to hunt for something out of His mouth which they could use as a charge against Him.

HERE three charges are levelled against the Scribes.

(i) They were experts in the law; they laid upon men the thousand and one burdens of the ceremonial law; but they did not keep them themselves, because they were experts in evasion. Here are some of their evasions. The limit of a Sabbath day's journey was 2,000 cubits (1,000 yards) from a man's residence. But if a rope was tied across the end of the street, the end of the street became his residence and he could go 1,000 yards beyond that; if on the Friday evening he left at any given point enough food for two meals that point technically became his residence and he could go 1,000 yards beyond that! One of the forbidden works on the Sabbath was the tying of knots, sailors' or camel drivers' knots, and knots in ropes. But a woman might tie the knot in her girdle. Therefore, if a bucket of water had to be raised from a well a rope could not be knotted to it, but a woman's girdle could, and it could be raised with that! To carry a burden was forbidden, but the codified written law lays it down,

" he who carries anything, whether it be in his right hand,
or in his left hand, or in his bosom, or on his shoulder is
guilty; but he who carries anything on the back of his
hand, with his foot, or with his mouth, or with his elbow,
or with his ear, or with his hair, or with his money bag
turned upside down, or between his money bag and his
shirt, or in the fold of his shirt or in his shoe, or in his
sandal is guiltless, because he does not carry it in the usual
way of carrying it out." It is incredible that men should
ever have thought that God could have laid down laws
like that, and that the working out of details like that was
a religious service and that the keeping of them was a
matter of life and death. But that was Scribal religion.
Little wonder that Jesus turned on the Scribes, and that
the Scribes regarded Him as an irreligious heretic.

(ii) The attitude of the Scribes to the prophets was
paradoxical. They professed a lip service and a deep
admiration for the prophets. But the only prophets they
admired were dead prophets; when they met a living one
they tried to kill him. They honoured the dead prophets
with tombs and memorials, but they dishonoured the living
ones with persecution and death. " Your new moons,"
said Isaiah, " and your appointed feasts my soul hateth."
" He hath shewed thee, O man, what is good," said Micah;
" and what doth the Lord require of thee but to do justly,
to love mercy and to walk humbly with thy God?" That
was the essence of the prophetic message; and that was
the very antithesis of Scribal teaching. No wonder the
Scribes, with their external details, hated the prophets,
and Jesus walked in the prophetic line. The murder of
Zacharias is described in 2 Chronicles 24: 20, 21.

(iii) The Scribes shut the people off from scripture.
Their interpretation of scripture was so fantastic that
it was impossible for the ordinary man to understand it.
In their hands scripture became a book of riddles. In
their mistaken ingenuity they refused to see its plain
meaning themselves, and they would not let anyone else

see it either. The scriptures had become the perquisite of the expert and a dark mystery to the common man.

None of this is so very out of date. There are still those who demand from others standards which they themselves refuse to satisfy. There are still those whose religion is nothing other than legalism. There are still those who make the word of God so difficult that the seeking mind of the common man is bewildered and does not know what to believe or to whom to listen.

THE CREED OF COURAGE AND OF TRUST
Luke 12: 1-12

> In the meantime, when the people had been gathered together in their thousands, so that they trampled on each other, Jesus began to say first of all to His disciples, " Be on your guard against the leaven of the Pharisees, which is hypocrisy. There is nothing covered up which will not be unveiled, and there is nothing secret which shall not be known. All, therefore, that you have spoken in the dark shall be heard in the light; and what you have spoken into someone's ear in the inner room will be proclaimed on the housetops. I tell you, my friends, do not be afraid of those who kill the body and who after that are not able to do anything further. I will warn you whom you are to fear—fear Him who after He has killed you has authority to cast you into hell. Yes, I tell you, fear Him! Are not five sparrows sold for two farthings? And yet not one of them is forgotten before God. But as for you—even the hairs of your head are all numbered. Do not be afraid. You are of more value than many sparrows. I tell you, everyone who acknowledges me before men, him will the Son of Man acknowledge before the angels of God; but he who denies me before men will be denied before the angels of God. If anyone speaks a word against the Son of Man it will be forgiven him; but he who speaks irreverently of the Holy Spirit will not be forgiven. When they bring you before Synagogues and rulers and those set in authority, do not worry how you will defend yourself or about what defence you will make, or about what you will say, for the Holy Spirit will teach you in that same hour what you ought to say."

WHEN we read this passage we are reminded again of the Jewish definition of preaching. As we saw, the Jews called preaching Charaz, which means *stringing pearls*. This passage, too, is a passage of pearls strung together, without the close connections which modern preaching demands. But in this passage there are certain dominant ideas.

(i) It tells us of the *forbidden sin*, which is *hypocrisy*. The word *hypocrite* began by meaning *someone who answers*; and *hypocrisy* originally meant *answering*. First the words were used of the ordinary flow of question and answer in any talk or in any dialogue; then they began to be connected with question and answer *in a play*. From that they went on to be connected with *acting a part*. *Hypocrisy is acting a part*. The hypocrite is never genuine; he is always play-acting. The basis of hypocrisy is insincerity. God would rather have a blunt, honest sinner, than someone who puts on an act of goodness.

(ii) It tells of the *correct attitude to life* which is an attitude of *fearlessness*. There are two reasons for that fearlessness. (*a*) Man's power over man is strictly limited to this life. A man can destroy another man's life *but not* his soul. In the 1914-18 war *Punch* had a famous cartoon in which it showed the German Emperor saying to King Albert of Belgium, " So now you have lost everything "; and back came Albert's answer, " But not my soul! " On the other hand, God's power is such that it can blot out a man's very self and soul. It is, therefore, only reasonable to fear God rather than to fear men. It was said of John Knox, as his body was being lowered into the grave, " Here lies one who feared God so much that he never feared the face of man." (*b*) God's care is the most detailed of all care. To God we are never lost in the crowd. Matthew says, "Are not two sparrows sold for a farthing? " (Matthew 10: 29). Here Luke says, "Are not *five* sparrows sold for *two farthings?* " If you were prepared to spend two farthings you got not four, but five sparrows. One was flung into the bargain as having no value at all. Not even the sparrow on which men set not a farthing's value is forgotten before God. The very hairs of our head are numbered. It has been computed that a blonde person has about 145,000 hairs; a dark-haired person, 120,000; and a person with red hair, 90,000! The Jews were so impressed with the individual care of God that they said that every blade of grass had its guardian angel. None of us needs to fear for each one of us can say, " God cares for *me*."

(iii) It tells us of *the unforgivable sin* which is the sin against the Holy Spirit. Both Matthew and Mark record that Jesus spoke about this sin immediately after the Scribes and Pharisees had attributed His cures to the prince of devils instead of to God (Matthew 12: 31, 32; Mark 3: 28, 29). These men could look at the very grace and power of God and call it the work of the devil. To understand this we must remember that Jesus was talking about the Holy Spirit as *the Jews* understood that conception, not in the full Christian sense, about which His audience at that time obviously knew nothing. To a Jew God's Spirit had two great functions. Through the Spirit God told His truth to men, and it was by the action of the Spirit in a man's mind and heart that he could recognize and grasp God's truth. Now, if a man for long enough refuses to use any faculty he will lose it. If we refuse to use any part of the body long enough it atrophies. Darwin tells how when he was a young man he loved poetry and music; but he so devoted himself to biology that he completely neglected them. The consequence was that in later life poetry meant nothing to him, and music was only a noise, and he said that if he had his life to live over again he would see to it that he would read poetry and listen to music so that he would not lose the faculty of enjoying them. Just so we can lose the faculty of recognizing God. By repeatedly refusing God's word, by repeatedly taking our own way, by repeatedly shutting our eyes to God and closing our ears to Him, we can come to a stage when we do not recognize God when we see Him, when to us evil becomes good and good becomes evil. That is what happened to the Scribes and Pharisees. They had so blinded and deafened themselves to God that when God came they called Him the devil. Why is that the unforgivable sin? Because in such a state *repentance is impossible*. If a man does not even realize that he is sinning, if goodness no longer makes any appeal to him, then he cannot repent. God has not shut him out. By his repeated refusals he has shut himself out. And that means that the one man who can never have committed the unforgivable sin is the man who fears that he has, for once a man has committed it, he is so dead to God that he would be conscious of no sin at all.

(iv) It tells us of *the rewarded loyalty*. The reward of loyalty is no material thing. The reward is that in heaven Jesus will say of us, " This was my man. Well done! "

(v) It tells us of *the help of the Holy Spirit*. In the Fourth Gospel the favourite title of the Holy Spirit is the *Paraclete*. *Parakletos* means *someone who stands by to help*. It can be used of a witness, or an advocate to plead our cause. In the day of trouble there need be no fear, for on such a day no less a person than the Holy Spirit of God stands by to help.

THE PLACE OF MATERIAL POSSESSIONS IN LIFE
Luke 12: 13-30

One of the crowd said to Jesus, " Teacher, tell my brother to divide the inheritance with me." He said to him, " Man, who appointed me a judge or an arbitrator over you? " He said to them, " Watch and guard yourself against the spirit which is always wanting more; for even if a man has an abundance his life does not come from his possessions." He spoke a parable to them. " The land," He said, " of a rich man bore good crops. He kept thinking what he would do. ' What will I do,' he said, ' because I have no room to gather in my crops? ' So he said, ' This is what I will do. I will pull down my barns and I will build bigger ones, and I will gather there all my corn and all my good things; and I will say to my soul, Soul, you have many good things laid up for many years. Take your rest, eat, drink and enjoy yourself.' But God said to him, ' Fool! This night your soul is demanded from you; and, the things you prepared—who will get them all? ' So is he who heaps up treasure for himself and is not rich towards God."

Jesus said to His disciples, " I therefore tell you, do not worry about your life—about what you are to eat; nor about your body—about what you are to wear. For your life is something more than food, and your body than clothing. Look at the ravens. See how they do not sow or reap; they have no store-house or barn; but God feeds them. How much more valuable are you than the birds? Which of you, by worrying about it, can add a few inches to his span of life? If, then, you cannot do the littlest thing why worry about the other things? Look at the lilies. See how they grow. They do not work; they do not spin; but, I tell you, not even Solomon in all his glory was clothed like one of these. If God so clothe the grass in the field, which is there to-day and which to-morrow is cast into the oven, how much more will He clothe you, O you of little faith? Do not you seek what you are to eat and what you are to drink; do not be tossed about in a storm of anxiety. The peoples of the world seek for all these things. Your Father knows that you need them. But seek His Kingdom and all these things will be added to you. Do not fear, little flock, because it is your Father's will to give you the Kingdom. Sell your possessions and give alms. Make yourselves purses which never grow old, a treasure in the heavens that does not fail, where a thief does not come near and a moth does not destroy. For where your treasure is there your heart will also be."

IT was not uncommon for people in Palestine to take their unsettled disputes to respected Rabbis; but Jesus refused to be mixed up in anyone's disputes about money. But out of that request there came to Jesus an opportunity to lay down what His followers' attitude to material things should be. Jesus had something to say both to those who had an abundant supply of material possessions and to those who had not.

(i) To those who had an abundant supply of possessions Jesus spoke this parable of the Rich Fool. Two things stand out about this man. (*a*) *He never saw beyond himself.* There is no parable which is full of the words, I, me, my and mine. A schoolboy was once asked what parts of speech *my* and *mine* are. He answered, " Agressive pronouns." The rich fool was aggressively self-centred. It was said of a self-centred young lady, " Edith lived in a little world, bounded on the north, south, east and west by Edith." The famous criticism was made of a self-centred person, " There is too much ego in his cosmos." When this man had a superfluity of goods the one thing that never even entered his head was to give any away. The man's whole attitude is the very reverse of Christianity. Instead of denying himself he aggressively affirmed himself; instead of finding his happiness in giving he tried to conserve it by keeping. John Wesley's rule of life was to *save* all he could and *give* all he could. When he was at Oxford he had an income of £30 a year. He lived on £28 and gave £2 away. When his income increased to £60, £90 and £120 a year, he still lived on £28 and gave the balance away. The Accountant-General for Household Plate demanded a return from him. His reply was, " I have two silver tea spoons at London and two at Bristol. This is all the plate which I have at present; and I shall not buy any more, while so many around me want bread." The Romans had a proverb which said that money was like sea-water; the more a man drank the thirstier he became. And so long as a man's attitude is that of the rich fool his desire will always be to get more—and that is the reverse of the Christian way. (*b*) *He never saw beyond this world.* All his plans were made on the basis of life in this world. There is a story of a conversation between a young and ambitious lad and an older man who knew life. " I will," said the young man, " learn my trade." " And then? " said the older man. " I will set up in business." " And then? " " I will make my fortune." " And then? " " I suppose that I shall grow old and retire and live on my money." "And then?" "Well, I suppose that some day I will die." "*And then?*" came the last stabbing question. The man who never remembers that there is another world is destined some day for the grimmest of grim shocks.

(ii) But Jesus had something to say to those who had few possessions. In all this passage the thought which Jesus forbids is *anxious thought* or *worry*. Jesus never ordered any man to live in a shiftless, thriftless, reckless way. What He did tell a man to do was to do his best and then to leave the rest to God. The lilies that Jesus spoke of were the scarlet anemones of the hills of Palestine. After one of the infrequent showers of summer rain, the mountain side would be scarlet with them; and they bloomed one day and died. Wood was scarce in Palestine, and it was the dried grasses and wild flowers that were used to feed the oven fire. " If," said Jesus, " God looks after the birds and the flowers, how much more will He care for you? " Jesus said, " Seek first the Kingdom of God." We saw that God's Kingdom was a state on earth in which God's will was as perfectly done as it is in heaven. So Jesus says, " Bend all your life to obeying God's will and rest content with that." Jesus said, " So many people give all their effort to heap up things which in their very nature cannot last. Work for the things which last forever. things which you need not leave behind when you leave this earth, but which you can take with you." In Palestine wealth was often in the form of costly raiment; the moths could get at the fine clothes and leave them ruined. But if a man clothes his soul with the garments of honour and purity and goodness, nothing on earth can injure them. if a man seeks the treasures of heaven his heart will be fixed on heaven; but if he seeks the treasures of earth his heart will be thirled to earth—and some day, inevitably, he must say good-bye to them, for, as the grim Spanish proverb has it, " There are no pockets in a shroud."

BE PREPARED

Luke 12: 35-48

" Let your loins be girt and your lamps burning. Be like men who are waiting for their master to come home from the wedding feast, so that, when he comes and knocks, they will open to him immediately. Happy are those servants whom the master will come and find awake. This is the truth that I tell you—he will gird himself; he will make them recline at table; and he will come and serve them. Happy are they if he finds them so, even if he comes in the second or third watch. Know this—that if the house-holder knew at what time the thief would come he would have been awake and he would not have allowed his home to be broken into. So you must show your-selves ready, for the Son of Man comes at an hour you do not expect."

Peter said, " Lord are you speaking this parable to us or to everyone? " The Lord said, " Who, then, is the faithful and wise steward, whom the master will set over the administration of his house to give them their ration of food at the right time? Happy is that servant whom the master will come and find acting like this. I tell you truly that he will put him in charge of all his possessions. But if that servant says in his heart, ' My master is delayed in coming,' and if he begins to beat the men servants and the maid servants, and to eat and drink and get drunk, the master of that servant will arrive on a day on which he is not expecting him and at an hour which he does not know, and he will cut him in pieces and he will place his part with the unfaithful. That servant who knew the will of his master, and who failed to have things ready, and to act in accordance with that will, will be beaten with many stripes. But he who did not know, even if he did things that deserved stripes, will be beaten with few stripes. To whom much is given, from him much will be required; and men will demand much from him to whom much was entrusted."

THIS passage has two senses. In its narrower sense it refers to the Second Coming of Jesus Christ; in its wider sense it refers to the time when God's summons enters man's life. It is at its widest a call to prepare to meet our God. The whole praise is for the servant who is ready. The long flowing robes of the east were a hindrance to work; and when a man prepared to work he gathered up his robes under his girdle to leave himself free for activity. The eastern lamp was like a cotton wick floating in a sauce-boat of oil. Always the wick had to be kept trimmed, and the lamp had to be kept replenished or the light would go out. No man can tell the day or the hour when eternity will invade time, and when God's summons will come. How, then, would we like God to find us?

(i) We would like God to find us *with our work completed.* Life for so many of us is filled with loose ends. There are the things undone and the things half done; the things put off and the things not even attempted. The great men had always the sense of a task that must be finished. Keats wrote,

" When I have fears that I may cease to be
    Before my pen has glean'd my teeming brain."

Robert Louis Stevenson wrote,

" The morning drum-call on my eager ear
    Thrills unforgotten yet; the morning dew
    Lies yet undried along my field of noon.

But now I pause at whiles in what I do,
    And count the bell, and tremble lest I hear
    (My work untrimmed) the sunset gun too soon."

It was Jesus Himself who said, " I have finished the work which Thou gavest me to do " (John 17: 4). No man should ever lightly leave undone a task he ought to have finished, or might have finished, before night falls.

(ii) We would like God to find us *at peace with our fellow-men.* It would be a haunting thing to pass from this world at bitterness with some fellow-man. No man should let the sun go down upon his wrath (Ephesians 4: 26), least

of all the last sun of all, and he never knows which sun
will be his last.

(iii) We should like God to find us *at peace with Himself*.
It will make all the difference at the last whether we feel
that we are going out to a stranger or to an enemy, or
whether we are going to fall asleep in the arms of God.

In the second section of this passage Jesus drew the
picture of the wise and the unwise steward. In the east
the steward had almost unlimited power. He was himself
a slave, yet he had control of all the other slaves. A trusted
steward ran a master's house for him, and administered
his estate. The unwise steward made two mistakes.

(i) He said, *I will do what I like while my master is away*.
He forgot that the day of reckoning must come, and would
come when he least expected it. We have a habit of dividing
life into compartments. There is the part of life in which
we remember that God is present; and there is the part
of life in which we never think of God at all. We tend to
draw a line between the activities which are sacred and the
activities which are secular. But if we really know what
Christianity means we will know that for us there is no
part of life when the master is away. We are working
and living forever in our great task-master's eye.

(ii) He said, *I have plenty of time to put things right before
the master comes*. There is nothing so fatal as to feel that
we have plenty of time. Jesus Himself said, " I must work
the works of Him that sent me while it is day; the night
cometh when no man can work " (John 9: 4). Dennis
Mackail tells how, when Sir James Barrie was old, he
would never make arrangements or give invitations for
a distant date. " Short notice now! " he would say. One
of the most dangerous days in a man's life is when he
discovers the word to-morrow.

The passage finishes with the warning that knowledge
and privilege always bring responsibility. Sin is doubly
sinful to the man who knew better; failure is doubly
blameworthy in the man who had every chance to do well.

THE COMING OF THE SWORD

Luke 12: 49-53

> Jesus said, " I came to cast fire upon the earth. And
> what do I wish? Would that it were already kindled!
> there is an experience through which I must pass; and
> now I am under tension until it is accomplished! Do
> you think I came to give peace in the earth? Not that, I
> tell you, but division! From now on in one house there
> will be five people divided—three against two, and two
> against three. They will be divided, father against son,
> and son against father, mother against daughter, and
> daughter against mother, mother-in-law against her
> daughter-in-law, and daughter-in-law against her
> mother-in-law."

To those who were learning to regard Jesus as the Messiah,
The Anointed One of God, these words would come like
a bleak shock. They regarded the Messiah as the conqueror
and king; and they regarded the Messianic age as a golden
time.

(i) In Jewish thought fire is almost always the symbol
of *judgment*. So, then, Jesus regarded the coming of His
Kingdom as a time of judgment. The Jews firmly believed
that God would judge the nations by one standard and
themselves by another; that, in fact, the very fact that a
man was a Jew would be enough to absolve him from the
judgment of God. However much our wishful thinking
wishes to eliminate the element of judgment from the
message of Jesus Christ it remains stubbornly and unal-
terably there.

(ii) The Authorised Version translates verse 50, " I
have a baptism to be baptised with." The Greek verb
baptizein means *to dip*. In the passive it means to be
submerged. Often it is used metaphorically. For instance,
it is used of a ship sunk beneath the waves and submerged.
It can be used of a man submerged in drink, and therefore
dead-drunk. It can be used of a scholar submerged by
an examiner's questions, as we say in our modern idiom,
sunk. But above all it is used of a man being submerged in

173

passing through some grim and terrible experience—of someone who can say, "All the waves and billows are gone over me." That is the way in which Jesus uses it here. "I have," He said, "a terrible experience through which I must pass; and life is full of tension until I pass through it and emerge triumphantly from it." The Cross was ever before His eyes. How different from the Jewish idea of God's King! Jesus came, not with avenging armies and flying banners, but to give His life a ransom for many.

> There was a Knight of Bethlehem,
>   Whose wealth was tears and sorrows,
> His men-at-arms were little lambs,
>   His trumpeters were sparrows.
> His castle was a wooden Cross
>   On which He hung so high;
> His helmet was a crown of thorns,
>   Whose crest did touch the sky.

(iii) His coming would inevitably mean divisions. In point of fact it did. That was one of the great reasons why the Romans hated Christianity—because it tore families in two. Over and over again a man had to decide whether he loved his kith and kin or Christ better. The essence of Christianity is that loyalty to Christ has to take precedence of the dearest loyalties of this earth. A man must be prepared to count all things but loss for the excellence of Jesus Christ.

WHILE YET THERE IS TIME

Luke 12: 54-59

> Jesus said to the crowds, "When you see a cloud rising in the west, immediately you say, 'Rain is coming.' And so it happens. When you feel the south wind blowing, you say, 'There will be scorching heat.' And so it happens. Hypocrites! you can read the signs of the face of the earth and the sky. How can you not read the signs of this time? Why do you

not for yourselves judge what is right? When you are going with your adversary to the magistrate, make an effort to come to an agreement with him on the way, lest he drag you to the judge, and the judge will hand you over to the officer, and the officer will throw you into prison. I tell you, you will not come out from there until you have paid the last farthing."

THE Jews of Palestine were weatherwise. When they saw the clouds forming in the west, over the Mediterranean Sea, they knew that the rain was on the way. When the south wind blew from the desert they knew that the sirocco-like wind, was coming. But those who were so wise to read the signs of the sky could not, or would not, read the signs of the times. If they had been able to do so they would have seen that the Kingdom of God was on the way.

Jesus used a very vivid illustration. He said, "When you are threatened with a law-suit, come to an agreement with your adversary before the matter comes to court, for if you do not you will have imprisonment to endure and a fine to pay." Note that the whole assumption is that the defendant has a bad case which will inevitably go against him. "Every man," Jesus implied, "has a bad case in the presence of God; and if a man is wise, he will make his peace with God while yet there is time."

Jesus, and all His great servants, have always been obsessed with the urgency of time. Andrew Marvell spoke of always hearing "time's wingèd chariot hurrying near." There are some things a man cannot afford to put off; above all he cannot afford to delay making his peace with God.

We read in the last verse of paying to the last *farthing*. We have already come across several references to money; and it will be useful if we collect the information about Jewish coinage in the time of Jesus. In order of value the principal coins were as follows:

The *Lepton; Lepton* means the *thin one*; it was the smallest coin, and was worth one sixteenth of a penny. It was the widow's mite (Mark 12: 42). It is also the coin mentioned here.

The *Quadrans* was worth two lepta, therefore it was one-eighth of penny. It is mentioned in Matthew 5: 26.

The *Assarion* was worth a little more than a halfpenny. It is mentioned in Matthew 10: 29 and Luke 12: 6.

The *Denarius* was worth about 8d. It was a day's pay for a working man (Matthew 20: 2); and it was the coin that the Good Samaritan left with the innkeeper (Luke 10: 25).

The *Drachma* was a silver coin worth about 9d. It was the coin which the woman lost and searched for (Luke 15: 8).

The *Didrachma* or *Half-shekel* was worth about 2s. It was the amount of the Temple Tax which everyone had to pay. It was also for thirty didrachmae—about £3— that Judas betrayed Jesus.

The *Shekel* was worth about 4s., and was the coin found in the fish's mouth (Matthew 17: 27).

The *Mina* is the coin mentioned in the Parable of the Pounds (Luke 19: 11-27). It was equal to 100 drachmae; and was, therefore, worth about £4.

The *Talent* was not so much a coin but a weight of silver worth £240. It is mentioned in Matthew 18: 24 and in the Parable of the Talents (Matthew 25: 14-30).

SUFFERING AND SIN

Luke 13: 1-3

At this time some men came and told Jesus about the Galilaeans whose blood Pilate had mingled with their sacrifices. " Do you think," He answered, " that these Galilaeans were sinners above all the Galilaeans because this happened to them? I tell you, No! But unless you repent you will all perish in like manner.

Or, as for the eighteen on whom the tower in Siloam
fell—do you think they were debtors to God beyond
all those who dwell in Jerusalem? I tell you, No!
But unless you repent you will perish in the same way.''

WE have here references to two disasters about which
we have no definite information and about which we can
only speculate. First, there is the reference to the Galilaeans
whom Pilate murdered in the middle of their sacrifices.
As we have seen, Galilaeans were always liable to get
involved in any political trouble that might arise, because
they were a highly inflammable people. Just about this
time Pilate had been involved in serious trouble. He had
decided very rightly that Jerusalem needed a new and
improved water supply. He proposed to build it and,
to finance it, he proposed to use certain Temple monies.
It was a laudable object, and a more than justifiable expen-
diture. But at the very idea of spending Temple monies
like that, the Jews were up in arms. When the mobs
gathered, Pilate instructed his soldiers to mingle with them.
The soldiers had cloaks over their battle dress so that they
were disguised. They were instructed to carry cudgels
rather than swords. At a given signal they were to fall
on the mob and disperse them. This was done, but the
soldiers dealt with the mob with a violence far beyond
their instructions and a considerable number of people
lost their lives. Almost certainly Galilaeans would be
involved in that. We know that Pilate and Herod were at
enmity, and only became reconciled after Pilate had sent
Jesus to Herod for trial (Luke 23: 6-12). And it may well
be that it was just this incident, involving the murder of
Galilaeans by Pilate, which provoked that enmity. As
for the eighteen on whom the tower in Siloam fell, they
are still more obscure. The Authorised Version uses the
word *sinners* of them also; but, as the margin shows,
it should not be *sinners* but debtors. Maybe we have a
clue here. It has been suggested that they had actually
taken work on Pilate's hated aqueducts. If so, any money

they earned was due to God and should have been voluntarily handed over, because it had already been stolen from God; and it may well be that popular talk had declared that the tower had fallen on them because of the work they had consented to do.

But there is far more than an historical problem in this passage. The Jews rigidly connected sin and suffering. Eliphaz had long ago said to Job, " Who ever perished being innocent? " (Job 4: 7). This was a cruel and a heart-breaking doctrine, as Job knew well. And Jesus utterly denied it in the case of the individual person. As we all know very well it is often the greatest saints who have to suffer most. But Jesus went on to say that if His hearers did not repent they too would perish. What did He mean by that? One thing is clear—Jesus foresaw and foretold the destruction of Jerusalem, which happened in A.D. 70 (cp. Luke 19: 21-24). Jesus knew well that if the Jews went on with their intrigues, their rebellions, their plottings, their political ambitions, they were simply going to commit national suicide; He knew that in the end Rome would step in and obliterate the nation; and that is precisely what happened. So what Jesus meant was this, if the Jewish nation kept on seeking an earthly kingdom and rejecting the Kingdom of God they could only come to one end.

To put the matter like that leaves a, at first sight, paradoxical situation. It means that we cannot say that individual suffering and sin are inevitably connected, but we can say that national sin and suffering are so connected. The nation which chooses the wrong ways will in the end suffer for it. But the individual is in very different case. The individual is not an isolated unit. He is bound up in the bundle of life. Often he may object, and object violently, to the course his nation is taking; but when the consequence of that course comes he cannot escape being involved in it. The individual is not an isolated unit, and is often caught up in a situation which he did not make; his suffering is often not his fault; but the nation is a unit and chooses its own policy and will reap the fruit of it. It is always dangerous to attribute human suffering to human sin; but it is always safe to say that the nation which rebels against God is on the way to disaster.

THE GOSPEL OF THE OTHER CHANCE AND THE THREAT OF THE LAST CHANCE

Luke 13: 6-10

> Jesus spoke this parable, "A man had a fig-tree planted in his vineyard. He came looking for fruit on it and did not find it. He said to the keeper of the vineyard, 'Look you—for the last three years I have been coming and looking for fruit on this fig-tree, and I still am not finding any. Cut it down! Why should it use up the ground?' 'Lord,' he answered him, 'let it be this year too, until I dig round about it and manure it, and if it bears fruit in the coming year, well and good; but if not, you will cut it down.'"

HERE is a parable at one and the same time lit by grace and close packed with warnings.

(i) The fig-tree occupied *a specially favoured position.* In Palestine it was not unusual to see fig-trees, thorn-trees and apple-trees in vineyards. The soil was so shallow and poor that trees were grown wherever there was soil to grow them; but the fact remains the fig-tree had a more than average chance; and it had not proved worthy of it. Repeatedly, directly and by implication, Jesus reminded men that they would be judged according to the opportunities they had. C. E. M. Joad once said of this, our own generation, "We have the powers of gods and we use them like irresponsible schoolboys." Never was a generation entrusted with so much, and, therefore, never was a generation so answerable to God.

(ii) Clearly the parable teaches us that *uselessness invites disaster.* It has been claimed that the whole process of evolution in this world is to produce useful things, and that that which is useful will go on from strength to strength in the economy of evolution, while that which is useless will surely be eliminated. The most searching question we can be asked is, " Of what use were you in this world? "

(iii) Further, the parable teaches that *nothing which only takes out can survive.* The fig-tree was drawing strength and sustenance from the soil; and in return it was producing nothing. That was precisely its sin. In the last analysis, there are two kinds of people in this world— those who take out more than they put in, and those who put in more than they take out. In one sense we are all in debt to life. We came into life at the peril of someone else's life; and we would never have survived without the care of those who loved us. We have inherited a Christian civilization and a freedom which we did not create. There is laid on us the duty of handing things on even better than we found them. " Die when I may," said Abraham Lincoln, " I want it said of me that I plucked a weed and planted a flower wherever I thought a flower would grow." Once a student was being shown bacteria under the microscope. He could actually see one generation of these microscopic living things being born, dying and another being born to take its place. He saw, as he had never seen before, how one generation succeeds another. " After what I have seen," he said, " I pledge myself never to be a weak link." If we take that pledge we will fulfil the obligation of putting into life at least as much as we take out.

(iv) This parable tells us of *the gospel of the second chance.* A fig-tree normally takes three years to reach maturity. If it is not fruiting by that time it is not likely to fruit. But this fig-tree was given a second chance. It is always Jesus' way to give a man chance after chance. Peter and Mark and Paul would all gladly have witnessed to that. God is infinitely kind to the man who falls and rises again.

(v) But this parable makes it quite clear that *there is a final chance*. If we refuse chance after chance, if God's appeal and challenge come again and again in vain the day comes, not when God has shut us out, but when we by deliberate choice have shut ourselves out from God. God save us from that!

MERCY MORE THAN LAW

Luke 13: 13-17

> Jesus was teaching in one of the Synagogues on the Sabbath; and—look you—there was a woman there who had a spirit of weakness for eighteen years. She was bent together and could not straighten up properly. When Jesus saw her He called her to Him. "Woman," He said, "you are set free from your weakness"; and He laid His hands upon her; and immediately she was straightened. The president of the Synagogue was vexed that Jesus had healed on the Sabbath. "Are there not six days," he said to the crowd, "in which work ought to be done? Come and be healed on them and not on the Sabbath day." "Hypocrites!" the Lord answered. "Does each one of you not loose his ox or his ass from the manger on the Sabbath, and lead him out and give him drink? And as for this woman, a daughter of Abraham, whom —look you—Satan bound for eighteen years, should she not have been loosed from this bond on the Sabbath day?" And, as He said this, His opponents were put to shame, and all the crowd rejoiced at the glorious things that were done by Him.

THIS is the last time that we ever hear of Jesus being in a Synagogue, and it is clear that, by this time, the authorities were watching His every action, and waiting to pounce upon Him whenever they got the chance. Jesus healed the woman who for eighteen years had not been able to straighten her bent body; and then the president of the Synagogue intervened. He had not even the courage to speak directly to Jesus. He addressed his protest to the

waiting people, although it was meant for Jesus. Jesus
had healed on the Sabbath; technically healing was work;
and, therefore, Jesus had broken the Sabbath. But Jesus
answered His opponents out of their own law. The Rabbis
abhorred cruelty to dumb animals and, even on the Sabbath,
it was perfectly legal to loose beasts from their stalls and
to water them. Jesus demanded, " If you can loose a
beast from a stall and water him on the Sabbath day,
surely it is right in the sight of God to loose this poor
woman from her infirmity."

(i) The president of the Synagogue, and those like him,
were *people who loved systems more than they loved people.*
They were more concerned that their own petty little
laws should be observed than that a woman should be
helped and healed. One of the great problems of a developed
civilization is the relationship of the individual to the system.
In times of war the individual vanishes. A man ceases
to be a man and becomes a member of such and such an
age group or the like. Certain men are lumped together,
not as individuals, but as living ammunition who are, in
the terrible word, expendable. A man becomes an item in a
statistical list. Sidney and Beatrice Webb, afterwards
Lord and Lady Passmore, were two great economists
and statistical experts; but H. G. Wells said of Beatrice
Webb that the trouble about her was that " she saw men
as specimens walking." In Christianity the individual
always comes before the system. It is true to say that
without Christianity there can be no such thing as democ-
racy, because Christianity alone guarantees and defends
the value of the ordinary and the individual man. If ever
Christian principles were banished from political and
economic life there would be nothing left to keep at bay
the totalitarian state where the individual is lost in the
system, and only exists, not for his own sake, but for the
sake of the system. Strangely enough, this worship of
systems very commonly invades the Church. There are
many Church people—it would be a mistake to call them

Christian people—who are more concerned with the method of Church government than they are with the worship of God and the service of men. It is all too tragically true that more trouble and strife arises in Churches over legalistic details of procedure than for any other reason. In the world, and in the Church, we are constantly in peril of loving systems more than we love God and more than we love men.

(ii) Jesus' whole action in this matter makes it clear that it is not God's will that any human being should suffer one moment longer than is absolutely necessary. The Jewish law was that it was perfectly legal to help someone on the Sabbath who was in actual danger of his life. If Jesus had postponed the healing of this woman until the morrow no one could have criticised Him; but Jesus insisted that suffering must not be allowed to continue until to-morrow if it could be helped to-day. Over and over again in life some good and kindly scheme is held up until this or that regulation is satisfied, or this or that technical detail worked out. He gives twice who gives quickly, as the Latin proverb has it. No helpful deed that we can do to-day should be postponed until to-morrow.

THE EMPIRE OF CHRIST

Luke 13: 18, 19

> So Jesus said to them, " To what is the Kingdom of God like, and to what will I compare it? It is like a grain of mustard seed, which a man took and cast into his garden; and it grew until it became a tree, and the birds of the air found a lodging in its branches."

THIS is an illustration which Jesus used more than once, and which He used for different purposes. In the east mustard is not a garden herb but a field plant. It does literally grow to be a tree. A height of seven or eight feet was common, and a traveller tells how once he came across a mustard plant which was twelve feet high, and which overtopped a horse and its rider. It is common to see a cloud of birds around such trees, for they love the little black mustard seeds.

Matthew (13: 31, 32) also relates this parable with a different emphasis. His version is,

> Jesus offered them another parable. " The Kingdom of Heaven is like a grain of mustard seed, which a man took and sowed in his field. It is the smallest of all seeds, but, when it has grown, it is greater than all herbs, and becomes a tree, so that the birds of the air come and find a lodging in its branches."

The point of the parable in Matthew and in Luke is quite different. Matthew stresses *the smallness of the seed* which Luke never even mentions; and Matthew's point is that the greatest things can, and do, start from the smallest beginnings and so does the Kingdom of Heaven. Luke's version leads up to the birds finding a lodging place in the branches. In the east the regular symbol of a great empire was a mighty tree; and the subject nations who found shelter and protection within it are typified by birds in the branches (cp. Ezekiel 31: 6; 17: 23). As we have seen more than once Luke is the universalist who dreamed of a world for Christ; and so Luke's point is that the Kingdom of God will grow into a vast empire in which all kinds of men and nations will come together, and in which they will find the shelter and the protection of God. There is much in Luke's conception that we would do well to learn.

(i) There is room in the Empire of the Kingdom for *a wide variety of beliefs*. No man and no Church has a monopoly of all truth. To think ourselves right and everyone else wrong can lead to nothing but trouble and bitterness and strife. So long as all these beliefs are stemmed in Christ they are all facets of God's truth.

(ii) There is room in the Empire of the Kingdom for *a wide variety of experiences*. We do infinite harm when we try to standardize Christian experience, and when we insist that all men must come to Christ in the same way. One man may have a sudden shattering experience and may be able to point to the day and the hour, and the very minute, when God invaded his life. Another man's heart may open to Christ normally and naturally, and without crisis, as the petal of the lint-bell opens to the sun. Both experiences come from God and both men belong to God.

(iii) There is room in the Empire of the Kingdom for *a wide variety of ways of worship*. One man finds touch with God in an elaborate ritual and in a splendid liturgy; another finds God in the bare simplicities. There is no right or wrong here. It is the glory of the Church that within its fellowship somewhere a man will find the worship that brings him to God. Let him find it, but let him not think his way the only way and let him not criticize another's way.

(iv) There is room in the Empire of the Kingdom for *all kinds of people*. The world has its labels and its distinctions and its barriers. But in the Kingdom there is no distinction between rich and poor, small and great, famous and unknown. The Church should be the only place in the world where all distinctions are gone.

(v) There is room in the Empire of God *for all nations*. There are still in the world barriers like the colour bar. A famous Test Match cricketer, whose autograph crowds struggle to get, can still be barred from a London hotel. A writer tells how in America she had lunch with Paul Robeson and his wife, and was thrilled to lunch with the great singer and actor. She moved on to stay with friends at Chicago. She was full of this experience, but her story of it was received very coldly. She asked why. The answer was, " If I were you, I would not talk too much about lunching with Paul Robeson." " Why? " she asked, " surely he is one of the world's great artists.". " That may be," was the answer, " but Paul Robeson's a nigger."

In Revelation 21: 16 we are given the dimensions of the Holy City. It is a square each of whose sides is 12,000 furlongs. 12,000 furlongs is 1,500 miles; and the area of a square whose sides are 1,500 miles is 2,250,000 square miles! There is room in the city of God for all the world and more.

THE LEAVEN OF THE KINGDOM

Luke 13: 20, 21

> Again Jesus said, " To what will I liken the Kingdom of God? It is like leaven, which a woman took and hid in three measures of meal, until the whole was leavened."

THIS is an illustration which Jesus took from His own home. In those days bread was baked at home. Leaven was a little piece of fermented dough which had been kept over from the last baking and had fermented in the keeping. Leaven is regularly used in Jewish thought for influence. Usually it is used for bad influence, because the Jews identified fermentation with putrefaction, and leaven stood for rottenness. Jesus had seen Mary take a little bit of leaven and put it in the dough. He had seen the whole character of the dough changed by that little bit of leaven. " That," He said, " is how my Kingdom comes." There are two interpretations of this parable. From the first of them the following points emerge.

(i) The Kingdom of Heaven starts *from the smallest beginnings*. The leaven was very small but it changed the whole character of the mass of the dough. We well know how in any court, or committee, or board one person can be a focus of trouble or a centre of peace. The Kingdom of Heaven starts from the dedicated lives of individual men and women. It may be that in the place where we work or live we are the only professing Christian. That is God giving us the task to be the leaven of the Kingdom there.

(ii) The Kingdom of Heaven *works unseen*. We cannot see the leaven working, but all the time it is doing its transforming work. The Kingdom is on the way. Anyone who knows a little history will be bound to see that. Seneca, than whom the Romans had no higher thinker, could write, " We strangle a mad dog; we slaughter a fierce ox; we plunge the knife into sickly cattle lest they taint the herd; children who are born weakly and deformed we drown." In A.D. 60 that was the normal thing. Things like that cannot happen to-day because slowly, but inevitably, the Kingdom is on the way.

(iii) The Kingdom of Heaven *works from inside*. Until the leaven got into the dough it was powerless to help; it had to get right inside. We will never change men from the outside. New houses, new conditions, better material things only change the surface. It is the task of Christianity to make, not new things, but new men. And once the new men are created the new world will surely follow. That is why the Church is the most important institution in the world, for it is the factory where *men* are produced.

(iv) The power of the Kingdom *comes from outside*. The dough had no power to change itself. Neither have we. We have tried and failed. To change life we need a power outside and beyond us. We need the master of life, and He is forever waiting to give to us also the secret of victorious living.

The second interpretation of this parable insists that so far from working unseen the work of the leaven is manifest to all because it turns the dough into a bubbling, seething mass. So, then, the leaven stands for the disturbing power of Christianity. In Thessalonica it was said of the Christians, " The people who have turned the world upside down have come here too " (Acts 17: 6). Religion is never dope; it never sends people comfortably to sleep; it never makes them placidly accept the evils that should be striven against. Real Christianity is the most revolutionary thing in the world, for it works a revolution in the individual life and in all society. " May God," said Unamuno the great Spanish mystic, " deny you peace and give you glory." The Kingdom of Heaven is the leaven which fills a man at one and the same time with the peace of God and the divine discontent which will not rest until the evils of earth are swept away by the changing, revolutionizing power of God.

THE RISK OF BEING SHUT OUT

Luke 13: 22-30

> Jesus continued to go through towns and villages, teaching and making His way to Jerusalem. " Lord," someone said to Him, "are those who are to be saved few in number? " He said to them, " Keep on striving to enter through the narrow door, because many, I tell you, will seek to enter in and will not be able to. Once the master of the house has risen and shut the door, and when you begin to stand outside and knock, saying, ' Lord, open to us,' he will answer you, ' I do not know where you come from.' Then you will begin to say, ' We have eaten and drunk in your presence and you taught in our streets.' He will say, ' I tell you, I do not know where you come from. Depart from me all you who are workers of iniquity.' There will be weeping and gnashing of teeth there, when you will see Abraham and Isaac and Jacob in the Kingdom of God and yourselves cast out. And they will come from the east and from the west, and from the north and from the south, and take their places at table in the Kingdom of God. And—look you— there are those who are last who will be first, and there are those first who will be last."

WHEN this questioner asked his question he would certainly do so on the assumption that the Kingdom of God was for the Jews only, and that Gentiles would all be shut out. Jesus' answer must have come as a shock to him.

(i) Jesus declared that entry to the Kingdom can never be automatic, and that it is the result and the reward of a struggle. " Keep on striving to enter," said Jesus. The word that is used for *striving* is the word from which the English word *agony* is derived. The struggle to enter in must be so intense that it can be described as an agony of soul and spirit. We run a certain danger. It is easy to think that, once we have become members of the Church by profession, we have reached the end of the road, that then we can, as it were, sit back like those who have arrived and who have achieved their goal. There is no such finality in the Christian life. A man must ever be going forward or necessarily he is going backward. The Christian way is like a climb up a mountain pathway towards a peak which will never be reached in this world. It was said of two gallant climbers who died on Mount Everest, "When last seen they were going strong for the top." It was inscribed on the grave of an Alpine guide who had died on the mountain-side, " He died climbing." For the Christian life is ever an upward and an onward way.

(ii) The defence of these people was, " We ate and drank in your presence, and you taught in our streets." There are those who seem to think that just because they are members of a Christian civilisation all is well. They would differentiate between themselves and the poor heathen in their ignorance and their blindness. But the man who lives in a Christian civilisation is not necessarily a Christian. He may be enjoying all its benefits; he certainly is living on the Christian capital which others before him have built up; but that is no reason for sitting back content and sure that all is well. It is a challenge which asks us, " What did you do to initiate all this? What have you done to preserve and develop it? " We cannot live on borrowed goodness.

(iii) There will be surprises in the Kingdom of God. Those who were very prominent in this world may have to be very humble in the next; those whom no one noticed here may be the princes of the world to come. There is a story of a woman who in this world had been used to every luxury and to all respect. She died, and when she arrived in heaven an angel was sent to conduct her to her house. They passed many a lovely mansion, and the woman thought that each one, as they came to it, must be the one allotted to her. When they had passed through the main streets of heaven they came to the suburbs and the outskirts where the houses were much smaller; and on the very fringe they came to a house which was little more than a hut. "That is your house," said the conducting angel. "What," said the woman, "that! I cannot live in that." "I am sorry," said the angel, "but that is all that we could build for you with the materials you sent up." The standards of heaven are not the standards of earth. Earth's first will often be last, and earth's last will often be first.

COURAGE AND TENDERNESS

Luke 13: 31-35

> At that hour some Pharisees came to Jesus. "Depart," they said to Him, "and get on your way from this place, because Herod is out to kill you." "Go," He said, "and tell that fox, look you, I cast out demons and I work cures to-day and to-morrow, and on the third day my work is perfected. I must be on my way to-day, and to-morrow and the next day, because it is not possible for a prophet to perish out of Jerusalem. Jerusalem! Jerusalem! Killer of the prophets! Stoner of those who sent to you! How often I wanted to gather together your children as a hen gathers her brood under her wings—and you would not! Look you, your house is desolate. I tell you, you will not see me until you shall say, 'Blessed is He who comes in the name of the Lord.'"

BECAUSE of the insight that it gives to us into the life of Jesus, as it were behind the scenes, this is one of the most interesting passages in Luke's gospel.

(i) It gives us the, at first sight, surprising information that not all the Pharisees were hostile to Jesus. Here we have some of them actually warning Him that He was in danger, and advising Him to seek safety. It is true that from the gospels we do get a one-sided picture of the Pharisees. The Jews themselves knew very well that there were good and bad Pharisees. They divided them into seven different classes. (i) *The Shoulder Pharisees.* These wore their good deeds on their shoulder, and performed them to be seen of men. (ii) *The Wait-a-little Pharisees.* They could always find a good excuse for putting off a good deed until to-morrow. (iii) *The Bruised or Bleeding Pharisees.* No Jewish Rabbi could be seen talking to any woman on the street, not even his wife, or mother or sister. But certain of the Pharisees went further. They would not even look at a woman on the street; they even shut their eyes to avoid seeing a woman; they, therefore, knocked into walls and houses and bruised themselves; and then exhibited their bruises as special badges of extraordinary piety. (iv) *The Pestle and Mortar or Hump-backed Pharisees.* They walked bent double in a false and cringing humility; they were the Uriah Heeps of Jewish religion. (v) *The Ever-reckoning Pharisees.* They were ever reckoning up their good deeds and, as it were, striking a balance-sheet of profit and loss with God. (vi) *The Timid or Fearing Pharisees.* They went ever in the fear of the wrath of God. They were, as it was said of Burns, not helped but haunted by their religion. (vii) *The God-loving Pharisees.* They were copies of Abraham and lived in faith and charity. There may have been six bad Pharisees for every good one; but this passage shows that even amongst the Pharisees there were those who admired and respected Jesus.

(ii) This passage shows us Jesus talking to a king. Herod Antipas, King of Galilee, was out to stop Jesus. To the Jew the fox was a symbol of three things. First, the fox was regarded as the sliest of animals. Second, it was regarded as the most destructive of animals. Third, the fox was the symbol of a worthless and insignificant man. It takes a brave man to call the reigning king a fox. It is told that Latimer was once preaching in Westminster

Abbey when Henry the king was one of the congregation. In the pulpit he soliloquised, " Latimer! Latimer! Latimer! Be careful what you say. The king of England is here! " Then he went on, " Latimer! Latimer! Latimer! Be careful what you say. The King of Kings is here." Jesus took His orders from God, and he would not shorten his work by one day to please or to escape any earthly king.

(iii) The lament over Jerusalem is a most important passage, because it is another of these passages which shows how little we really know of Jesus' life. It is quite clear that Jesus could never have spoken like this, unless, prior to this, He had more than once gone with His offer of love to Jerusalem; and in the first three gospels there is no word or indication of any such visits. Once again it is clear that in the gospels we have the merest sketch of Jesus' life. There is nothing which hurts so much as to go to someone and offer love, and to have that offer rejected and spurned. It is life's bitterest tragedy to give one's heart to someone only to have it broken. That is what happened to Jesus in Jerusalem; and still He comes to men, and still men reject Him. But the fact remains that to reject the love of God is in the end to be in peril of the wrath of God.

UNDER THE SCRUTINY OF HOSTILE MEN

Luke 14: 1-6

On the Sabbath day Jesus had gone into the house of one of the rulers who belonged to the Pharisees to eat bread; and they were watching Him. And—look you—there was a man before Him who had dropsy. Jesus said to the Scribes and Pharisees, " Is it lawful to heal on the Sabbath? Or, is it not? " They kept silent. So He took him and healed him and sent him away. He said to them, " Suppose one of you has an ass or an ox, and it falls into a well, will he not immediately pull it out, even if it is on the Sabbath day? " And they had no answer to these things.

IN the gospel story there are seven incidents in which
Jesus healed on the Sabbath day. In Luke's gospel we
have already studied the story of the healing of Simon's
wife's mother (4: 38); of the man with the withered
hand (6: 6); and of the woman who was bent for eighteen
years (13: 14). To these John adds the story of the healing
of the paralytic at the pool of Bethesda (John 5: 9); and
of the man born blind (John 9: 14). Mark adds one more—
the healing of the demon-possessed man in the Synagogue
at Capernaum (Mark 1: 21). Anyone would think that a
record like that would have made a man beloved of all;
but it is the tragic fact that every miracle of healing that
Jesus wrought on the Sabbath day only made the Scribes
and Pharisees more certain that He was a dangerous and
irreligious law-breaker who must at all costs be stopped.
If we are to understand what happened to Jesus it is
essential to remember that the orthodox Jews of His day
regarded Him as a law-breaker. He healed on the Sabbath;
therefore He worked on the Sabbath; therefore He broke
the law.

On this occasion a Pharisee invited Him to a meal on
the Sabbath. The law had its meticulous and detailed
regulations about Sabbath meals. Of course no food could
be cooked on the Sabbath; that would have been to work.
All food had to be cooked on the Friday; and, if it was
necessary to keep it hot, it must be kept hot in such a way
that it was not cooked any more! So it is laid down that
food to be kept warm for the Sabbath must not be put
into " oil dregs, manure, salt, chalk or sand, whether
moist or dry, nor into straw, grape-skins, flock or vegetables,
if these are damp, though it may be if they are dry. It may
be, however, put into clothes, amidst fruits, pigeons'
feathers and flax tow." It was the observance of regulations
like that that the Pharisees and Scribes regarded as religion.
No wonder they could not understand Jesus!

It is by no means impossible that the Pharisees
" planted " the man with the dropsy in this house on this

occasion to see what Jesus would do. They were watching Him; and the word used for *watching* is the word that is used for "interested and sinister espionage." Jesus was under scrutiny.

Without hesitation Jesus healed the man. He knew perfectly well what they were thinking; and He quoted their own law and practice to them. Open wells were quite common in Palestine, and were not infrequently the cause of accidents. (cp. Exodus 21: 33). It was perfectly allowable to rescue a beast which had fallen in. Jesus, with searing contempt, demands how, if it be right to help an animal on the Sabbath, it can be wrong to help a man.

This passage tells us certain things about Jesus and about His enemies.

(i) It shows us the serenity with which Jesus met life. There is nothing more trying than to be under constant and critical scrutiny. When that happens to most people they lose their nerve and, even more often, they lose their temper. They become irritable, and there may be greater sins than irritability, but there is none which causes more pain and heartbreak. But even in things which would have broken men's spirit Jesus remained serene. If we live with Him, He can make us like Himself.

(ii) It is to be noted that Jesus never refused any man's invitation of hospitality. To the end He never abandoned hope of men. To hope to change them, or even to appeal to them, might be the forlornest of forlorn hopes, but He would never let a chance go. He would not refuse even an enemy's invitation. It is as clear as daylight that we will never make our enemies our friends if we refuse to meet them and to talk with them.

(iii) The most amazing things about the Scribes and Pharisees is their staggering lack of a sense of proportion. They would go to endless trouble to formulate and to obey their petty rules and regulations; and yet they would count it a sin to ease a sufferer's pain on the Sabbath day. If a man had one prayer to pray he might well pray to be

given a sense of proportion. The things which disturb
the peace of congregations are seldom big things and are
often trifles. The things which divide men from men, and
which destroy friendships, are often little things to which
no sensible man, in his saner moments, would allow any
importance. The little things can bulk so largely that they
can fill the whole horizon. Only if we put first things first
will all things take their proper place—and love comes
first.

THE NECESSITY OF HUMILITY

Luke 14: 7-11

> Jesus spoke a parable to the invited guests, for He
> noticed how they chose the first places at the table.
> " When you are bidden by someone to a marriage
> feast," He said, " do not take your place at table in
> the first seat, in case someone more distinguished
> than you has been invited by him, for in that case,
> the man who invited you will come and say to you,
> ' Give place to this man.' And then, with shame,
> you will begin to take the lowest place. But, when
> you have been invited, go and sit down in the lowest
> place, so that, when the man who has invited you
> comes he will say to you, ' Friend, come up higher.'
> Then you will gain honour in front of all who sit at table
> with you. For he who exalts himself will be humbled,
> and he who humbles himself will be exalted."

JESUS chose a homely illustration to point an eternal
truth. If a quite undistinguished guest arrived early at a
feast and annexed the top place, and if a more distinguished
person then arrived, and the man who had usurped the
first place was told to step down, a most embarrassing
situation would result. If, on the other hand, a man
deliberately slipped into the bottom place, and was then
asked to occupy a more distinguished place, his humility
would gain him all the more honour.

Humility has always been one of the inevitable characteristics of great men. When Thomas Hardy was so famous
that any newspaper would gladly have paid enormous
sums for his work, he used sometimes to send to a newspaper a poem; and always with it he enclosed a stamped
and addressed envelope for the return of his manuscript
should it be rejected. Even in his greatness he was humble
enough to think that his work might be turned down.
There are many stories and legends of the humility of
Principal Cairns. He would never enter a room, or go on
to a platform, first. He always said, " You first, I follow."
Once, as he came on to a platform, there was a great burst
of applause in welcome. He stood aside and let the man
after him come first, and began himself to applaud. He
never dreamed that the applause could possibly be for him;
he thought that it must be for the other man. It is only
the little man who is self-important.

How can we retain our humility?

(i) We can retain it by realizing the facts. How ever
much we know we know very little compared with the
sum total of knowledge. How ever much we have achieved
we have achieved very little in the end. However important we may believe ourselves to be, when death
removes us, or, when we retire from our position, life and
work will go on just the same.

(ii) We can retain it by comparison with the perfect.
It is when we go and see or hear the expert that we realize
how poor our own performance is. Many a man has
decided to burn his clubs after a day at the Golf Open
Championship. Many a man has decided never to appear
in public again after hearing a master musician perform.
Many a preacher has been humbled almost to despair
when he has heard a real saint of God speak. And if we
set our lives beside the life of the Lord of all good life, if
we see our unworthiness in comparison with the radiance
of His stainless purity, then pride will die and self-satis-
faction will be shrivelled up.

DISINTERESTED CHARITY

Luke 14: 12-14

> Jesus said to the man who had invited Him, " Whenever you give a dinner or a banquet, do not call your friends, or your brothers, or your kinsfolk or your rich neighbours, in case they invite you back again in return and you receive a repayment. But when you give a feast, invite the poor, the maimed, the lame and the blind. Then you will be happy, because they cannot repay you. You will receive your repayment at the resurrection of the righteous."

HERE is a searching passage, because it demands that we should examine the motives behind our generosity, and our charity and all our giving.

(i) A man may give from a sense of duty.

> He dropped a penny in the plate
> And meekly raised his eyes,
> Glad the week's rent was duly paid
> For mansions in the skies.

Our giving may be given to God and to man much in the same way as we pay our income tax—as the satisfaction of a grim duty which we cannot escape.

(ii) A man may give purely from motives of self-interest. Consciously or unconsciously he may regard his giving as an investment. He may regard each gift he gives as an entry on the credit side of his account in the ledger of God. Such giving, so far from being generosity, is simply rationalized selfishness.

(iii) A man may give in order to feel superior. Such giving can be a cruel thing. It can hurt the recipient much more than a blunt refusal would. When a man gives like that he stands on his little eminence and looks down. He may even with the gift throw in a short and smug lecture. It would be better not to give at all than to give merely to gratify one's own vanity and one's own desire for power. The Rabbis had a saying that the best kind of giving was when the giver did not know to whom he was giving, and when the receiver did not know from whom he was receiving.

(iv) A man may give because he cannot help it. That is the only real way to give. The law of the Kingdom is this—that if a man gives to gain a reward he will receive no reward; but if a man gives with no thought of reward his reward is certain. The only real giving is the giving which is the uncontrollable outflow of love. Once Dr. Johnson cynically described gratitude as " a lively sense of favours to come." The same definition could equally apply to certain forms of giving. God gave because God so loved the world—and so must we.

THE KING'S BANQUET AND THE KING'S GUESTS

Luke 14: 15-24

> When one of those who were sitting at table with Jesus heard this. he said, " Happy is the man who eats bread in the Kingdom of God." Jesus said to him, " There was a man who made a great banquet, and who invited many people to it. At the time of the banquet he sent his servants to say to those who had been invited, ' Come, because everything is now ready.' With one accord they all began to make excuses. The first said to him, ' I have bought a field, and I must go out and see it. Please have me excused.' Another said, ' I have bought five yoke of oxen, and I am on my way to try them out. Please have me excused.' Another said, ' I have married a wife, and, therefore, I cannot come.' So the servant came and told his master these things. The master of the house was enraged, and said to his servant, ' Go out quickly to the streets and lanes of the town and bring here the poor, and the maimed, and the blind and the lame.' The servant said, ' Sir, your orders have been carried out and there is still room.' So the master said to his servant, ' Go out to the roads and to the hedges, and compel them to come in, so that my house may be filled. For I tell you that none of these men who were invited shall taste of my banquet.' "

THE Jews had a series of ever-recurring conventional pictures of what would happen when God broke into history, and when the golden days of the new age arrived. One of these pictures was the picture of the Messianic Banquet. On that day God would give a great feast to His own people at which Leviathan, the sea monster, would be part of the food. It is of that banquet that the man who spoke to Jesus was thinking. When he spoke of the happiness of those who would be guests at that banquet he was thinking of Jews, and of Jews only, for the average, orthodox Jew would never have dreamed that the Gentiles and the sinners would find a place at the feast of God. Jesus knew that, and that is why Jesus spoke this parable. In Palestine, when a man made a feast, the day of it was announced long beforehand, and the invitations were sent out and accepted; but the hour of it was not announced; and when the day came and all things were ready, servants were sent out to summon the already invited guests. To accept the invitation beforehand and then to refuse it when the day came was a grave and serious insult. In the parable the master stands for God. The originally invited guests stand for the Jews. Throughout all their history they had looked forward to the day when God would break in; and when He did, they tragically refused His invitation. The poor people from the streets and lanes stand for the tax-gatherers and sinners who welcomed Jesus in a way in which the orthodox never did. Those gathered in from the roads and the hedges stand for the Gentiles for whom there was still ample room at the feast of God. As Bengel, the great commentator put it, " both nature and grace abhor a vacuum," and when the Jews refused God's invitation and left His table empty, the invitation went out to the Gentiles.

There is one sentence in this parable which has been sadly misused. " Go out," said the master, " and compel them to come in." Long ago Augustine used that text as a justification for religious persecution. It was used as a defence, and even a command, to coerce people into the Christian faith. It was used as a defence for the inquisition, the thumb-screw, the rack, the threat of death and imprisonment, the campaigns against the heretics, for all those things which are the shame of Christianity. Beside it we should always set another text—The love of Christ constrains us. (2 Corinthians 5: 14.) In the Kingdom of God there is only one compulsion—the compulsion of love.

But though this parable spoke with a threat to the Jews who had refused God's invitation, and with an undreamed of glory to the sinners and the outcasts, and the Gentiles who had never dreamed of receiving it, there are in it truths which are forever permanent, and which are as new as to-day. In the parable the invited guests made their excuses, and men's excuses do not differ so very much to-day.

(i) The first man said that he had bought a field, and was going to see it. He allowed the claims of business to usurp the claims of God. It is still possible for a man to be so immersed in this world that he has no time to worship, and even no time to pray.

(ii) The second man said that he had bought five yoke of oxen, and that he was going to try them out. He let the claims of novelty usurp the claims of Christ. It often happens that when people enter into new possessions they become so taken up with them that the claims of worship and of God get crowded out. People have been known to acquire a motor car, and then to say, " We used to go to Church on a Sunday, but now that we have got the car we go off to the country for the day." It is perilously easy for a new game, a new hobby, even a new friendship to take up even the time that should be kept for God.

(iii) The third man said, with even more finality than the others, " I have married a wife, and I cannot come." One of the wonderful merciful laws of the Old Testament laid it down, " When a man hath taken a new wife, he shall not go out to war, neither shall he be charged with any business, but he shall be free at home one year, and shall cheer up his wife which he hath taken." (Deuteronomy 24: 5.) No doubt that very law was in this man's mind. It is one of the tragedies of life when good things, the best of things, can crowd the claims of God out of life. There is no lovelier thing than a home, and yet a home was never meant to be used selfishly. They live best together who live with God; they serve each other best who also serve their fellow men; the atmosphere of a home is most lovely when those who dwell within it never forget that they are also members of the great family and household of God.

The Banquet of the Kingdom

Before we leave this passage we must note this, that the whole of it, verses 1 to 25, has all to do with feasts and banquets. It is a most significant thing that Jesus thought of His Kingdom and His service in terms of a feast. The symbol of the Kingdom was the happiest thing that human life can give. Surely this is the final condemnation of the Christian who is afraid to enjoy himself. There has always been a type of Christianity which has taken all the colour out of life. Julian spoke of those pale-faced, flat-breasted Christians for whom the sun shone and they never saw it. Swinburne slandered Christ by saying,

> " Thou hast conquered, O pale Galilæan,
> The world has grown gray at thy breath."

Ruskin, who was brought up in a rigid and a narrow home, tells how he was given a jumping-jack as a present, and how a pious aunt took it away from him, saying that toys were no things for a Christian child. Even so great and sane and healthy a scholar as A. B. Bruce said that you could not conceive of the child Jesus playing games when He was a boy, or smiling when He was a man. W. M. Macgregor, in his Warrack Lectures, speaks with the scorn, of which he was such a master, about one of John Wesley's few mistakes. He founded a school at Kingswood, near Bristol. He laid it down that no games were to be allowed in the school or in the grounds, because " he who plays when he is a child will play when he is a man." There were no holidays. The children rose at 4 a.m. and spent the first hour of the day in prayer and meditation, and on Friday they fasted until three in the afternoon. W. M. Macgregor characterizes the whole set up as " nature-defying foolishness." We must always remember that Jesus thought of the Kingdom in terms of a feast. A gloomy Christian is a contradiction in terms. Locke, the great philosopher, defined laughter as " a sudden glory." There is no healthy pleasure which is forbidden to a Christian man, for a Christian is like a man who is forever at a wedding feast.

ON COUNTING THE COST

Luke 14: 25-33

Great crowds were on the way with Jesus. He turned and said to them, " If any man comes to me and does not hate his father and mother, and wife and children, and brothers and sisters, and even his own life too, he cannot be my disciple. Whoever does not carry his cross and come after me cannot be my disciple. Which of you, if he wishes to build a tower, does not first sit down and reckon up the expense, to see whether he has enough to finish it? This he does lest, when he has laid the foundation and is unable to complete the work, all who see him begin to mock him, saying, ' This man began to build and was unable to finish the job.' Or, what king when he is going to engage battle with another king, does not first sit down and take counsel, whether he is able with ten thousand men to meet him who comes against him with twenty thousand? If he finds he cannot, while he is still distant, he sends an embassy and asks for terms of peace. So, therefore, everyone of you who does not bid farewell to all his possessions cannot be my disciple."

WHEN Jesus said this He was on His way to Jerusalem. He knew that He was on His way to the Cross; the crowds who were with Him thought that He was on His way to an empire. That is why He spoke to them like this. In the most vivid way possible He told them that the man who would follow Him was not on the way to worldly power and glory, but must be ready for a loyalty which would sacrifice the dearest things in life, and for a suffering which would be like the agony of a man upon a cross. We must not take the words of Jesus with a cold and unimaginative literalness. Eastern language is always as vivid as the human mind can make it. When Jesus tells us to hate our nearest and dearest, he does not mean that literally. He means that no love in life can compare with the love we must bear to him.

There are two suggestive truths within this passage.

(i) It is possible to be a follower of Jesus without being a disciple; to be a camp follower without being a soldier of the king; to be a hanger-on in some great work without pulling one's weight. Once someone was talking to a great scholar about a younger man. He said, " So and so tells me that he was one of your students." The teacher answered devastatingly, " He may have attended my lectures, but he was not one of my students." There is a world of difference between attending lectures and being a student. It is one of the supreme handicaps of the Church that in the Church there are so many distant followers of Jesus and so few real disciples.

(ii) It is a Christian's first duty to count the cost of following Christ. The tower which the man was going to build was probably a vineyard tower. Vineyards were often equipped with towers from which watch was kept against thieves who might steal the harvest. An unfinished building is always a humiliating thing. In Scotland, we can, for instance, think of that weird structure called " M'Caig's Folly " which stands behind Oban. In every sphere of life a man is called upon to count the cost. In the introduction to the marriage ceremony the minister states what marriage is, and then says, " It is, therefore, not to be entered upon lightly or unadvisedly, but thoughtfully, reverently, and in the fear of God." First a man and woman must count the cost. No man need become a student unless he will count the cost of learning. It is so with the Christian way. But if a man is daunted by the high demands of Christ let him remember that he is not left to fulfil them alone. He who called him to the steep road will walk with him every step of the way and will be there at the end to meet him.

THE INSIPID SALT

Luke 14: 34, 35

> Jesus said, " Salt is a fine thing; but if salt has become insipid, by what means shall its taste be restored? It is fit neither for the land nor the dunghill. Men throw it out. He who has an ear to hear, let him hear."

JUST sometimes Jesus speaks with a threat in His voice. When a person is always carping, and criticizing, and complaining, his irritable anger ceases to have any significance or any effect. But when someone whose accent is the accent of love suddenly speaks with a threat we are bound to listen. What Jesus is saying here is this—when a thing loses its essential quality, and when it fails to perform the essential duty for which it was created, it becomes useless and is fit for nothing but to be thrown away. In this passage Jesus uses salt as a symbol of the Christian life. What, then, are its essential qualities? In Palestine salt had three characteristic uses.

(i) Salt was used as *a preservative*. Salt is the earliest of all preservatives. The Greeks used to say that salt could put a new soul into dead things. Without salt the thing

putrefied and went bad; with salt its freshness was pre-
served. That must mean that true Christianity must
act as a preservative against the corruption of the world.
The individual Christian must be the conscience of his
fellows; and the Church must be the conscience of the
nation. The Christian must be such that in his presence
no doubtful language will be used, no questionable stories
told, no dishonourable action suggested. He must be like
a cleansing antiseptic in the circle in which he moves.
The Church must be such that she speaks fearlessly against
all evils, and supports fearlessly all good causes. She must
be such that she will never hold her peace through fear or
favour of men.

(ii) Salt was used as *a flavouring*. Food, without salt,
can be revoltingly insipid. The Christian, then, must be
the man who brings flavour into life. The Christianity
which acts like a shadow of gloom and a wet blanket is no
true Christianity. The Christian is the man who, by his
courage, his hope, his cheerfulness and his kindness brings
a new flavour into life.

(iii) Salt was used *on the land*. It was used to make it
easier for all good things to grow. The Christian must be
such that he makes it easier for people to be good, and
harder to be bad. We all know people in whose company
there are certain things we would not and could not do;
and equally we all know people in whose company we might
well stoop to things which by ourselves we would not do.
There are those fine souls in whose company it is easier to
be brave, and cheerful and good. The Christian must
carry with him a breath of heaven in which the fine things
flourish and in which the evil things shrivel up.

That is the function of the Christian; if he fails in his
function there is no good reason why he should exist at
all; and we have already seen that in the economy of God
uselessness invites disaster. He who has an ear to hear,
let him hear.

THE SHEPHERD'S JOY

Luke 15: 1-7

> The tax-collectors and sinners were all coming near to Jesus to hear Him, and the Pharisees and Scribes were murmuring, saying, " This man welcomes sinners and eats with them."
>
> He spoke this parable to them. " What man of you," he said, " who has a hundred sheep, and who hast lost one of them, does not leave the ninety-nine in the wilderness and go after the one that is lost until he finds it? And when he finds it, rejoicing he lays it on his shoulders; and when he comes home he calls together his friends and neighbours, saying to them, ' Rejoice with me because I have found my sheep which was lost.' I tell you that just so there will be joy in heaven over one sinner who repents more than over ninety-nine just people who have no need of repentance."

THERE is no chapter of the New Testament so well known and so dearly loved as the fifteenth chapter of Luke's gospel. It has been called " the gospel in the gospel," as if it contained the very distilled essence of the good news which Jesus came to tell.

These parables of Jesus arose out of a perfectly definite situation. It was an offence to the Scribes and Pharisees that Jesus companied and associated with men and women who, by the orthodox, were labelled as sinners. The Pharisees gave to people who did not keep the law a general classification. They called them *The People of the Land*. There was a complete barrier between the Pharisees and The People of the Land. To marry a daughter to one of them was like exposing her, bound and helpless, to a lion. The Pharisaic regulations laid it down, " When a man is one of the People of the Land, entrust no money to him, take no testimony from him, trust him with no secret, do not appoint him guardian of an orphan, do not make him the custodian of charitable funds, do not accompany him on a journey." A Pharisee was forbidden to be the guest of any such man, or to have him as his guest. He was

even forbidden, so far as it was possible, to have any
business dealings with him, or to buy anything from him
or sell anything to him. It was the deliberate Pharisaic
aim to avoid every contact with The People of the Land,
the people who did not observe the petty details of the
law. Obviously, they would be shocked to the core at the
way in which Jesus companied with people who were not
only rank outsiders, but sinners, contact with whom would
necessarily defile. We will understand these parables
more fully if we remember that the strict Jews said, not
" There is joy in heaven over one sinner who repents,"
but, " There is joy in heaven over one sinner who is obliterated before God." They looked sadistically forward not
to the saving but to the destruction of the sinner.

So Jesus told them the parable of the lost sheep and the
shepherd's joy. The shepherd in Judæa had a hard and
dangerous task. Pasture was scarce. The narrow central
plateau was only a few miles wide, and then it plunged
down to the wild cliffs and the terrible devastation of the
desert. There were no restraining walls, and the sheep
would wander. George Adam Smith wrote of the shepherd,
" On some high moor across which at night the hyænas
howl, when you meet him, sleepless, far-sighted, weather-
beaten, armed, leaning on his staff and looking out over
his scattered sheep, everyone of them on his heart, you
understand why the shepherd of Judæa sprang to the
front in his people's history; why they gave his name to
the king and made him the symbol of providence; why
Christ took him as the type of self-sacrifice." The shepherd
was personally responsible for the sheep. If a sheep was
lost the shepherd must at least bring home the fleece to
show how it had died. These shepherds were experts at
tracking, and could follow the straying sheep's footprints
for miles across the hills. There was not a shepherd for
whom it was not all in the day's work to lay down his life
for his sheep. Many of the flocks were communal flocks,
belonging, not to individuals, but to villages. There would

be two or three shepherds in charge. Those whose flocks
were safe would arrive home on time, and they would
bring news that one shepherd was still out on the mountain
side searching for a sheep which was lost. The whole
village would be upon the watch, and then, when, in the
distance, they saw the shepherd striding home with the
lost sheep across his shoulders there would rise from the
whole community a shout of joy and of thanksgiving.
That is the picture that Jesus drew of God; that, said
Jesus, is what God is like. God is as glad when a lost
sinner is found as a shepherd is when a strayed sheep is
brought home. As a great saint said, " God, too, knows
the joy of finding things that have gone lost."

There is a wondrous thought here. It is the truly
tremendous truth that God is kinder than men. The
orthodox would write off the tax-collectors and the sinners
as being beyond the pale, and as deserving of nothing but
destruction. Not so God. Men may give up hope of a
sinner. Not so God. God loves the folk who never stray
away; but in His heart there is the joy of joys when one
lost one is found and comes home; and it would be a
thousand times easier to come back to God than to come
home to the bleak criticism of men.

> Souls of men! why will ye scatter
>   Like a crowd of frightened sheep?
> Foolish hearts! why will ye wander
>   From a love so true and deep?
>
> Was there ever kindest shepherd
>   Half so gentle, half so sweet,
> As the Saviour who would have us
>   Come and gather round His feet?
>
> For the love of God is broader
>   Than the measure of man's mind;
> And the heart of the Eternal
>   Is most wonderfully kind.

THE COIN A WOMAN LOST AND FOUND

Luke 15: 8-10

Or, what woman who has ten silver pieces, if she loses one piece, does not light a lamp and sweep the house and search carefully until she finds it? And when she has found it she calls together her friends and neighbours, saying, " Rejoice with me because I have found the silver piece which I lost." Even so, I tell you, there is joy in the presence of the angels of God over one sinner who repents.

THE coin in question in this parable was a silver drachma which was worth about 9d. It would not be difficult to lose a coin in a Palestinian peasant's house, and it might take a long search to find it. The Palestinian houses were very dark, for they were lit by one little circular window not much more than about eighteen inches across. The floor was beaten earth covered with dried reeds and rushes; and to look for a coin on a floor like that was very much like looking for a needle in a haystack. The woman swept the floor in the hope that she might see the coin glint, or hear it tinkle as it fell among the rushes.

There are two reasons why the woman may have been so eager to find the coin.

(i) It may have been a matter of sheer necessity. 9d. does not sound very much, but it was a little more than a whole day's wage for a working man in Palestine. These people lived always on the edge of things, and very little stood between them and real hunger and starvation. The woman may well have searched with intensity because if she did not find the family would not eat.

(ii) But there may be a much more romantic reason than that. In Palestine the mark of a married woman was a head-dress made of ten silver coins linked together by a silver chain. For years maybe a girl would scrape and save to amass her ten coins, for the head-dress was almost the equivalent of her wedding ring. When she had it it was so inalienably hers that it could not even be taken from her for debt. It may well be that it was one of these coins that the woman in the parable lost, and she searched for it as any woman would search if she had lost her marriage ring.

In either case it is easy to think of the joy of the woman when at last she saw the glint of the elusive coin, and when she held it in her hand again. God, said Jesus, is like that. The joy of God, and of all the angels, when one sinner comes home is like the joy of a home when a coin which has stood between them and starvation has been lost and is found; it is like the joy of a woman who loses her most precious possession, which had a value far beyond money, and then finds it again. No Pharisee had ever dreamed of a God like that. A great Jewish scholar has admitted that this is the one absolutely new thing which Jesus taught men about God—that God actually sought and searched for men. The Jew might have agreed that if a man came crawling home to God in self-abasement and knelt before God praying for pity he might find it; but the Jew would never have conceived of a God who went out to search for sinners. It is our glory that we believe in the seeking love of God, because we see that love incarnate in Jesus Christ, the Son of God, who came to seek and to save that which was lost.

THE STORY OF THE LOVING FATHER

Luke 15: 11-32

Jesus said, " There was a man who had two sons. The younger of them said to his father, ' Father, give me the part of the estate which falls to me.' So his father divided his living between them. Not many days after, the son realized it all and went away to a far country, and there in wanton recklessness scattered his substance. When he had spent everything a mighty famine arose throughout that country and he began to be in want. He went and attached himself to a citizen of that country, and he sent him into his fields to feed pigs; and he had a great desire to fill

himself with the husks the pigs were eating; and no
one gave anything to him. When he had come to
himself, he said, ' How many of my father's hired
servants have more than enough bread, and I—I am
perishing here with hunger. I will get up and I will
go to my father, and I will say to him, " Father, I have
sinned against heaven and before you. I am no
longer fit to be called your son. Make me as one of
your hired servants."' So he got up and went to his
father. While he was still a long way away his father
saw him, and was moved to the depths of his being
and ran 'and flung his arms round his neck and kissed
him tenderly. The son said to him, ' Father, I have
sinned against heaven and before you. I am no longer
fit to be called your son.' But the father said to his
servants, ' Quick! Bring out the best robe and put
it on him; put a ring on his finger; put shoes on his
feet; and bring the fatted calf and kill it and let us
eat and rejoice, for this my son was dead and has come
back to life again; he was lost and has been found.'
And they began to rejoice.

"Now the elder son was in the field. When he came
near the house he heard the sound of music and
dancing. He called one of the slaves and asked what
these things could mean. He said to him, ' Your
brother has come, and your father has killed the fatted
calf because he has got him back safe and sound.'
He was enraged and refused to come in. His father
went out and urged him to come in. He answered
his father, ' Look you, I have served you so many
years and I never transgressed your order, and to me
you never gave a kid that I might have a good time
with my friends. But when this son of yours—this
fellow who consumed your living with harlots—came,
you killed the fatted calf for him.' ' Child,' he said
to him, ' you are always with me. Everything that is
mine is yours. But we had to rejoice and be glad, for
your brother was dead and has come back to life
again; he was lost and has been found.'"

Not without reason this has been called the greatest short
story in the world. Under Jewish law a father was not
free to leave his property as he liked. The elder son must
get two-thirds, and the younger one-third. (Deuteronomy
21: 17.) It was by no means unusual for a father to

distribute his estate before he died if he wished to retire from the actual management of affairs. But there is a certain heartless callousness in the request of the younger son. He said in effect, " Give me now the part of the estate I will get anyway when you are dead, and let me get out of this." The father did not argue. He knew that if the son was ever to learn he must learn the hard way; and he gave him his request. Without delay the son realized his share of the property and left home. He soon ran through the money; and he finished up feeding pigs, a task, that was forbidden to a Jew because the law said, " Cursed is he who feeds swine." Then Jesus paid sinning mankind the greatest compliment it has ever been paid. " *When he came to himself,*" said Jesus. Jesus believed that so long as a man was away from God and against God he was not truly himself; he was only truly himself when he was on the way home. Beyond a doubt Jesus did not believe in total depravity; he never believed that you could glorify God by blackguarding man. He believed that man was never essentially himself until he came home to God. So the son decided to come home, and to plead to be taken back not as a son but in the lowest rank of slaves, the hired servants, the men who were only day labourers. The ordinary slave was in some sense a member of the family, but the hired servant could be dismissed at a day's notice. He was not one of the family at all. So he came home; and, according to the best Greek text, his father never gave him the chance to ask to be a servant. He broke in before that. That robe stands for honour; the ring stands for authority, for if a man gave to another his signet ring it was the same as giving him the power of attorney; the shoes stand for a son as opposed to a slave, for children of the family were shod and slaves were not. The slave's dream in the negro spiritual is of the time when " all God's chillun got shoes," for shoes were the sign of freedom. And a feast was made that all might rejoice at the wanderer's return.

Let us stop there, and let us see the truth so far in this parable.

(i) The parable should never have been called the Parable of the Prodigal Son, for the son is not the hero. It should be called the Parable of the Loving Father, for it tells us rather about a father's love than a son's sin.

(ii) The parable tells us much about the forgiveness of God. The father must have been waiting and watching for the son to come home, for he saw him a long way away. When he came he forgave him with no recriminations. There is a way of forgiving when forgiveness is conferred as a favour; and worse, when someone is forgiven, but always by hint and by word and by threat his sin is held over him. Once Lincoln was asked how he was going to treat the rebellious southerners when they had finally been defeated and had returned to the Union of the United States. The questioner expected that Lincoln would take a dire vengeance, but he answered, " I will treat them as if they had never been away." It is the wonder of the love of God that God treats us like that.

But that is not the end of the story. There enters the elder brother who was actually sorry that his brother had come home. The elder brother stands for the self-righteous Pharisees who would rather have seen a sinner destroyed than saved. Certain things stand out about the elder brother.

(i) His whole attitude shows that his years of obedience to his father had been years of grim duty and not of loving service.

(ii) His whole attitude is one of utter lack of sympathy. He refers to his brother, not as *my brother* but as *your son*. He was the kind of self-righteous character who would cheerfully have kicked a man farther into the gutter when he was already down.

(iii) He had a peculiarly nasty mind. There is no mention of harlots until he mentions them. He, no doubt, suspected and accused his brother of the sins he himself would have liked to commit.

Once again we have the same amazing truth here, that it is easier to confess to God than it is to many a man; that God is more merciful in his judgments than many an orthodox man is; that the love of God is far broader than the love of man; and that God can forgive when men refuse to forgive. In face of a love like that we cannot be other than lost in wonder, love and praise.

Three lost things

We must finally note that these three parables are not simply three ways of stating the same thing. There is a difference. The sheep went lost through *sheer foolishness*. It did not think, and many a man would escape sin if he thought in time. The coin did not go lost at all; it was lost *through no fault of its own*. Many a man is lead astray, and God will not hold him guiltless who has taught another to sin. The son *deliberately went lost*, callously turning his back on his father. But the love of God can defeat the foolishness of man, the seductions of the tempting voices, and even the deliberate rebellion of the heart.

A BAD MAN'S GOOD EXAMPLE

Luke 16: 1-13

Jesus said to His disciples, " There was a rich man who had a steward. He received information against the steward which alleged that he was dissipating his goods. He called him, and said to him, ' What is this that I hear about you? Give an account of your stewardship, for you can no longer be steward.' The steward said to himself, ' What am I to do? I have not the strength to dig, and I am ashamed to beg. I know what I will do, so that, when I am removed from my stewardship, they will receive me into their houses.' So he summoned each of the people who owed debts to his master. To the first he said, ' How much do you owe

my master?' He said, ' Nine hundred gallons of oil.'
He said to him, ' Take your accounts and sit down
and write quickly, four hundred and fifty.' Then he
said to another ' And you—how much do you owe?'
He said, ' A thousand bushels of corn.' He said to
him, ' Take your accounts and write eight hundred.'
And the master praised the wicked steward because
he acted shrewdly; for the sons of this world are
shrewder in their own generation than the sons of
light. And, I tell you, make for yourselves friends
by means of your material possessions, even if they
have been unjustly acquired, so that when your money
goes done they will receive you into a dwelling which
lasts forever. He who is trustworthy in a very little
is also trustworthy in much; and he who is dishonest
in a very little is also dishonest in much. If you have
not shown yourself trustworthy in your ordinary
business dealings about material things, who will
trust you with the genuine wealth? If you have not
shown yourselves trustworthy in what belongs to
someone else, who will give you what is your own ?
No household slave can serve two masters, for either
he will hate the one and love the other, or he will hold
to the one and despise the other. You cannot be the
slave of God and of material things."

IT is quite clear that this is a difficult parable to interpret.
It is a story about as choice a set of rascals as one could
meet anywhere. The steward was a rascal. He was a
slave, but he was nonetheless in charge of the running of
his master's whole estate. In Palestine there were many
absentee landlords. The master may well have been one
of these, and his whole business may well have been entrusted to his steward's hands. The steward had followed
a career of embezzlement. The debtors were also rascals.
No doubt what they owed was rent. Rent in Palestine
was often paid to a landlord, not in money, but in kind.
It was often an agreed proportion of the produce of the
part of the estate which had been rented. The steward
knew that he had lost his job. He, therefore, had a brilliant
idea. He falsified the entries in the books so that the
debtors were debited with far less than they owed. This

would have two effects. First, the debtors would be grateful to him; and second, and much more effective, he had involved the debtors in his own misdemeanours, and, if the worst came to the worst, he was now in a strong position to exercise a little judicious blackmail! The master himself was something of a rascal, for, instead of being shocked at the whole proceeding, he appreciated the shrewd brain behind it, and actually praised the steward for what he had done. The difficulty of the parable is clearly seen from the fact that Luke attaches no fewer than four different morals or lessons to it.

(i) In verse 8 the lesson is that children of this world are wiser in their generation that the children of light. That means that, if only the Christian was as eager and ingenious in his attempt to attain goodness as the man of the world is in his attempt to attain money and comfort, he would be a better man. If only men would give as much attention to the things which concern their souls as they do to the things which concern their business, they would be better men. It is quite true that over and over again a man will expend twenty times the amount of time and money and effort on his pleasure, his hobby, his golf, his garden, his sport as he does on his church. Our Christianity will only begin to become real and effective when we spend as much time and effort on it as we do on our worldly activities.

(ii) In verse 9 the lesson is that material possessions should be used to cement the friendships wherein the real and permanent value of life lies. That could be done in two ways. (a) It could be done as it affects eternity. The Rabbis had a saying, " The rich help the poor in this world, but the poor help the rich in the world to come." Ambrose, commenting on the rich fool who built bigger barns to store his goods, said, " The bosoms of the poor, the houses of widows, the mouths of children are the barns which last forever." It was in any event a Jewish belief that charity given to poor people would stand to a man's credit in the world to come. A man's true wealth would not be in what he kept, but in what he gave away. (b) It could be done as it affects this world. A man can use his wealth selfishly, or he can use it to make life easier, not only for himself, but for his friends and his fellow men. How many a poor scholar is forever grateful to a rich man who gave or left money to found bursaries and scholarships which made a university career possible! How many a man is grateful to a better-off friend who saw him through some time of need in the most practical way! Possessions are not in themselves a sin, but they *are* a great responsibility, and the man who uses them to help his friends has gone far to discharge that responsibility.

(iii) In verses 10 and 11 the lesson is that a man's way of fulfilling a small task is the best proof of his fitness or unfitness to be entrusted with a bigger task. That is clearly true of earthly things. No man will be advanced to a higher position until he has given proof of his honesty and ability in a smaller position. But Jesus extends the principle to eternity. He says, " Upon earth you are in charge of things which are not really yours. You cannot take them with you when you die. They are only lent to you. You are only a steward over them. They cannot, in the nature of things, be permanently yours. On the other hand in heaven you will get what is really and eternally and essentially yours. And what you get in heaven depends on how you used the things of earth. What you will be given as your very own will depend on how you used the things of which you were only steward."

(iv) Verse 13 lays down the rule that no slave can serve two masters. The master possessed the slave, and possessed him *exclusively*. Nowadays, a servant or a workman can quite easily do two jobs, and work for two people. He can do one job in his working time and another in his spare time. He could, for instance, be a clerk by day and a musician by night. Many a man augments his income or finds his real interest in a spare time occupation. But a slave had no spare time; every moment of his day, and every ounce of his energy, belonged to his master. He had no time which was his own. So, serving God, can never be a part time or a spare time job. Once a man chooses to serve God every moment of his time and every atom of his energy belongs to God. God is the most exclusive of masters. We either belong to God totally and altogether, or not at all.

THE LAW WHICH DOES NOT CHANGE

Luke 16: 14-18

> When the Pharisees, who were characteristically fond of money, heard these things, they derided Jesus. So He said to them, " You are those who make yourselves look righteous before men, but God knows your hearts, because that which is exalted amongst men is an abomination before God.
>
> " The law and the prophets were until John; from then the good news of the Kingdom of God is proclaimed; and every one forces his way into it; but it is easier for heaven and earth to pass away than for one dot of the law to become invalid.
>
> " Everyone who divorces his wife and marries another commits adultery, and he who marries a woman who has been divorced from her husband commits adultery."

THIS passage falls into three sections.

(i) It begins with a rebuke to the Pharisees. It says that they *derided* Jesus. The word literally means that they turned up their noses at Jesus. The Jew tended to connect earthly prosperity and goodness. Wealth was a sign that a man was a good man. The Pharisees put on a parade of goodness; and they regarded material prosperity as a reward of that goodness; but the more they exalted themselves before men, the more they became an abomination to God. It is bad enough for a man to think himself a good man; but it is worse when he points to material prosperity as an unanswerable proof of his goodness.

(ii) Before Jesus the law and the prophets had been the final word of God; but Jesus came preaching the Kingdom. When He did so the most unlikely people, the tax-collectors and the sinners, came storming their way into the Kingdom even when the Scribes and Pharisees would have set up barriers to keep them out. But Jesus emphasized one thing. The Kingdom was not the end of the law. True, the little details and regulations of the ceremonial law were wiped out. But let no man think that Christianity offered an easy way in which no laws remained. The great laws stood unaltered and unalterable. Certain Jewish letters are very like each other; they are distinguished only by the serif, which is the little line at the top or bottom of a letter. Not even a serif of the great laws would pass away.

(iii) As an illustration of the law that would never pass away Jesus took the law of chastity. This very definite statement of Jesus must be read against the contemporary background of Jewish life. The Jew glorified fidelity and chastity. The Rabbis said, " All things can God overlook except unchastity." " Unchastity causes the glory of God to depart." A Jew must surrender his life rather than commit idolatry, murder or adultery. But the tragedy was that at this time the marriage bond was on the way to being destroyed. We must always remember that in the eyes of Jewish law a woman was a thing. A woman could only divorce her husband if he became a leper, or an apostate, or if he ravished a virgin. Otherwise a woman had no rights whatever and no redress, other than that the marriage dowry must be repaid if she was divorced. The law said, " A woman may be divorced with or without her will; a man only with his will." The Mosaic law (Deuteronomy 24: 1) said, " When a man hath taken a wife and married her, and it come to pass that she find no favour in his eyes because he hath found some uncleanness in her, then let him write her a bill of divorcement, and give it in her hand, and send her out of his house." The bill of divorce had to be signed before two witnesses and ran, " Let this be from me thy writ of divorce and letter of dismissal and deed of liberation, that thou mayest marry whatsoever man thou wilt." Divorce was as simple and easy as that. The matter turned on the interpretation of the phrase *some uncleanness* in the Mosaic regulation. There were two schools of thought. The school of Shammai said that that meant adultery, and adultery alone. The school of Hillel said that it could mean " if she spoiled a dish of food; if she spun in the street; if she talked to a strange man; if she was guilty of speaking disrespectfully of her husband's relations in his hearing; if she was a brawling woman," which was defined as a woman whose voice could be heard in the next house. Rabbi Akiba went so far as to say that a man could divorce his wife if he found a woman who was fairer than she. Human nature being what it is, it was the school of Hillel which prevailed, so that, in the time of Jesus, things were so bad that women refused to marry at all, and family life was in danger. Jesus here lays down the sanctity of the marriage bond. The saying is repeated in Matthew 5: 31, 32 where adultery is made the sole exception to the universal rule. We sometimes think that our own generation is bad, but Jesus lived in a generation when things were every bit as bad. If we destroy family life, we destroy the very basis of the Christian life; and Jesus here lays down the law which men will only relax at their peril.

THE PUNISHMENT OF THE MAN WHO NEVER NOTICED

Luke 16: 19-31

There was a rich man who dressed habitually in purple and fine linen, and who feasted in luxury every day. A poor man, called Lazarus, was laid at his gate. He was full of ulcerated sores, and he desired to satisfy his hunger from the things which fell from the rich man's table; more, the dogs used to come and lick his sores. The poor man died, and he was carried by the angels to the bosom of Abraham. The rich man died and was buried. And in hell, being in torture, he lifted up his eyes, and from far away he saw Abraham, and Lazarus in his bosom. He called out, " Father Abraham, have pity on me, and send Lazarus to me that he may dip the tip of his finger in water and cool my tongue, because I am in anguish in this fire." Abraham said, " Child, remember that you received in full your good things in your life-time, just as Lazarus received evil things. Now he is comforted, and you are in anguish; and, besides all this, between you and us a great gulf is fixed, so that those who wish to pass from here to you cannot do so, nor can any cross from there to us." He said, " Well then, I ask you, father, to send him to my father's house, that he may warn them, so that they, too, may not come to this place of torture." Abraham said, " They have Moses and the prophets. Let them listen to them." He said, " No, father Abraham; but if some one goes to them from the dead, they will repent." He said to them, " If they will not listen to Moses and the prophets, neither will they be convinced if some one should rise from the dead."

THIS is a parable constructed with such masterly skill that not one phrase is wasted. Let us look at the two characters in it.

(i) First, there is the rich man, who is usually called Dives, which is the Latin for rich. Every phrase adds something to the luxury in which he lived. He was clothed in purple and fine linen. That is the description of the robes of the High Priests, and such robes cost anything from £30 to £40, an immense sum in days when a working man's wage was about 9d. a day. He feasted in luxury every day. The word used for feasting is the word that is used for a glutton and a gourmet feeding on exotic and costly dishes. He did this *every day*. In so doing he definitely and positively broke the fourth commandment. That commandment does not only forbid work on the Sabbath; it also says *six days shalt thou labour* (Exodus 20: 9). In a country where the common people were

fortunate if they ate meat once in the week and where they
toiled for six days of the week, Dives is a figure of indolent
self-indulgence. Lazarus was waiting for the crumbs that
fell from Dives' table. In the time of Jesus there were
neither knives nor forks nor napkins. Food was eaten
with the hands and, in very wealthy houses, the hands
were cleansed by wiping them on hunks of bread, and then
the bread was thrown away. It was that bread which
Lazarus was waiting for. Dives is the picture of wealthy
luxury.

(ii) Second, there is Lazarus. Strangely enough Lazarus
is the only character in any of the parables who is given
a name. The name is the Latinized form of Eleazar, and
means *God is my help*. He was a beggar. He was covered
with ulcerated sores. So helpless was he that he could not
even ward off the street dogs, unclean animals, who pestered
him. Lazarus is the picture of helpless and abject poverty.

Such is the scene in this world, and then abruptly it
changes to the next, and there Lazarus is in glory and Dives
is in torment. What was the sin of Dives? He had not
ordered Lazarus to be removed from his gate. He had
had no objections to Lazarus receiving the bread that was
flung away from his table. He did not kick Lazarus in
the passing. He was not deliberately cruel to him. The
sin of Dives was that he never noticed Lazarus, that he
accepted Lazarus as part of the landscape, that he thought
it perfectly natural and inevitable that Lazarus should lie
in pain and hunger while he wallowed in luxury. As someone said, " It was not what Dives did that got him into
gaol; it was what he did not do that got him into hell."
The sin of Dives was that he could look on the world's
suffering and need, and feel no answering sword of grief
and pity pierce his heart; he looked at a fellow man,
hungry and in pain, and did nothing about it. His was
the punishment of the man who never noticed.

It seems hard that his request that his brothers should
be warned was refused. But it is the plain fact that if

men possess the truth of God's word, and if, wherever they look, there is sorrow to be comforted, need to be supplied, pain to be relieved, and if it moves them to no feeling and to no action, nothing will change them.

It is a terrible warning to remember that the sin of Dives was, not that he did wrong things, but that he did nothing.

LAWS OF THE CHRISTIAN LIFE

Luke 17: 1-10

Jesus said to His disciples, " It is impossible that snares to sin should not arise; but woe to him through whom they do arise! It would be better for him if a millstone were hung around his neck and he were thrown into the sea rather than that he should cause one of these little ones to trip up.

" Take heed to yourselves. If your brother sins, rebuke him; and if he repents, forgive him. Even if he sins against you seven times in the day, and if seven times he turns to you, saying, ' I repent,' you must forgive him."

The apostles said to the Lord, " Give us also faith! " The Lord said, " If you have faith as a grain of mustard seed, you would say to this sycamine tree, ' Be rooted up and be planted in the sea, and it would obey you.'

" If any of you has a slave ploughing or watching the flock, and the slave comes in from the field, will he say to him, ' Come at once and take your place at table '; or rather, will he not say to him, ' Get ready my evening meal, and gird yourself and serve me, until I eat and drink, and after that you shall eat and drink yourself '? Does he thank a servant because he has done what he was ordered to do? Even so, you too, when you have done everything you were ordered to do, say, ' We are unworthy servants. We have done what it was our duty to do.'"

THIS passage falls into four definite and disconnected sections.

(i) Verses 1 and 2 condemn the man who teaches others to sin. The Authorised Version talks in these verses about *offences*. The Greek word is exactly the same word as the

English word *scandal* (skandalon). This word has two
meanings. (*a*) It originally meant the bait-stick in a
trap, the stick which an animal, lured by the bait, might
touch, and so be caught in the trap. (*b*) It then came
to mean any stumbling-block placed in a man's way to
trip him up. Jesus said that it was impossible to construct
a world with no temptations; but woe to that man who
taught another to sin, or who took away another's innocence.
Every one must be given his first invitation to sin, his first
push along the wrong way. Kennedy Williamson tells of
an old man who was dying. Something was obviously
worrying him. He told them at last what it was. " When
I was a lad," he said, " I often played on a wide common.
Near its centre two roads met and crossed, and, standing
at the cross-roads, was an old ricketty sign-post. I remember
one day twisting it round in its socket, thus altering the
arms, and making them point in the wrong direction; and
I've been wondering ever since how many travellers were
sent on the wrong road by me." God will not hold the man
guiltless, who, on the road of life, sends a younger or a
weaker brother on the wrong way.

(ii) Verses 3 and 4 speak of the necessity of forgiveness
in the Christian life. It tells us to forgive seven times.
The Rabbis had a saying that if any man forgave another
three times, he was a perfect man. The Christian standard
takes the Rabbinic standard and doubles it and adds one.
It is not a matter of calculated arithmetic. It simply
means that the Christian standard of forgiveness must
immeasurably exceed the best the world can achieve.

(iii) Verses 5 and 6 tell us that faith is the greatest force
in the world. We must again remember that it was the
eastern custom to use language in the most vivid possible
way. This saying means that even that which looks completely impossible becomes possible, if it is approached
with faith. We have only to think of the number of
scientific marvels, of the number of surgical operations,
of the feats of endurance which to-day have been achieved,

and which less than fifty years ago would have been regarded as impossible. If we approach a thing, saying, 'It can't be done,' it will not be done; if we approach it, saying, 'It must be done,' the chances are that it will be done. We must always remember that we approach no task alone, but that with us there is God and all the power of God.

(iv) Verses 7-10 tell us that we can never put God in our debt, and that we can never have any claim on God. When we have done our best we have only done our duty; and a man who has done his duty has only done what, in any event, he could be compelled to do.

> Were the whole realm of Nature mine,
>   That were an offering far too small;
> Love so amazing, so divine,
>   Demands my soul, my life, my all.

It may be possible to satisfy the claims of *law*; but every lover knows that nothing he can ever do can satisfy the claims of *love*.

THE RARITY OF GRATITUDE

Luke 17: 11-19

> When Jesus was on the way to Jerusalem, He was going along between Samaria and Galilee; and, as He entered a village, ten lepers, who stood far off, met Him. They lifted up their voices and said, "Jesus, Master, have pity upon us." When He saw them, He said, "Go, and show yourselves to the priests." And as they went they were cleansed. When one of them saw that he was cured, he turned back, glorifying God with a great voice. He fell on his face at Jesus' feet and kept on thanking Him. And he was a Samaritan. Jesus said, "Were the ten not cleansed? The nine—where are they? Were none found to turn back and give glory to God except this foreigner?" And He said to him, "Rise and go! Your faith has made you well."

At this time Jesus was on the border between Galilee and Samaria. He was met by a band of ten lepers. We know that the Jews had no dealings with the Samaritans, and yet in this band there was at least one Samaritan. Here is an example of one great law of life. A common misfortune had broken down the racial and the national barriers. In the common tragedy of their leprosy they had forgotten that they were Jews and Samaritans and remembered only that they were men in need. It is said that if a flood surges over a piece of country, and the wild animals congregate on some little bit of higher ground, you will see standing together animals who are natural enemies, and, who, at any other time, would have done their best to kill each other. Surely one of the things which should draw all men together is their common need of God.

The lepers stood afar off. (cp. Leviticus 13: 45, 46; Numbers 5: 2). There was no specified distance at which they should stand, but we know that at least one authority laid it down, that, when the wind was blowing from the leper to the healthy person, the leper should stand at least fifty yards away. Nothing could better show the utter isolation in which lepers lived.

There is no story in all the gospels which so poignantly shows man's ingratitude. The lepers had come to Jesus with a desperate longing; He had cured them, and nine never came back to give thanks. So often, once a man has got what he wants, he never comes back.

(i) So often children are ungrateful to their parents. There is a time in life when a week's neglect would have killed us. Of all living creatures man requires longest to become able to meet the needs which are essential for life. There were long years when we were dependent on parents for literally everything. And yet the day comes when an aged parent is a nuisance; and few young people ever think of repaying the debt they owe. As King Lear said in the day of his own tragedy,

226

" How sharper than a serpent's tooth it is
To have a thankless child! "

(ii) So often we are ungrateful to our fellow men. There are few of us who have not at some time owed a very great deal to some fellow man. There are few of us who, at the moment, believed that we would ever forget; and there are few of us who in the end satisfied the debt of gratitude that we owe. If often happens that a friend, a teacher, a doctor, a surgeon does something for us which it is impossible to repay. The tragedy of life is that we do not even try to repay it.

Blow, blow, thou winter wind,
Thou art not so unkind
As man's ingratitude.

(iii) So often we are ungrateful to God. In some time of bitter need we pray with desperate intensity; the time passes and we forget God. So many of us never even give to God a grace before meat. He gave us His only Son, and so often we never give to Him even a word of thanks. The best thanks we can give God is to try to deserve His goodness and His mercy a little better. " Bless the Lord, O my soul, and *forget not all his benefits*." (Psalm 103: 2.)

THE SIGNS OF HIS COMING

Luke 17: 20-37

When Jesus was asked by the Pharisees when the Kingdom of God was coming, He answered them, " The Kingdom of God does not come with signs that you can watch for; nor will they say, ' Look here!' or ' Look there!' For—look you—the Kingdom of God is within you."
He said to His disciples, " Days will come when you will long to see one of the days of the Son of Man and you will not see it. And they will say to you,

' Look there! Look here!' Do not depart, and do not
follow them. For, as the flashing lightning lights up
the sky from one side to another, so shall be the Son
of Man in His day. But, first He must suffer many
things and must be rejected by this generation. Even
as it was in the days of Noah, so it will be in the days
of the Son of Man. They were eating, they were
drinking, they were marrying, they were being given
in marriage, until the day on which Noah entered
the ark and the flood came and wiped them all out.
In the same way, so it was in the days of Lot. They
were eating, they were drinking, they were buying,
they were selling, they were planting, they were
building, but, on the day on which Lot went out of
Sodom, fire and brimstone rained from heaven and
wiped them all out. It will be the same on the day
on which the Son of Man is revealed. If, on that day,
anyone is on the housetop, and his goods are in the
house, let him not come down to take them. In the
same way, if anyone is in the field, let him not turn
back. Remember Lot's wife! Whoever seeks to gain
his life will lose it, but whoever loses it will preserve
it alive. This is the truth I tell you—on that night
there will be two in one bed. One will be taken and
the other will be left. Two women will be grinding
together. One will be taken and the other left.''
They said to Him, " Where, Lord? " He said to them,
" Where the body is, there the vultures will be gathered
together."

HERE are two very difficult passages.

In verses 20 and 21 Jesus answered the question of
the Pharisees as to when the Kingdom of God would come.
He said that it would not come with signs that you can
watch for. The word he used is the word that is used for
a doctor watching a patient for symptoms of some disease
which he suspects. We are not quite sure what Jesus
went on to say. The Greek may mean two things. (a) It
may mean, The Kingdom of God is within you. That is to
say, the Kingdom of God works in men's hearts. The
Kingdom of God is to produce not new things, but new
people. It is not a revolution in material things that we

are to look for, but a revolution in the hearts of men. (b) It may mean, The Kingdom of God is among you. That would refer to Jesus Himself. He was the very embodiment of the Kingdom, and they did not recognize Him. It was as if He said, " The whole offer and the whole secret of God are here—and you will not accept it."

Verses 22-37 speak of the Second Coming of Jesus. Out of this difficult passage we can only pick the things which are certain—and in truth they are enough.

(i) There will be times when the Christian will long for the coming of Christ. Like the martyred saints he will cry out, " How long? " (Revelation 6: 10.) But he will need to learn to light a candle of patience, and to wait. God takes His own time.

(ii) The coming of Christ is certain, but the time of that coming is quite unknown. Speculation is vain and useless People will come with false prophecies and false predictions. We must not leave our ordinary work to follow them. The best way that Christ can come upon a man is when a man is faithfully and humbly and watchfully doing his duty. As a great commentator said, " No man will forsee it, and all men will see it."

(iii) When that day comes the judgments of God will operate, and, of two people who, all their lives, lived side by side, one will be taken and the other will be left. There is a warning here. Intimacy with a good person does not necessarily guarantee our own salvation. " No man can deliver his brother." Is it not often true that a family is apt to leave the duties of church membership to one member of the family? Is it not often true that many a husband leaves the duties of the Church to his wife? The judgment of God is an individual judgment. We cannot discharge our duty to God by proxy, nor even by association. Often one will be taken and another left.

(iv) When they asked Jesus when all this would happen, He answered by quoting a well-known proverb. " Where the body is, there the vultures will be gathered together."

That simply meant that a thing would happen when the necessary conditions were fulfilled. That means for us that God will bring Jesus Christ again in His good time. We cannot know that time; we dare not speculate about it. We must live so that whenever He comes, at morning, at midday or at evening, He may find us ready.

UNWEARIED IN PRAYER

Luke 18: 1-8

> Jesus spoke a parable to them to show that it is necessary always to pray and not to lose heart. " There was a judge," He said, " in a town who neither feared God nor respected man. There was a widow in the same town who kept coming to him and saying, ' Vindicate me against my adversary.' For some time he refused. But afterwards he said to himself, ' Even though I neither fear God nor respect man, because she bothers me, I will vindicate this widow, lest by her constant coming she exhausts me.' " The Lord said, " Listen to what the unjust judge says. And shall God not vindicate His own chosen ones who cry to Him day and night, even though He seem to wait for long? But when the Son of Man comes will He find faith on earth? "

THIS parable tells of the kind of thing which could, and often did, happen in Palestine. There are two characters in it.

(i) There is the judge. He was clearly not a Jewish judge. All ordinary Jewish disputes were taken before the elders, and not into the public courts at all. If, under Jewish law, a matter was taken to arbitration, one man could not constitute a court. There were always three judges, one chosen by the plaintiff, one by the defendant, and one independently appointed. This judge was one of these paid magistrates appointed either by Herod or by the Romans. Such judges were notorious. Unless a plaintiff had influence and money to bribe his way to a verdict he had no hope of ever getting his case settled.

They were said to pervert justice for a dish of meat. People even punned on their title. Officially they were called *Dayyaneh Gezeroth*, which means judges of prohibitions or punishments. Popularly they were called *Dayyaneh Gezeloth*, which means robber judges.

(ii) The widow was the symbol of all who were poor and defenceless. It was obvious that she, without resource of any kind, had no hope of ever extracting justice from such a judge. But she had one weapon—the weapon of persistence. It is quite possible that what the judge in the end feared was actual physical violence. The word translated, lest she *exhausts* me can, and does mean, lest she *give me a black eye*. It is possible to close a person's eye in two ways—either by sleep or assault and battery! In any event, in the end, her persistence won the day.

This parable is like the Parable of the Friend at Midnight. It does not *liken* God to an unjust judge; it *contrasts* God to such a person. In this parable Jesus was saying, " If, in the end, an unjust and rapacious judge can be wearied into giving a widow woman justice, *how much more* will God, who is a loving Father, give His children what they need ? "

That is true, but we must ever remember that that is no reason why we should expect to get whatever we pray for. Often a father has to refuse the request of a child, because he knows that what the child asks would hurt rather than help. God is like that. We do not know what is to happen in the next hour, let alone the next week, or month, or year. Only God sees time whole, and, therefore, only God knows what is good for us *in the long run*. That is why Jesus said that we must never be discouraged in prayer. That is why He wondered if men's faith would stand the long delays before the Son of Man should come. We will never grow weary in prayer, and our faith will never falter if, after we have offered to God *our* prayers and requests, we add the perfect prayer, *Thy* will be done.

THE SIN OF PRIDE

Luke 18: 9-14

> Jesus spoke this parable to some who were self-
> confidently sure that they were righteous and who
> despised others. " Two men went up to the Temple
> to pray. The one was a Pharisee, the other, a tax-
> collector. The Pharisee stood and prayed thus with
> himself, ' O God, I thank Thee, that I am not as the
> rest of men, thieves, unjust, adulterers, or even as
> this tax-collector. I fast twice a week. I give a tenth
> of all that I get.' The tax-collector stood afar off,
> and would not lift even his eyes to heaven, and kept
> beating his breast and said, ' O God, be merciful, to
> me—the sinner.' I tell you, this man went down to
> his house accepted with God rather than the other,
> because everyone who exalts himself will be humbled,
> but he who humbles himself will be exalted."

IN Palestine the devout observed three prayer times
daily—9 a.m., 12 midday and 3 p.m. Prayer was held to
be specially efficacious if it was offered in the Temple, and
so at these hours many went up to the Temple courts to
pray. Jesus told of two men who thus went to pray.

(i) There was a Pharisee. He did not really go to pray
to God. He prayed *with himself*. True prayer is always
offered to God and to God alone. A certain American
cynically described a preacher's prayer as " the most
eloquent prayer ever offered to a Boston audience." The
Pharisee was really giving himself a testimonial before
God. The Jewish law prescribed only one absolutely
obligatory fast—that on the Day of Atonement. But
those who wished to gain special merit fasted also on
Mondays and Thursdays. It is noteworthy that these
were the market days when Jerusalem was full of country
people. Those who fasted whitened their faces and appeared in dishevelled clothes, and those days gave their
piety the biggest possible audience. The Levites were to
receive a tithe of all a man's produce (Numbers 18: 21;
Deuteronomy 14: 22). But this Pharisee tithed everything, even things which there was no obligation to tithe.

His whole attitude was not untypical of the worst in Pharisaism. There is a recorded prayer of a certain Rabbi which runs like this, "I thank, Thee, O Lord my God, that Thou hast put my part with those who sit in the Academy, and not with those who sit at the street-corners. For I rise early, and they rise early; I rise early to the words of the law, and they to vain things. I labour, and they labour; I labour and receive a reward, and they labour and receive no reward. I run, and they run; I run to the life of the world to come, and they to the pit of destruction." It is on record that Rabbi Simeon ben Jochai once said, "If there are only two righteous men in the world, I and my son are these two; if there is only one, I am he!" The Pharisee did not really go to pray; he went to inform God how good he was.

(ii) There was the tax-collector. He stood afar off, and would not even lift his eyes to God. The Authorised Version does not even do justice to his humility for he prayed, "O God, be merciful to me—*the* sinner," as if he was not merely *a* sinner, but *the* sinner *par excellence.* "And," said Jesus, "it was that heart-broken, self-despising prayer which won him acceptance before God."

There are certain things about prayer which this parable unmistakably tells us.

(i) No man who is proud can pray. The gate of heaven is so low that none can enter it save upon his knees. All that a man can say is,

" None other Lamb, none other Name,
    None other Hope in heaven or earth or sea,
  None other Hiding-place from guilt and shame,
    None beside Thee."

(ii) No man who despises his fellow men can pray. In prayer we do not lift ourselves above our fellow men. We remember that we are one of a great army of sinning, suffering, sorrowing humanity, all kneeling before the throne of the mercy of God.

(iii) True prayer comes from setting our lives beside the life of God. No doubt all that the Pharisee said was true. He did fast; he did meticulously give tithes; he was not as other men are; still less was he like that tax-collector. But the question is not, " Am I as good as my fellow men? " The question is, " Am I as good as God? " Once I made a journey in the train down to England. As we passed through the Yorkshire moors I saw a little whitewashed cottage and it seemed to me to shine with an almost radiant whiteness. Some days later I made the journey back to Scotland. The snow had fallen, and was lying deep all around. We came again to the little white cottage, but this time its whiteness seemed drab and soiled and almost grey—in comparison with the virgin whiteness of the driven snow. It all depends what we compare ourselves with. And when we set our lives beside the wonder of the life of Jesus, and beside the holiness of God, then all that is left to say is, " God be merciful to me—the sinner."

THE MASTER AND THE CHILDREN

Luke 18: 15-17

> People were bringing even their babies to Jesus that He might touch them. When the disciples saw it they rebuked them. But Jesus called them to Him saying, " Let the little children come to me, and don't stop them, for of such is the Kingdom of God. This is the truth I tell you—whoever does not receive the Kingdom of God as a little child shall not enter into it."

IT was the custom in Palestine for mothers to bring their children to some distinguished Rabbi on their first birthday that he might bless them. That is what the mothers wanted for their children from Jesus. We are not to think that the disciples were hard and cruel. It was kindness that made them act as they did. Remember where Jesus was going. He was on the way to Jerusalem to die upon a Cross. The disciples could see upon His face the inner tension of His heart; and they did not want Jesus to be bothered. Often at home we say to some little child, " Don't bother your Daddy; he's tired and worried to-night." That is exactly how the disciples felt about Jesus. It is one of the loveliest things in all the gospel story that Jesus had time for the children when He was on the way to Jerusalem to die.

When Jesus said that it was of the child-like that the Kingdom of God was composed, what did He mean? What were the qualities of the child of which He was thinking?

(i) The child has not lost *the sense of wonder*. Tennyson tells of going, early one morning, into the bedroom of his little grandson, and of seeing the child " worshipping the sunbeam playing on the bedpost." As we grow older we begin to live in a world which has grown old and gray and tired. The child lives in a world with a sheen on it, a world in which God is always near.

(ii) The child's whole life is founded on *trust*. When we are young we never doubt where the next meal is to come from, or where our clothes will be found. We go out to school certain that the home will be there when we return, and all things ready for our comfort. When we go on a journey we never doubt that the fare will be paid, and that our parents know the way and will take us safely there. The child's trust in his parents is absolute—as ours should be in our great Father—God.

(iii) The child is naturally *obedient*. True, he often disobeys and grumbles at his parents' bidding. But his instinct is to obey. He knows very well that he should not disobey. He is not happy when he has been disobedient. In his heart of hearts his parents' word to him is law. Even so, so should we be with God.

(iv) The child has an amazing faculty of *forgiveness*. Almost all parents are unjust to their children. We demand from them a standard of obedience, of good manners, of refined language, of diligence which we seldom satisfy ourselves. Time and again we scold them for doing the very things we do ourselves. If others treated us in the way we treat our children in the matter of plain justice we would never forgive. But the child forgives and forgets, and does not even realize it when he is very young. It would be so much lovelier a world if we could forgive as a child forgives.

To keep alive the sense of wonder, to live in unquestioning trust, instinctively to obey, to forgive and to forget—that is the childlike spirit, and that is the passport to the Kingdom of God.

THE MAN WHO WOULD NOT PAY THE PRICE

Luke 18: 18-30

A ruler asked Jesus, " Good teacher, what shall I do to inherit eternal life?" Jesus said to him, " Why do you call me good? There is none good except one—God. You know the commandments—do not commit adultery, do not kill, do not steal, do not bear false witness, honour your father and your mother." He said, " From my youth I have kept all these." When Jesus heard that He said to him, " You still lack one thing. Sell everything you have got and distribute it to the poor, and you will have treasure in heaven. And come! Follow me!" When he heard these things he was very sad, because he was exceedingly rich. When Jesus saw him He said, " How hard it is for those who have riches to enter into the Kingdom of God! It is easier for a camel to go through the eye of a needle than for a rich man to enter the Kingdom of God." Those who heard Him said, " And who can be saved?" He said, " The things which are impossible with men are possible with God." Peter said, " Look you—we have left our private possessions and have followed you." He said to them, " This is the truth I tell you—there is no one who has left house, or wife, or brother, or parents or children for the sake of the Kingdom of God who will not get it all back many times over in this time, and, in the age that is coming, eternal life."

THIS ruler addressed Jesus in a way which, for a Jew, was without parallel. In all the religious Jewish literature there is no record of any Rabbi being addressed as, " Good teacher." The Rabbis always said " there is nothing that is good but the law." To address Jesus in such a way savoured of almost fulsome flattery. So Jesus began by driving him and his thoughts back to God. Jesus was always sure that His own power, and His own message, came to Him from God. When the nine lepers failed to return, Jesus' grief was, not that they had forgotten to come back to say thanks to Him, but that they had not come back to glorify God. (Luke 17: 18.)

It was indisputable that this ruler was a good man, but he felt within his heart and soul that in his life there was something lacking. Jesus' command to him was that if he wanted to find all that he was searching for in life he must sell all his possessions and distribute them to the poor and follow Him. Why did Jesus make this demand specially from this man? When the man whom Jesus had cured in the country of the Gerasenes wished to follow Him, He told him to stay at home. (Luke 8: 38, 39.) Why this very different advice to this ruler? There is a gospel called the *Gospel according to the Hebrews* most of which is lost; but in one of the fragments which remain there is an account of this incident which gives us a clue. " The other rich man said to Jesus, ' Master, what good thing must I do really to live? ' Jesus said to him, ' Man, obey the law and the prophets.' He said, ' I have done so.' Jesus said to him, ' Go, sell all that you possess, distribute it among the poor, and come, follow me! ' The rich man began to scratch his head because he did not like this command. The Lord said to him, ' Why do you say that you have obeyed the law and the prophets? For it is written in the law, " You must love your neighbour as yourself," and look you—there are many brothers of yours, sons of Abraham, who are dying of hunger, and your house is full of many good things, and not one single thing goes out of it to them.'

And He turned and said to Simon, his disciple, who was sitting beside Him, ' Simon, son of Jonas, it is easier for a camel to go through the eye of a needle than for a rich man to enter the Kingdom of Heaven.' '' There we have the secret and the tragedy of this rich ruler. He was living utterly selfishly. He was rich, and yet he gave nothing away. His real God was comfort, and the thing he really worshipped was his own possessions and his wealth. That is why Jesus told him to give it all away. There is many a man who uses such wealth as he has to bring comfort and joy and good to his fellow men; but this man used it for nobody but himself. If a man's god is that to which he gives all his time, his thought, his energy, his devotion, then wealth was his god. If he was ever to find happiness he must be done with all that and live for others with the same intensity as he had so long lived for himself.

Jesus went on to say that it was easier for a camel to go through the eye of a needle than for a rich man to enter the Kingdom of God. Quite often the rabbis talked of an elephant trying to get through the eye of a needle as a picture of something fantastically impossible. But Jesus' picture may have one of two origins. (i) It is said that beside the great gate into Jerusalem through which traffic went there was a little gate just wide and high enough for a man to get through. It is said that that little gate was called the needle's eye, and the picture is that of a camel trying to struggle through that little gate. (ii) The Greek word for a camel is *kamelos*. In this age of Greek there was a tendency for the vowel sounds to become very like each other, and there was another word which would sound almost exactly the same—the word *kamilos*, which means *a ship's hawser*. It may well be that what Jesus said was that it would be easier to thread a needle with a ship's hawser than for a rich man to enter the Kingdom of God. Why should it be so? The whole tendency of possessions is to shackle a man's thoughts to this earth. He has so big a stake in earth that he never wants to leave it, and never thinks of anything else. It is not a sin to have much wealth—but it is a great danger to the soul and a great responsibility.

Peter pointed out that he and his fellow disciples had left all to follow Jesus; and Jesus promised them that no man would ever give up anything for the Kingdom of God but he would be repaid many times over. It is the experience of all Christian folk that that is true. Once someone, thinking of the trials he had endured, and the sorrows he had borne, how he had lost his wife and ruined his health in Africa, said to David Livingstone, " What sacrifices you have made! " Livingstone answered, " Sacrifices? I never made a sacrifice in all my life." For the man who walks the Christian way there may be things the world calls hard, but, beyond them all and through them all, there is a peace which the world cannot give, and cannot take away, and a joy that no man taketh from him.

THE WAITING CROSS

Luke 18: 31-34

> Jesus took The Twelve and said to them, " Look you—we are going up to Jerusalem, and everything that was written through the prophets about the Son of Man will be fulfilled. He will be handed over to the Gentiles; and He will be mocked and cruelly treated; and spat upon; and they will scourge Him and kill Him; and on the third day He will rise again." But they did not understand these things; this word was hidden from them; and they did not grasp what was being said.

THERE are two kinds of courage. There is the courage of the man who, suddenly and without warning, is confronted with some emergency or some crisis, and who unhesitatingly and even recklessly flings himself into it without time to think. There is the courage of the man who sees the terrible situation looming ahead, and who knows that

nothing short of flight can avoid it, and who goes stead-
fastly and inflexibly on. There is no question which is the
higher courage. Many a man is capable of the heroic
action on the spur of the moment; it takes a man of
supreme courage to go on to face something which haunts
him for days ahead, and which, by turning back, he could
escape. In a novel a writer paints a picture of two children
walking along the road playing their children's games.
The one said to the other, "When you're walking along the
road, do you ever pretend that there is something terrible
just around the next corner waiting for you; and you've
got to go and face it? It makes it so exciting." With
Jesus it was no game of let's pretend. It was the grim
truth that there was something terrible waiting for Him.
He knew what crucifixion was like; He had seen it; and
yet He went on. If Jesus was nothing else He would still
be one of the most heroic figures of all time.

In face of Jesus' frequent warning of what was going to
happen to Him in Jerusalem we must often have wondered
why, when the Cross came, it was such a shock and such
a shattering blow to His disciples. The truth is that they
simply could not take in what He was saying to them.
They were obsessed with the idea of a conquering King;
they still clung to that hope that He would let loose His
power in Jerusalem and blast His enemies off the face of
the earth. Here is a great warning to every listener.
There are none so blind as those who refuse to see. The
human mind has a way of listening only to what it wants
to hear. There is a kind of wishful thinking which in its
heart of hearts believes that the unpleasant truth cannot
be true, and that the thing it does not want to happen
cannot happen. A man must ever struggle against the
human tendency to hear only what he wants to hear.

One thing more we must note. Jesus never foretold
the Cross without foretelling the Resurrection. He knew
that the shame lay before Him, but He was equally certain
that the glory lay before Him too. He knew what the

malice of men could do, but He knew also what the power of God could do. It was in the certainty of ultimate victory that He faced the apparent defeat of the Cross. He knew that without a cross there can never be any crown.

THE MAN WHO WOULD NOT BE SILENCED

Luke 18: 35-43

> When Jesus was approaching Jericho, a blind man was sitting by the wayside begging. When he heard the crowd passing through he asked what it meant. They told him, " Jesus of Nazareth is passing by." He shouted, " Jesus, Son of David, have pity on me! " Those who were going on in front rebuked him and told him to be quiet, but he cried all the more, " Son of David, have pity on me." Jesus stood, and ordered him to be brought to Him. When he had come near He asked him, " What do you want me to do for you? " He said, " Lord, that I may receive my sight." Jesus said to him, " Receive your sight; your faith has made you well." And immediately he received his sight and followed Him glorifying God, and, when the people saw it, they all gave praise to God.

THE one thing which stands out in this story is the sheer, desperate persistence of the blind man. Jesus was on His way to Jerusalem to the Passover. At such a time pilgrims travelled in bands together. One of the commonest ways for a Rabbi to teach was to discourse as he walked. That was what Jesus was doing, and the rest of the pilgrim band were crowding close around Him, not to miss anything that He might say. As such a pilgrim band passed through a village or a town those who themselves could not go to the feast lined the wayside to see the pilgrims pass and to bid them godspeed on the way. It was amongst the crowd that the blind man was sitting. When he heard the murmur of the crowd he asked what was happening, and he was told that Jesus was passing by. Immediately he cried out to Jesus for help and healing. Thereupon everyone tried to silence him. The people round Jesus were missing what Jesus was saying because of the clamour of this blind man. But the man would not be silenced. He shouted again. The word used for the shouts of the blind man is quite different in verse 39 from verse 38. In verse 38 the word describes an ordinary loud shout to attract attention. In verse 39 the word is the word used to describe the instinctive shout of ungovernable emotion, a scream, an almost animal cry. The word well shows the utter desperation of the man. So Jesus stopped, and the blind man found the healing he so passionately desired.

This story tells us two things.

(i) It tells us something about the blind man. He was determined to come face to face with Jesus. Nothing would stop him. He refused to be silent, and he refused to be restrained. His sense of need drove him relentlessly into the presence of Jesus. If a man wants a miracle that is the spirit that he must show. It is not just a gentle, sentimental longing that really taps the power of God; but the passionate, intense desire of the very depths of the human heart will never be disappointed.

(ii) It tells us something about Jesus. Jesus at the moment was discoursing to the crowd like any rabbi. But at the blind man's cry of need He stopped, the discourse forgotten. For Jesus it was always more important to act than to talk. Words always took second place to deeds. Here was a human soul in need. Discourse must end and action begin. Someone has said that so many teachers are like men throwing chatty remarks to a man drowning in a tempestuous sea. Jesus was never like that; He did not talk; He leaped to the rescue of the man. There is many a man who could not put two sentences together, but others love him for he is kind. Men may respect an orator, but they love a man with helping hands. Men admire a man with a great mind, but they love a man with a big heart.

THE GUEST OF THE MAN WHOM ALL MEN DESPISED

Luke 19: 1-10

> Jesus entered Jericho and was passing through it. And—look you—there was a man called Zacchæus by name, and he was commissioner of taxes, and he was rich. He was seeking to see who Jesus was, and he could not for the crowd, because he was short in height. So he ran on ahead and climbed up into a sycomore tree, for He was to pass that way. When Jesus came to the place He looked up and said to him, " Zacchæus! Hurry and come down! for this very day I must stay at your house." So he hurried and came down, and welcomed Him gladly; and when they saw it they all murmured, " He has gone in to be the guest of a man who is a sinner." Zacchæus stood and said to the Lord, " Look you—half of my goods, Lord, I hereby give to the poor. If I have taken anything from any man by fraud I give it back to him four times over." Jesus said to him, " To-day salvation has come to this house, because he also is a son of Abraham; for the Son of Man came to seek and to save that which was lost."

JERICHO was a very wealthy, and a very important town. She lay in the Jordan valley, and she commanded both the approach to Jerusalem and the crossings of the river which gave access to the lands east of the Jordan. She had a great palm forest and world famous balsam groves which perfumed the air for miles around. Her gardens of roses were known far and wide. Men called her " The City of Palms." Josephus called her " a divine region," " the fattest in Palestine." The Romans carried her dates and balsam to world-wide trade and fame. All this combined to make her one of the greatest taxation centres in Palestine. We have already seen the taxes which the tax-collectors collected, and the wealth which they rapaciously acquired (Luke 5: 27-32). Zacchæus was a man who had reached the top of his profession, and he was also the best hated man in the district. There are three stages in the story of Zacchæus.

(i) Zacchæus was wealthy, but he was not happy. Inevitably he was lonely, for he had chosen a way that made him an outcast. He had heard of this Jesus who welcomed tax-collectors and sinners, and he wondered if He would have any word for him. Despised and hated by men, Zacchæus was reaching after the love of God.

(ii) Zacchæus determined to see Jesus, and he would let nothing stop him. For Zacchæus, to mingle with the crowd at all was a courageous thing to do, for many a man would take the chance to get a nudge, or kick, or push at this little tax-collector. It was an opportunity not to be missed. Zacchæus would be black and blue with bruises that day. He could not see—the crowd took an ill delight in making sure that he could not see. So he ran on ahead and climbed a fig-mulberry tree. A traveller describes the tree as being like " the English oak, and its shade is most pleasing. It is consequently a favourite wayside tree . . . It is very easy to climb, with its short trunk and its wide lateral branches forking out in all directions." Things were not easy for Zacchæus, but the little man had the courage of desperation.

(iii) Zacchæus took steps to show all the community that he was a changed man. When Jesus announced that He would stay that day at his house, and when he discovered that he had found a new and wonderful friend, immediately Zacchæus took a decision. He decided to give half of his goods to the poor; the other half he did not intend to keep to himself but to use to make restitution for the frauds of which he had been self-confessedly guilty. In his restitution he went far beyond what was legally necessary. Only if robbery was a deliberate and violent act of destruction was a fourfold restitution necessary. (Exodus 22: 1.) If it had been ordinary robbery, and the original goods were not restorable, double the value had to be repaid. (Exodus 22: 4, 7.) If voluntary confession was made, and voluntary restitution offered, the value of the original goods had to be paid, plus one-fifth. (Leviticus 6: 5;

Numbers 5: 7.) Zacchæus was determined to do far more
than the law demanded. He showed by his deeds that he
was a changed man. Dr. Boreham has a terrible story.
There was a meeting in progress at which several women
were giving their testimony. One woman kept grimly
silent. She was asked to testify, and she refused. She was
asked why, and she answered, " Four of these women who
have just given their testimony owe me money, and I and
my family are half-starved because we cannot buy food."
A testimony is utterly worthless unless it is backed by
deeds which guarantee its sincerity. It is not a mere change
of words which Jesus Christ demands, but a change of life.

(iv) So the story ends with the great words, The Son of
Man came to seek and to save that which was lost. We
must always be careful how we regard the meaning of
this word *lost*. In the New Testament it does not mean
damned or doomed. It simply means *in the wrong place*.
A thing is lost when it has got out of its own place into the
wrong place, and when we find such a thing, we return
it to the place it ought to occupy. A man is lost when he
has wandered away from God; and he is found when once
again he takes his rightful place as an obedient child in
the household and the family of his Father.

THE KING'S TRUST IN HIS SERVANTS

Luke 19: 11-27

As they were listening to these things Jesus went on
to tell them a parable because He was near Jerusalem,
and they were thinking that the Kingdom of God was
going to appear immediately. So He said, " There
was a noble man who went into a distant country to
receive a kingdom for himself and then to return.
He called ten of his own servants and gave them £5
each and said to them, ' Trade with these until I
come.' His citizens hated him, and they despatched
an embassy after him, saying, ' We do not wish this
man to be king over us.' When he had received the

kingdom and had returned, he ordered the servants to whom he had given the money to be called to him, that he might know what they had made by trading with it. The first came and said, ' Sir, your £5 has produced £50.' So he said to him, ' Well done, good servant! Because you have shown yourself faithful in a little thing, you shall have authority over ten cities.' And the second came and said to him also, ' Sir, your £5 has made £25.' He said to him also, ' You, too, are to be promoted over five cities.' Another came to him and said, ' Sir, here is your £5, which I was keeping laid away in a towel, for I was afraid of you, because I know that you are a hard man. You take up what you did not put down and you reap what you did not sow.' He said to him, ' Out of your own mouth I judge you, wicked servant. You knew that I am a hard man, taking up what I did not put down, and reaping what I did not sow. You ought, therefore, to have given my money to the bankers, so that when I came, I would have received it plus interest.' He said to those standing by, ' Take the £5 from him and give it to him who has £50.' ' They said to him, ' Sir, he has £50.' I tell you, that to everyone who has it will be given; but from him who has not, even what he has will be taken away. But as for these my enemies, who did not wish to have me as their king—bring them here and hew them to pieces in my presence."

THIS parable is quite unique among the parables of Jesus, because it is the only parable part of whose story is based on an actual historical event. It tells about a king who went away to receive a kingdom, and whose subjects did their best to stop him receiving it. When Herod the Great died in 4 B.C. he left his kingdom divided between Herod Antipas, Herod Philip and Archelaus. That division had to be ratified by the Romans, who were the overlords of Palestine, before it became effective. Archelaus, to whom Judæa had been left, went to Rome to persuade Augustus to allow him to enter into his inheritance, whereupon the Jews sent an embassy of fifty men to Rome to inform Augustus that they did not wish to have him as king. In point of fact, Augustus confirmed him in his inheritance, though without the actual title of king. Anyone in Judæa.

on hearing the parable, would immediately remember the historical circumstances on which it was based. The parable of the King and his servants tells us about certain great facts of the Christian life.

(i) It tells us of the king's *trust*. He gave his servants the money and then he went away and left them to use it as they could and as they thought best. He did not in any way interfere with them, or, as it were, stand over them. He left them entirely to their own devices. That is the way in which God trusts us. Someone has said, " The nicest thing about God is that He trusts us to do so much by ourselves."

(ii) It tells us of the king's *test*. As always, this trust was a test. The king's test was whether or not a man was faithful and reliable in little things. Sometimes a man justifies a certain large inefficiency in the ordinary routine affairs of life by claiming that " he has a mind above trifles." God has not. It is precisely in these routine duties that the tests of God are testing men. There is no example of this like Jesus Himself. Of His thirty-three years of life Jesus spent thirty in Nazareth. Had He not discharged with absolute fidelity the tasks of the carpenter's shop in Nazareth, and the obligation of being the bread-winner of the family, God could never have given Him the supreme task of being the Saviour of the world.

(iii) It tells us of the king's *reward*. The reward that the faithful servants received was not a reward which they could enjoy by sitting down and folding their hands and doing nothing. The one was put over ten cities and the other over five. The reward of work well done was more work to do. The greatest compliment we can pay a man is to give him ever greater, and ever harder tasks to do. The great reward of God to the man who has satisfied the test is more trust.

(iv) The parable concludes with one of the inexorable laws of life. To him who has, more will be given; from him who has not, what he has will be taken away. If a man plays a game, if he goes on practising at it, he will play it with ever greater efficiency; if he does not, he will lose even the small knack and ability he had. If we discipline and train our bodies they will grow ever fitter and stronger; if we do not they grow fat and flabby, and we lose even the strength we had. If a schoolboy is learning Latin, if he goes on with his learning, the wealth and riches of Latin literature will open wider and wider to him; if he does not go on learning, he will forget even the Latin he knew. If we really strive after goodness, if we master this and that temptation, new vistas and new heights of goodness are ever open to us; if we give up the battle and take the easy way even the resistance power we once possessed will be lost and we will slip from even the little height to which we had attained. There is no such thing as standing still in the Christian life. We either get more or lose what we had. We either advance to greater heights or slip back every day.

THE ENTRY OF THE KING

Luke 19: 28-40

When Jesus had said these things, He went on ahead on the way up to Jerusalem. When He had come near Bethphage and Bethany, which is near the mount called the Mount of Olives, He despatched two of His disciples. " Go to the village opposite," He said. " As you come into it, you will find tethered a colt upon which no man has ever sat. Loose it and bring it here. And if any one asks you, ' Why are you loosing this colt?' you will say, ' The Lord needs it.' " Those who had been despatched went off, and found everything exactly as He had told them. And as they were loosing the colt, its owners said to them, "Why are you loosing the colt?" They said, " The Lord needs it "; and they brought it to Jesus. They flung their garments on the colt, and mounted Jesus on it. As He went they strewed their garments on the road. When He was now drawing near, at the descent from the Mount of Olives, the whole crowd of the disciples began to rejoice, and to praise God with shouts for all the deeds of power they had seen, saying, " Blessed is the King who comes in the name of the Lord! Peace in heaven and glory in the heights! " Some of the Pharisees who were in the crowd said to Him, " Teacher, rebuke your disciples." " I tell you," He answered, " if these keep silent, the stones will cry out."

FROM Jerusalem to Jericho was only twenty miles, and now Jesus had almost reached His goal. Jerusalem, His journey's end, lay just ahead. The prophets had a regular custom of which they made use again and again. When words were of no effect, when people refused to take in and to understand the spoken message, the prophets resorted to some dramatic action which put their message into a picture which none could fail to see. We will get examples of such dramatic prophetic actions in I Kings II: 29-31; Jeremiah 13: 1-11; 27: 1-11; Ezekiel 4: 1-3; 5: 1-4. It was just such a dramatic action which Jesus planned now. He proposed to ride into Jerusalem in such a way that the very action would be an unmistakable claim to be the Messiah, God's Anointed King. We have to note certain things about this entry into Jerusalem.

(i) It was carefully planned. It was no sudden, impulsive action. Jesus did not leave things until the last moment. He had His arrangement with the owners of the colt. *The Lord needs it* was a pass-word chosen long ago.

(ii) It was an act of glorious defiance, and of superlative courage. By this time there was a price on Jesus' head. (John II: 57). It would have been natural that, if He was going into Jerusalem at all, He should have slipped in unseen and hidden Himself in some secret place in the back streets. But He entered in such a way as to focus the whole lime-light upon Himself, and to occupy the centre of the stage. It is a breath-taking thing to think of a man with a price upon his head, an outlaw, deliberately riding into a city in such a way that every eye was fixed upon him. It is impossible to exaggerate the sheer courage of Jesus.

(iii) It was a deliberate claim to be king. It was a deliberate fulfilling of the picture in Zechariah 9: 9. But even in this Jesus underlined the kind of kingship which He claimed. The ass in Palestine was not the lowly beast that it is in this country. It was a noble beast. Only in war did kings ride upon a horse; when they came in peace they came upon an ass. So Jesus by this action came as the king who comes to His people in love and in peace, and not as the conquering hero, in martial splendour, whom the mob expected and awaited.

(iv) It was one last appeal. In this action Jesus came, as it were with pleading hands outstretched, saying, " Even now, will you not take me as your King? " Before the hatred of men engulfed Him, once again He confronted men with love's last invitation.

THE PITY AND THE ANGER OF JESUS

Luke 19: 41-48

> When Jesus had come near, and when He saw the city, He wept over it. " Would that, even to-day," He said, " you recognised the things which would give you peace! But as it is, they are hidden from your eyes; for days will come upon you when your enemies will cast a rampart around you, and will surround you, and will hem you in on every side, and they will dash you and your children within you to the ground, and they will not leave one stone upon another within you, because you did not recognise the day when God visited you."
>
> And He entered into the Temple and began to cast out those who were selling. " It is written," He said to them, " My house shall be a house of prayer, but you have made it a brigands' cave."
>
> And He taught daily in the Temple. The chief priests and the scribes sought to kill Him, as did the chief men of the nation; and they could not discover anything they could do to Him, for all the people, as they listened to Him, hung upon His words.

In this passage there are three separate incidents.

(i) There is Jesus' lament over Jerusalem. From the descent of the Mount of Olives there is a magnificent view of Jerusalem in which the whole city lies full displayed to the sight. As Jesus came to that turn in the road He stopped and wept over Jerusalem. Jesus knew what was going to happen to the city. The Jews were even then embarking upon a career of political manœuvre and intrigue which ended in the destruction of Jerusalem in A.D. 70, when the city was so devastated that a plough was drawn across the midst of it. The tragedy was that if only they had abandoned their dreams of political power and had taken the way of Christ it need never have happened. The tears of Jesus are the tears of God when He sees the needless pain and suffering in which men involve themselves through their foolish rebellion against His will.

(ii) There is the cleansing of the Temple. Luke's account of it is very summary. Matthew's is a little fuller (Matthew 21: 12, 13). Why did Jesus, who was the very incarnation of love, act with such violence to the money changers and the sellers of animals in the Temple courts? First, let us look at the money changers. Every male Jew had to pay a Temple tax every year of half a shekel. That was equal to about 1s. 2d., but, in evaluating it, it must be remembered that that was equal to two days' pay for a working man. A month before the Passover booths were set up in all the towns and villages and it could be paid there; but by far the greater part of it was actually paid by the pilgrims in Jerusalem when they came to the Passover Feast. In Palestine all kinds of currencies were in circulation, and, for ordinary purposes, they were all—Greek, Roman, Tyrian, Syrian, Egyptian—equally valid. But this tax had to be paid either in exact half shekels of the Sanctuary or in ordinary Galilæan shekels. That is where the money changers came in. To change a coin of exact value they charged one *maah*, which was equal to 2d. If a larger coin was tendered a charge of one *maah* was made for the requisite half shekel and of another *maah* for the giving of change. It has been computed that these money changers made a profit of between £8,000 and £9,000 per annum. It was a deliberate ramp, and an imposition on poor people who could least of all afford it. Second, let us look at the sellers of animals. Almost every visit to the Temple involved its sacrifice. Victims could be bought outside at very reasonable prices ; but the Temple authorities had appointed inspectors, for a victim must be without spot and blemish. It was, therefore, far safer to buy victims from the booths officially set up in the Temple. But there were times when a pair of doves would cost as much as 15s. inside the Temple and considerably less than 1s. outside. Again, it was a deliberately planned victimization of the poor pilgrims. It was nothing more or less than legalized robbery. Still worse, these Temple shops were known as the Booths of Annas, and were the property of the family of the High Priest. That is why Jesus was brought first before Annas when He was arrested (John 18: 13). Annas was delighted to gloat over this Jesus, who had struck such a blow at his evil monopoly. Jesus cleansed the Temple with such violence, because the Temple traffic was being used to exploit helpless men and women. It was not simply that the buying and selling interfered with the dignity and the solemnity of worship. It was that the very worship of the house of God was being used to exploit the worshippers. It was the passion for social justice which burned in Jesus' heart when He took this drastic step.

(iii) There is something almost incredibly audacious in the action of Jesus in teaching in the Temple courts when there was a price on His head. This was sheer defiance. At the moment the authorities could not arrest Him, for the people hung upon His every word. But every time He spoke He took His life in His hands, and He knew well that it was only a matter of time until the end should come. The courage of the Christian should match the courage of his Lord. He left us an example that we should never be ashamed to show whose we are and whom we serve.

BY WHAT AUTHORITY?

Luke 20: 1-8

> One day, while Jesus was teaching the people in the Temple and telling them the good news, the chief priests and scribes, with the elders came up and said to Him, " Tell us, by what authority do you do these things? Or, who is it who gives you this authority? " He said to them, " I, too, will ask you for a statement. Tell me, was the baptism of John from heaven or from men? " They discussed it with each other. " If," they said to each other, " we say, ' From heaven,' He will say, ' Why did you not believe in him?' But, if we say, ' From men,' all the people will stone us, for they are convinced that John was a prophet." So they answered that they did not know where it was from. Jesus said to them, " Neither do I tell you by what authority I do these things."

THIS chapter describes what is usually called *The Day of Questions*. It was a day when the Jewish authorities, in all their different sections, came to Jesus with question after question designed to trap Him, and when, in His wisdom, He answered them in such a way that He routed them, and left them speechless, and without an answer.

The first question is put by the chief priests, the scribes and the elders. The chief priests were a body of men composed of ex-High Priests and of members of these families from which the High Priests were drawn. The phrase describes the religious aristocracy of the Temple. The three sets of men—chief priests, scribes and elders— were the component parts of the Sanhedrin, the supreme Council and governing body of the Jews; and we may well take it that this is a question concocted and raised by the Sanhedrin with a view to formulating a charge against Jesus.

No wonder they asked Him by what authority He did these things! To ride into Jerusalem as He did, and then to take the law into His own hands and cleanse the Temple as He did, required some explanation. To the orthodox Jews of the day, Jesus' calm assumption of authority was at all times an amazing thing. No Rabbi ever delivered a judgment or made a statement without giving his authorities. He would say, " There is a teaching that . . ." Or he would say, " This was confirmed by Rabbi So and So when he said . . ." But none would have claimed that utterly independent authority with which Jesus moved among men. What they wanted was that Jesus should say bluntly and directly that He was the Messiah and the Son of God. Then they would have a ready-made charge of blasphemy, and could arrest Him on the spot. But He would not give that answer, for His hour was not yet come.

The answer of Jesus is sometimes described as a clever debating answer, used simply to score a point like a shrewd debater. But it is far more than that. He asked them to answer the question, " Whence came the authority of John the Baptist? Was it human, or was it divine?" Now the whole point is that their answer to Jesus' question would answer their own question. Every one knew how John had regarded Jesus, and how he had considered himself only the fore-runner of the one who was the Messiah. If they agreed that John's authority was divine then they had also to agree that Jesus was the Messiah, because John had said so. If they denied it the people would rise against them. Jesus' answer in fact asks the question, " Tell me—where do you think yourself I got my authority?" He did not need to answer their question if they answered his.

To face the truth may confront a man with a sore and a difficult situation; but to refuse to face it confronts a man with a tangle out of which there is no escape. The emissaries of the Pharisees refused to face the truth, and they had to withdraw, frustrated and discredited with the crowd.

A PARABLE WHICH WAS A CONDEMNATION

Luke 20: 9-18

Jesus began to speak this parable to the people. " A man planted a vineyard and let it out to tenants, and went

254

away for a long time. At the proper time he despatched a servant to the tenants so that they might give him his share of the fruit of the vineyard. The tenants beat him and sent him away empty-handed. He went on to send another servant. They beat him, too, and maltreated him, and sent him away empty-handed. He went on to send a third. This one they wounded and threw out. The owner of the vineyard said, ' What am I to do? I will send my beloved son. It may be they will respect him.' When the tenants saw him they said to each other, ' This is the heir. Let us kill him so that the inheritance will be ours.' And they flung him out of the vineyard and killed him. What, then, will the owner of the vineyard do to them? He will come, and he will destroy these tenants, and will give the vineyard to others." When they heard this, they said, " God forbid!" He looked at them and said, "What, then, is this which stands written—' The stone which the builders rejected, this has become the head of the corner? Everyone who falls against that stone will be shattered; but if it falls on anyone it will wipe him out as the wind blows the chaff away.' "

THIS is a parable whose meaning is crystal clear. The vineyard stands for the nation of Israel. (cp. Isaiah 5: 1-7.) The tenants are the rulers of Israel into whose hands the nation was entrusted. The messengers are the prophets who were disregarded, persecuted and killed. The son is Jesus Himself. And the doom is that the place which Israel should have occupied is to be given to others.

The story itself is the kind of story which could, and did happen. Judæa in the time of Jesus was in the throes of economic trouble and labour unrest. There was many an absentee landlord who let out his lands in just such a way. The rent was seldom paid in money. It was either a fixed amount of produce, irrespective of the success or the failure of the harvest, or, it was a percentage of the crop, whatever it might be.

In its teaching this is one of the richest of the parables. It tells us certain things about man.

(i) It tells us of *human privilege*. The tenants did not make the vineyard. They entered into possession of it.

The owner did not stand over them with a whip. He went away and left them to work in their own way.

(ii) It tells us of *human sin*. The sin of the tenants was that they refused to give the owner his due, and that they wished to control that which it was the sole right of the owner to control. Sin consists in the failure to give God His proper place in life and in usurping the power which should be His.

(iii) It tells of *human responsibility*. For long enough the tenants were left to their own devices; but the day of reckoning came. Soon or late a man is called upon to give account for that which was committed to his charge.

The parable tells us certain things about God.

(i) It tells us of the *patience* of God. The owner did not strike at the first sign of rebellion on the part of the tenants. He gave them chance after chance to do the right thing. There is nothing so wonderful as the patience of God. If any man had created the world he would have taken his hand, and, in exasperated despair, he would have wiped it out long ago.

(ii) It tells us of the *judgment* of God. The tenants thought that they could presume on the patience of the master, that, to use the modern phrase, they could get away with it. But God has not abdicated. However much a man may seem to get away with it, the day of reckoning comes. As the Romans put it, " Justice holds the scales with an even and a scrupulous balance and in the end she will prevail."

The parable tells us something about Jesus.

(i) It tells us that *He knew what was coming*. He did not come to Jerusalem hugging a dream that even yet He might escape the Cross. Open eyed, and unafraid, He went on. When Achilles, the great Greek hero, was warned by the prophetess Cassandra that, if he went out to battle, he would surely die, he answered, " Nevertheless I am for going on." For Jesus there was no turning back.

(ii) It tells us that *He never doubted God's ultimate triumph*. Beyond the power of wicked men there stood the undefeatable majesty of God. Wickedness may seem for a time to prevail, but it cannot in the end escape its punishment.

> Careless seems the great Avenger, history's pages but record
> One death grapple in the darkness, 'twixt old systems and the Word;
> Truth forever on the scaffold, Wrong forever on the throne,
> Yet that scaffold sways the future, and behind the dim unknown,
> Standeth God within the shadows, keeping watch above His own.

(iii) It lays down most unmistakably *Jesus' claim to be the Son of God*. In it deliberately He removes Himself from the succession of the prophets. They were servants. He is *the Son*. In this parable He made a claim that none could fail to see to be God's Chosen King.

The quotation about the stone which the builders rejected comes from Psalm 118: 22, 23. It was a favourite quotation in the early Church as a description of the death and resurrection of Jesus. (cp. Acts 4: 11; I Peter 2: 7.)

CAESAR AND GOD

Luke 20: 19-26

> The Scribes and chief priests tried to lay hands on Jesus at that very hour; and they feared the people, for they realized that He spoke this parable to them. They watched for an opportunity, and they despatched spies, who pretended that they were genuinely concerned about the right thing to do, so that they might fasten on what He said and be able to hand Him over to the power and the authority of the governor. They asked Him, " Teacher, we know that you speak and

257

teach rightly, and you are no respecter of persons. Is it lawful for us to pay tribute to Cæsar? Or not? " He saw their subtle deception and said to them, " Show me a shilling piece. Whose image and inscription is on it? " They said, " Cæsar's." " Well then," He said to them, " give to Cæsar what belongs to Cæsar, and give to God what belongs to God." There was nothing in this statement that they could fasten on to in the presence of the people. They were amazed at His answer, and they had nothing to say.

HERE the emissaries of the Sanhedrin returned to the attack. They suborned men to go to Jesus and to ask a question as if it was really troubling their consciences. The tribute to be paid to Cæsar was a poll-tax of one *denarius*, about 9d., per year. Everyone from 14 to 65 had to pay that simply for the privilege of existing. This tribute was a burning question in Palestine, and had been the cause of more than one rebellion. It was not the merely financial question which was at stake. The tribute was not regarded as a heavy imposition, and was in fact no real burden at all. The issue at stake was this—the fanatical Jews claimed that they had no king but God, and held that it was wrong to pay tribute to anyone other than God. The question was a religious question, for which there were many who were willing to die. So, then, these emissaries of the Sanhedrin attempted to impale Jesus on the horns of a dilemma. If He said that the tribute should not be paid, they would at once report Him to Pilate and arrest would follow as the night the day. If He said that it should be paid, He would alienate many of His supporters, especially the Galilæans, whose support was so strong. Jesus answered them on their own grounds. He asked to be shown a *denarius*. Now, in the ancient world, the sign of kingship was the issue of currency. For instance, the Maccabees had immediately issued their own currency whenever Jerusalem was freed from the Syrians. Further, it was universally admitted that to have the right to issue currency carried with it the right to impose taxation. If a man had the right to put his image and superscription on a coin, *ipso facto* he had acquired the right to impose taxation. So Jesus said, " If you accept Cæsar's currency and use it, you are bound to accept Cæsar's right to impose taxes "; " *but*," He went on, " there is a domain in which Cæsar's writ does not run and which belongs wholly to God."

(i) If a man lives in a state, and enjoys all the privileges of a state, he cannot divorce himself from that state. The more honest a man is, the better citizen he will be. There should be no better and no more conscientious citizens of any state than Christians; and one of the tragedies of modern life is that Christians will not take their part in the government of the state. If they abandon their responsibilities, and leave materialistic politicians to govern the country, they cannot complain about what is happening and what will happen.

(ii) Nonetheless it remains true that in the life of the Christian, God has the last word and not the state. The voice of conscience is louder than the voice of any man-made laws. The Christian is at once the servant and the conscience of the state. Just because he is the best of citizens he will refuse to do what a Christian citizen cannot do. He will at one and the same time fear God and honour the king.

THE SADDUCEES' QUESTION

Luke 20: 27-40

Some of the Sadducees, who say that there is no resurrection, came to Jesus and asked Him, " Teacher, Moses wrote to us that, if a man's married brother dies without leaving any children, his brother must take his wife and raise up descendants for his brother. Now there were seven brothers. The first took a wife and died childless. The second and the third also took her; and in the same way the whole seven left no children and died. Later the wife died too. Whose wife will she be at the resurrection, for the seven had her to wife?" Jesus said to them, " The sons of this age marry and are married. But those who are deemed worthy to obtain that age and the resurrection from the dead neither marry or are married, for they cannot die any more, for they are like angels and they are sons of God, for they are the sons of the resurrection. That the dead are raised even Moses indicated in the passage about the bush, when he called the Lord, the God of Abraham, the God of Isaac and the God of Jacob. God is not the God of the dead but of the living, for all live to Him." Some of the Scribes said, " Teacher, you have spoken well "; and they no longer dared to ask Him any question.

WHEN the emissaries of the Sanhedrin had been finally silenced the Sadducees appeared on the scene. The whole point of their question depends on two things. (i) It depends upon the levirate law of marriage. (Deuteronomy 25: 5.) According to that law if a man died childless, his brother must marry the widow and beget children to carry on the line. It is far from likely that that law was operative in the time of Jesus, but it was included in the Mosaic regulations, and therefore the Sadducees regarded it as binding. (ii) It depends upon the beliefs of the Sadducees. Sadducees and Pharisees are often mentioned together, but in beliefs they were poles apart. (a) The Pharisees were entirely a religious body. They had no political ambitions, and were content with any government which allowed them to carry out the ceremonial law. The Sadducees were few but very wealthy. The priests and the aristocrats were nearly all Sadducees. They were the governing class; and they were largely collaborationist with Rome. It usually happens that the wealthy are collaborationist in any occupied country simply because they do not wish to lose their wealth, their comfort and their place, and are prepared to collaborate in order to keep them. (b) The Pharisees accepted the scriptures plus all the thousand detailed regulations and rules of the oral and ceremonial law, such as the Sabbath law and the laws about hand washing. The Sadducees accepted only

the written law of the Old Testament. And in the Old
Testament they stressed only the law of Moses and set
no store on the prophetic books. (c) The Pharisees believed
in the resurrection from the dead and in angels and spirits.
The Sadducees held that there was no resurrection from
the dead and that there were no angels or spirits. (d) The
Pharisees believed in fate. They believed that a man's
life was planned and ordered by God. The Sadducees
believed in unrestricted free-will. (e) The Pharisees
believed in and hoped for the coming of the Messiah; the
Sadducees did not. For them the coming of the Messiah
would have been a disturbance of their carefully ordered
lives. The Sadducees, then, came with this question about
who would be the husband in heaven of the woman who
was married to seven different men. They regarded such
a question as the kind of thing that made belief in the
resurrection of the body ridiculous. Jesus gave them an
answer which has a permanently valid truth in it. He said
that we must not think of heaven in terms of this earth.
Life there will be quite different, because we will be quite
different. It would save a mass of misdirected ingenuity,
and not a little heartbreak, if we ceased to speculate on
what heaven is like and left things to the love of God.

But Jesus went further. As we have said, the Sadducees
did not believe in the resurrection of the body. They
declared they could not believe in it because there is no
information about it, still less any proof of it, in the books
of the law which Moses was held to have written. So far
no Rabbi had been able to meet them on that ground;
but Jesus did. He pointed out that Moses himself had
heard God say, " I am the God of Abraham, the God of
Isaac and the God of Jacob " (Exodus 3: 1-6), and that it
was impossible that God should be the God of the dead.
Therefore Abraham and Isaac and Jacob are still alive.
Therefore there is such a thing as the resurrection of the
body. No wonder the Scribes declared it to be a good

answer, for Jesus had met the Sadducees on their own ground and had defeated them.

It may well be that we find this an arid passage. It deals with questions which were burning questions in the time of Jesus by arguments which a Rabbi would find completely convincing but which are not convincing to the modern mind. But out of this very aridity there emerges one great truth for anyone who teaches or who wishes to commend Christianity to his fellows. *Jesus used arguments that the people He was arguing with could understand.* He talked to people in their own language; He met them on their own grounds; and that is precisely why the common people heard Him gladly. Sometimes, when one reads religious and theological books, one feels that all this may be true but it would be quite impossible to present it to the non-theologically minded man who, in the world and the Church, is in an overwhelming majority. Jesus used language and arguments which people could, and did, understand; He met people with their own vocabulary, on their own grounds, and with their own ideas. We will be far better teachers of Christianity, and far better witnesses for Christ, when we learn to do the same.

THE WARNINGS OF JESUS

Luke 20: 41-44

> Jesus said to them, " How does David say that the Christ is his son? For David himself says in the Book of Psalms, ' The Lord said to my Lord, sit at my right hand until I make your enemies your footstool.' So David calls Him Lord, and how can He be his son? "

IT is worth while taking this little passage by itself for it is a passage which to us is very difficult to understand. The most popular title of the Messiah was Son of David. That is what the blind man at Jericho called Jesus (Luke 18: 38, 39), and that is how the crowds addressed Him at

His entry into Jerusalem (Matthew 21: 9). Here Jesus seems to cast doubts on the validity of that title. The quotation is from Psalm 110: 1. In Jesus' time all the Psalms were attributed to David, and this Psalm was taken to refer to the Messiah. In it David says that He heard God speak to His Anointed One, and tell Him to sit at His right hand until His enemies became His footstool; and in it David calls the Messiah *My Lord*. How can the Messiah be at once David's son and David's Lord?

Jesus was doing here what He so often tried to do. He was trying to correct the popular ideas of the Messiah. The popular idea of the Messiah was that under him the golden age would come and Israel would become the greatest nation in the world. It was a dream of political power. How was that to happen? There were many ideas about that, but the popular idea was that some great descendant of David would come to this earth to be the invincible captain and king. So then the title *Son of David* was inextricably mixed up with world dominion, with military prowess, and with material conquest. Really what Jesus was saying here is, " You think of the coming Messiah as Son of David; so he is; *but He is far more*. He is Lord." He is telling men that they must revise their ideas of what Son of David means. They must abandon these fantastic dreams of world power, and visualize the Messiah as the Lord of the hearts and lives of men. He was implicitly blaming them for having too little an idea of God. It is always man's tendency to make God in his own image, and thereby to miss the full majesty of God.

THE LOVE OF HONOUR AMONG MEN

Luke 20: 45-47

> While all the people were listening, Jesus said to His disciples, " Beware of the Scribes who like to walk about in long robes, and who love greetings in the market places, and the chief seats in synagogues,

and the top place at banquets. They devour widows' houses and pretend to offer long prayers. These will receive the greater condemnation."

THE honours which the Scribes and Rabbis expected to receive, and did receive were quite extraordinary. They had rules of precedence all carefully drawn up. In the college, the most learned Rabbi took precedence; at a banquet, the oldest. It is on record that two Rabbis came in, after walking on the street, grieved and bewildered because more than one person had greeted them with, "May your peace be great," without adding, "My masters!" They claimed to rank even above parents. They said, "Let your esteem for your friend border on your esteem for your teacher, and let your respect for your teacher border on your reverence for God." "Respect for a teacher should exceed respect for a father, for both father and son owe respect to a teacher." "If a man's father and teacher have lost anything, the teacher's loss has the precedence, for a man's father only brought him into this world; his teacher, who taught him wisdom, brought him into the life of the world to come. . . . If a man's father and teacher are carrying burdens, he must first help his teacher, and afterwards his father. If his father and teacher are in captivity, he must first ransom his teacher, and afterwards his father." Such claims are almost incredible; it was not good for a man to make them; it was still less good for him to have them conceded to him. It was claims like that that the Scribes and Rabbis made.

Jesus also accused the Scribes of devouring widows' houses. A Rabbi was legally bound to teach for nothing. All Rabbis were supposed to have trades, and to support themselves by the work of their hands, while their teaching was given free. That sounds very noble, but it was deliberately taught that to support a Rabbi was an act of the greatest piety. "Whoever," they said, "puts part of his income into the purse of the wise is counted worthy of a seat in the heavenly academy." "Whosoever harbours a disciple of the wise in his house is counted as if he offered a daily sacrifice." "Let thy house be a place of resort to wise men." It is by no means extraordinary that impressionable women were the legitimate prey of the less scrupulous and more comfort-loving rabbis. At their worst, they did devour widows' houses.

The whole unhealthy business shocked and revolted Jesus. It was worse, because these men knew so much better and held so responsible a place within the life of the community. It is always a thing which God will condemn when a man uses a position of trust to further his own ends and to pander to his own comfort.

THE PRECIOUS GIFT

Luke 21: 1-4

> Jesus looked up and saw those who were putting their gifts into the treasury—rich people—and He saw a poor widow putting in half a farthing. So He said, "I tell you truly that this poor widow has put in more than all, for all these contributed to the gifts out of their abundance, but she, out of her need, has put in everything she had to live on."

In the Court of the Women in the Temple there were thirteen collecting boxes known as The Trumpets. They were shaped like trumpets with the narrow part at the top and the wider part at the foot. Each of the thirteen was assigned to offerings for a different purpose—for instance, for the wood that was used to burn the sacrifice, for the incense that was burned on the altar, for the upkeep of the golden vessels, and so on. It was near The Trumpets that Jesus was sitting. After the strenuous debates with the emissaries of the Sanhedrin and the Sadducees He was tired, and His head drooped between His hands. He looked up and He saw many people flinging their offerings into The Trumpets; and then there came a poor widow. All she had in the world was two *lepta*, two mites. A *lepton* was the smallest of all coins; the name means "the thin one." It was worth one-sixteenth of a penny; and, therefore, the offering of the widow woman was only half a farthing. But Jesus said that it far outvalued all the other offerings, because it was everything that she had.

There are two things which determine the value of any gift.

(i) There is *the spirit in which it is given*. A gift which is unwillingly extracted, a gift which is given with a grudge, a gift that is given for the sake of prestige or of self-display loses more than half its value. The only real gift is the gift which is the inevitable outflow of the loving heart, the gift which is given because the giver cannot help giving it.

(ii) There is *the sacrifice which it involves*. That which is a mere trifle to one man may be a vast sum to another. The gifts of the rich, as they flung their offerings into The Trumpets, did not really cost them much; but the two mites of the widow woman cost her everything she had. They no doubt gave having nicely calculated how much they could afford to give; she gave with that utterly reckless generosity which could give no more. Giving does not begin to be giving until it hurts. A gift only shows our love when we ourselves have had to do without something, or have had to work doubly hard, in order to give it. How few people give to God like that! Someone draws a picture of a man in church, lustily singing,

> Were the whole realm of Nature mine
>   That were an offering far too small;
> Love so amazing, so divine
>   Demands my life, my soul, my all,

while, all the time, he is carefully feeling the coins in his pocket to make sure that it is a sixpence and not a shilling that he will put into the collection which is immediately to follow.

He is an insensate man who can read the story of the widow and her two mites without searching and humiliating self-examination.

TIDINGS OF TROUBLE

Luke 21: 5-24

When some were speaking about the Temple, how it was adorned with lovely stones and offerings, Jesus said, " As for these things at which you are looking —days will come in which not one stone here will be left upon another, which will not be pulled down." They asked Him, " Teacher, when, then, will these things be? And what will be the sign when these things are going to happen? " He said, " Take care that you are not led astray. Many will come in my name, saying, ' I am He! ' and, ' The time is at hand! ' Do not go after them. When you hear of wars and upheavals, do not be alarmed; for these things must happen first; but the end will not come at once."

Then He said to them, " Nation will rise against nation, and kingdom against kingdom. There will be great earthquakes; in some places there will be famines and pestilences; there will be terrifying things, and great signs from heaven. Before all these things, they will lay hands upon you, and they will hand you over to the synagogues and prisons, and you will be brought before kings and governors for the sake of my name. It will all be an opportunity for you to bear witness to me. So, then, make up your minds not to prepare your defence beforehand, for I will give you a mouth and wisdom against which all your opponents will be unable to stand or argue. You will be handed over even by parents, and brothers, and kinsfolk and friends; some of you will be put to death; and you will be hated by all for the sake of my name. But not one hair of your head will perish. By your endurance you will win your souls.

"When you shall see Jerusalem encircled by armies, then know that the time of the desolation is at hand. At that time let those in Jerusalem flee to the mountains; let those who are in the midst of her go out of her; and let not those in the country districts enter into her, because these are days of vengeance, to fulfil all that stands written. Woe to those who, in those days, are carrying a child in the womb, or who have a babe at the breast. For great distress will be upon the earth and wrath upon all the people. They shall fall by the edge of the sword, and they will be taken away captive to all nations. Jerusalem will be trodden underfoot by the Gentiles, until the times of Gentiles are completed."

The Background of the Chapter

FROM verse 5 onwards this becomes a very difficult chapter. Its difficulty lies in the fact that beneath it there lie four different conceptions.

(i) There is the conception of *The Day of the Lord*. The Jews regarded time as being in two ages. There was *The Present Age*, which was altogether bad and evil, incapable of being cured, and fit only for destruction. There was *The Age to come*, which was the golden age of God and of Jewish supremacy. But in between the two there would be *The Day of the Lord*, which would be a terrible time of cosmic upheaval and destruction, the desperate birth-pangs of the new age. It would be a day of terror. " Behold the Day of the Lord cometh, cruel both with wrath and fierce anger, to lay the land desolate; and He shall destroy the sinners thereof out of it." (Isaiah 13: 9; cp. Joel 2: 1, 2; Amos 5: 18-20 ; Zephaniah 1: 14-18.) It would come suddenly. " The Day of the Lord cometh as a thief in the night." (I Thessalonians 5: 2; cp. 2 Peter 3: 10.) It would be a day when the world would be shattered. " The stars of the heaven and the constellations thereof shall not give their light; the sun shall be darkened in his going forth, and the moon shall not cause her light to shine. . . . Therefore will I shake the heavens, and the earth shall remove out of her place, in the wrath of the Lord of hosts, and in the day of His anger." (Isaiah 13: 10-13; cp. Joel 2: 30, 31; 2 Peter 3: 10.) The Day of the Lord was one of the basic conceptions of religious thought in the time of Jesus. Everyone knew these terrible pictures. In this passage verses 9, 11, 25, 26 take their imagery from that.

(ii) There is *the prophesied Fall of Jerusalem*. Jerusalem fell to the Roman armies in A.D. 70 after a desperate siege in which the inhabitants were actually reduced to cannibalism and in which the city had to be taken literally stone by stone. Josephus, the Jewish historian, says that the incredible numbers of 1,100,000 people perished in the siege, and 97,000 were carried away into captivity. The Jewish nation was obliterated; and the Temple was fired and became a desolation. In this passage verses 5, 6, 20-24 clearly refer to that event still to come.

(iii) There is *the Second Coming of Christ*. Jesus was sure that He was to come again, and the Early Church waited for that coming. It will often help us to under-stand the New Testament passages about the Second Coming if we remember that much of the older imagery which had to do with The Day of the Lord was taken and attached to it. In this passage verses 27 and 28 clearly refer to it. Before the Second Coming it was expected that many false claimants to be the Christ would arise, and great upheavals take place. In this passage verses 7, 8, 9 refer to that.

(iv) There is the idea of *persecution to come*. Jesus clearly foresaw and foretold the terrible things His people would have to suffer for His sake in the days to come. In this passage verses 12-19 refer to that.

This passage will become much more intelligible and valuable if we remember that beneath it there is not one consistent idea, but four allied conceptions.

The Passage

It was a comment on the splendour of the Temple that moved Jesus to prophesy. In the Temple the pillars of the porches and of the cloisters were columns of white marble, forty feet high, and each made of one single block of stone. Of the offerings, the most famous was the great vine made of solid gold, each of whose clusters was as tall as a man. The finest description of the Temple as it stood in the time of Jesus is in Josephus' book, *The Wars of the Jews*, in book 5, section 5. Josephus, at one point, writes, " The

outward face of the Temple in its front wanted nothing
that was likely to surprise either men's minds or their
eyes, for it was covered all over with plates of gold of
great weight, and, at the first rising of the sun, reflected
back a very fiery splendour, and made those who forced
themselves to look upon it to turn their eyes away, just as
they would have done at the sun's own rays. But the
Temple appeared to strangers, when they were at a distance,
like a mountain covered with snow, for, as to those parts
of it that were not gilt, they were exceeding white." To
the Jews it was unthinkable that the glory of the Temple
should be shattered to dust.

From this passage we learn certain basic things about
Jesus and about the Christian life.

(i) Jesus could read the signs of history. Others might
be blind to the approaching disaster but He saw the
avalanche about to descend. It is only when a man sees
things through the eyes of God that he sees them clearly.

(ii) Jesus was completely honest. "This," He said to
His disciples, "is what you must expect if you choose to
follow me." Once in the middle of a great struggle for
righteousness, an heroic leader wrote to a friend, "Heads
are rolling in the sand; come and add yours." Jesus
believed in men enough to offer them, not an easy way,
but a way for heroes.

(iii) Jesus promised that His disciples would never
meet their tribulations alone. It is the sheer evidence of
history that the great Christians have written over and
over again, when their bodies were in torture, and when
they were awaiting death, of sweet times with Christ.
A prison can be like a palace, a scaffold like a throne,
the storms of life like summer weather, when Christ is
with us.

(iv) Jesus spoke of a safety that overpasses the threats
of earth. "Not one hair of your head," He said, "will be
harmed." In the days of the 1914-18 war Rupert Brooke,
out of his faith and his ideal, wrote these lines:

We have found safety with all things undying,
  The winds, and morning, tears of men and mirth,
The deep night, and birds singing, and clouds flying,
  And sleep, and freedom, and the autumnal earth.
We have built a house which is not for Time's throwing,
  We have gained a peace unshaken by pain for ever.
War knows no power. Safe shall be my going,
  Secretly armed against all death's endeavour:
Safe though all safety's lost; safe where men fall;
And if these poor limbs die, safest of all.

The man who walks with Christ may lose his life, but he
can never lose his soul.

WATCH!

Luke 21: 25-37

And there will be signs in sun, and moon, and stars,
and on earth the nations will be in distress and will
not know what to do in the roaring of the sea and of
the wave, while men's hearts will swoon from fear
and from foreboding of the things that are coming
on the world. The power of the heavens will be shaken;
and then they will see the Son of Man coming in a
cloud, with power and much glory. When these
things begin to happen, look up and lift up your
hearts for your deliverance is near.

And He spoke this parable to them, " Look at the
fig-tree and all the trees; whenever they put out
their leaves, you see it for yourselves and you know that
the harvest is near. So, whenever you see these
things happening, you know that the Kingdom of
God is near. This is the truth I tell you, that this
generation will not pass away until all these things
have happened. The heaven and the earth will pass
away, but my words will not pass away."

Take care lest your hearts grow heavy with dissi-
pation and drunkenness and anxieties for the things
of this life, and lest that day come suddenly upon
you like a trap closing, for it will come upon all who
dwell upon the face of the earth. Be watchful at all
times, and keep praying that you may have strength

to escape all the things that are going to happen, and to be able to stand before the Son of Man.

During the days Jesus was teaching in the Temple, but at night He went out and stayed in the Mount called the Mount of Olives; and all the people came early in the morning to listen to Him in the Temple.

THERE are two main conceptions here.

(i) There is the conception of *the Second Coming of Jesus Christ*. There has always been much vain and useless argument and speculation about the Second Coming. When it will be, and what it will be like, are not ours to know. But the one great truth which it enshrines is this —that history is going somewhere. The Stoics regarded history as circular. They held that every three thousand years or so the world was consumed by a great conflagration, and that then it started all over again, and history repeated itself. That meant that history was going nowhere, and that men were tramping round on a kind of eternal treadmill. The Christian conception of history is that it has a goal and, at that goal, Jesus Christ will be Lord of all. That is all we know, and all we need to know.

(ii) There is stressed *the need to be upon the watch*. The Christian must never come to think that he is living in a permanent situation. He must be a man who lives in a permanent state of expectation. A novelist, in one of her books, has a character who will not stoop to certain things that others do. " I know," she said, " that some day the great thing will come into my life, and I want to keep myself fit to take it." We must live forever in the shadow of eternity, in the certainty that we are men who are fitting or unfitting themselves to appear in the presence of God. There can be nothing so thrilling as the Christian life.

(iii) Jesus spent the day amidst the crowds of the Temple; He spent the night beneath the stars with God. He won His strength to meet the crowds through His quiet time alone; He could face men because He came to men from the presence of God.

AND SATAN ENTERED INTO JUDAS

Luke 22: 1-6

> The Feast of Unleavened Bread, which is called the Passover, was near, and the chief priests and the Scribes searched to find a way to destroy Jesus, for they were afraid of the people. And Satan entered into Judas, who was called Iscariot, who belonged to the number of The Twelve. So he went away and discussed with the chief priests and captains how he might betray Jesus to them. They were glad, and they undertook to give him money. So he agreed, and he began to look for a suitable time to betray Him, when the mob were not there.

It was at the Passover time that Jesus came to Jerusalem to die. The Feast of Unleavened Bread is not, strictly speaking, the same thing as the Passover. The Feast of Unleavened Bread lasted for a week, from 15th to 21st Nisan (April), and the Passover itself was eaten on 15th Nisan. It commemorated the deliverance of the people of Israel from their slavery in Egypt (Exodus 12). On that night the angel of death smote the first-born son in every Egyptian family; but *he passed over* the homes of the Israelites, because the lintel of their doors was smeared with the blood of the lamb to distinguish them. On that night they left so quickly that, at their last meal, there was no time to bake bread with leaven. It was unleavened cakes they ate.

There were elaborate preparations for the Passover. Roads were repaired; bridges were made safe; wayside tombs were whitewashed lest the pilgrim should fail to see them, and so touch them and become unclean. For a month before, the story and the meaning of the Passover was the subject of the teaching of every Synagogue. Two days before the Passover there was in every house a ceremonial search for leaven. The householder took a candle and solemnly searched every nook and cranny in silence, and the last particle of leaven was thrown out. Every

273

male Jew, who was of age, and who lived within 15 miles of Jerusalem, was bound by law to attend the Passover. But it was the ambition of every Jew in every part of the world, at least once in his lifetime, to come to the Passover in Jerusalem. To this day, when Jews keep the Passover, in every land they pray that they may keep it next year in Jerusalem. Because of this, vast numbers came to Jerusalem at the Passover time. Cestius was governor of Palestine in the time of Nero, and Nero tended to belittle the importance of the Jewish faith. To convince Nero of it Cestius took a census of the lambs slain at one particular Passover time. Josephus tells us that the number was 256,500. Now, the law laid it down that the minimum number for a Passover celebration was 10. And that means that on that occasion, if these figures are correct, there must have been more than 2,700,000 pilgrims to the Passover. It was in a city crowded like that that the drama of the last days of Jesus was played out.

The atmosphere of the Passover time was always inflammable. The headquarters of the Roman government was at Cæsarea, and, normally, only a small detachment of troops was stationed at Jerusalem; but at the Passover time many more were drafted in. The problem which faced the Jewish authorities was how to arrest Jesus without provoking a riot. It was solved for them by the treachery of Judas. Satan entered into Judas. Two things stand out.

(i) Just as God is ever looking for men to be His instruments, so is Satan. A man can be the instrument of good or of evil, of God or of the devil. The Zoroastrians see this whole universe as the battle ground between the god of the light and the god of the dark, and, in that battle, a man must choose his side. We, too, know that a man can be the servant of the light or of the dark.

(ii) But it remains true that Satan could not have entered into Judas unless Judas had opened the door. There is no handle on the outside of the door of the human heart. It must be opened from within.

To every man there openeth
A high way and a low;
And every man decideth
The way his soul shall go.

It is in our own decision whether we will choose to be the instrument of Satan or the weapon in the hand of God. We can enlist in either service. God help us to choose aright!

THE LAST MEAL TOGETHER

Luke 22: 7-23

There came the day of the Feast of Unleavened Bread, on which the Passover had to be sacrificed. Jesus despatched Peter and John. " Go," He said, " and make ready the Passover for us that we may eat it." They said to Him, " Where do you want us to make it ready? " " Look you," He said to them, " when you have gone into the city, a man will meet you, carrying a jar of water. Follow him to the house into which he enters; and you will say to the master of the house, ' The Teacher says to you, " Where is the guest room that I may eat the Passover with my disciples? " ' And he will show you a big upper room, ready furnished. There, get things ready." So they went away and found everything just as He had told them; and they made ready the Passover.

When the hour came He took His place at table, and so did His disciples. " I have desired with all my heart," He said to them, " to eat this Passover with you before I suffer, for I tell you that I will not eat it until it is fulfilled in the Kingdom of God." He received the cup, and gave thanks, and said, " Take this and divide it among yourselves. For I tell you that from now on I will not drink of the fruit of the vine until the Kingdom of God has come." And He took the bread, and gave thanks, and broke it, and gave it to them, saying, " This is my body which is being given for you. Do this so that you will remember me." In the same way, after the meal, He took the cup saying, " This cup is the new covenant made at the price of my blood, which is shed for you. But—

look you—the hand of him who betrays me is on the table with me, for the Son of Man goes as it has been determined. But woe to that man by whom He has been betrayed "; and they began to question one another who of them it could be who was going to do this.

ONCE again Jesus did not leave things until the last moment; His plans were made. The better class houses had two rooms. The one room was on the top of the other; the house looked exactly like a small box placed on the top of a large one. The upper room was reached by an outside stair. During the Passover time all lodging in Jerusalem was free. The only pay a host might receive for letting lodgings to the pilgrims was the skin of the lamb which was eaten at the feast. A very usual use of an upper room was that it was the place where a Rabbi met with his favourite disciples to talk things over with them, and to open his heart to them. Jesus had taken steps to procure such a room. He sent Peter and John into the city to look for a man bearing a jar of water. To carry water was a woman's task. A man carrying a jar of water would be as easy to pick out as, say, a man using a lady's umbrella on a wet day. This was a pre-arranged signal between Jesus and a friend.

So the feast went on; and Jesus used the ancient symbols to give them a new meaning.

(i) He said of the bread, " This is my body." Herein is exactly what we mean by a sacrament. A sacrament is something, usually a very ordinary thing, which has acquired a meaning far beyond itself for him who has eyes to see and a heart to understand. There is nothing specially theological or mysterious about this. In the house of everyone of us there is a drawer full of things which can only be called junk, and yet we will not throw them out; we cannot make ourselves do so, because when we touch and handle, and look at them, they bring back to us this or that person, or this or that occasion. They are common things, but they have a meaning far beyond themselves. That is a sacrament. When Sir James Barrie's mother died, and when they were clearing up her belongings, they found that she had kept all the envelopes in which her famous son had sent her the cheques he so faithfully and lovingly sent. They were only old envelopes, but they meant much to her. That is a sacrament. When Nelson was buried in St. Paul's Cathedral a party of his sailors bore his coffin to the tomb. One who saw the scene writes, " With reverence, and with efficiency, they lowered the body of the world's greatest admiral into its tomb. Then, as though answering to a sharp order from the quarter deck, they all seized the Union Jack with which the coffin had been covered and tore it to fragments, and each took his souvenir of the illustrious dead." All their lives that little bit of coloured cloth would speak to them of the Admiral they had loved. That is a sacrament. The bread which we eat at the sacrament is common bread, but, for him who has a heart to feel and understand, it is the very body of Christ.

(ii) He said of the cup, " This cup is the new covenant made at the price of my blood." In the biblical sense, a covenant is a relationship between man and God. God graciously approached man; and man promised to obey, and to keep God's law. The whole matter is set out in Exodus 24: 1-8. Now the continuance of that covenant depends on man's keeping his pledge and obeying this law. Man could not and cannot do that; man's sin interrupts the relationship between man and God. All the Jewish sacrificial system was designed to restore that relationship by the offering of sacrifice to God to atone for sin. What Jesus said was this—" By my life, and by my death, I have made possible a new relationship between you and God. You are sinners. That is true. But because I died for you, God is no longer your enemy but your friend." It cost the life of Christ to restore the lost relationship of friendship between God and man.

(iii) Jesus said, " Do this and it will make you remember me." Jesus knew how easily the human mind forgets. The Greeks had an adjective which they used to describe time—" time," they said, " which wipes all things out," as if the mind of man were a slate, and time a sponge which wiped it clean. Jesus was saying, " In the rush and press of things you will forget me. Man forgets because he must, and not because he will. Come in sometimes to the peace and stillness of my house and do this again with my people—and you will remember."

It made the tragedy all the more tragic that at that very table there was one who was a traitor. Jesus Christ has at every communion table those who betray Him, for if, in His house, we pledge ourselves to Him, and then if, by our lives, we go out to deny Him, we too are traitors to His cause.

STRIFE AMONG THE DISCIPLES OF CHRIST

Luke 22: 24-30

> Strife arose amongst them about which of them was to be considered greatest. Jesus said to them, " The kings of the Gentiles exercise lordship over them, and those who have authority over them claim the title of Benefactor. It must not be so with you; but let him who is greatest among you be as the youngest; and let him who is the leader be as him who serves. Who is the greater? He who sits at table, or he who serves? Is it not he who sits at table? But I am among you as one who serves. You are those who have stayed with me in my tribulations; and I assign to you a kingdom, just as my Father has assigned one to me, that you may eat and drink at my table in my Kingdom; and you will sit upon thrones judging the twelve tribes of Israel."

IT is one of the most poignantly tragic things in the gospel story that the disciples could quarrel about precedence in the very shadow of the Cross. The seating arrangements at a Jewish feast were very definite. The table was arranged like a square with one side left open. At the top side of the square, in the centre, sat the host. On his right sat the guest of first honour; on his left the second guest; second on his right, the third guest; second on his left the fourth guest; and so on round the table. The disciples had been quarrelling about where they were to sit, for they had not yet rid themselves of the idea of an earthly kingdom. Jesus told them bluntly that the standards of His Kingdom were not the standards of this world. A king on earth was evaluated by the power he exercised. One of the commonest titles for a king in the east was *Euergetes*, which is the Greek for *Benefactor*. Jesus said, " It is not the king but the servant who obtains that title in my Kingdom."

(i) What the world needs is service. The odd thing is that the business world knows this. Bruce Barton points out that you will find by the road-side, over and over again, the sign, *Service Station*. It was the claim of one firm, " We will crawl under your car oftener and get ourselves dirtier than any of our competitors." The strange thing is that there is more argument about precedence, and more concern about people's " places " in the Church, than anywhere else. The world needs and recognizes service.

(ii) It is only the man who will consent to serve more than anyone else who will really rise high. It frequently happens that the ordinary worker will go home at 5.30 p.m. to forget his or her job until next morning, while the light will be burning in the office of the chief executive long after everyone else has gone home. Often passers-by would see the light burning in John D. Rockefeller's office when the rest of the building was in darkness. It is a law of life that service leads to greatness; and that the higher a man rises the greater the servant he must be.

(iii) We can found our life on giving or on getting; but the plain fact is that if we found it on getting we shall miss both the friendship of man and the reward of God, for no one ever loved a man who was always out for himself.

(iv) Jesus finished His warning by promising His disciples that those who had stood by Him through thick and thin would in the end reign with Him. God will be in no man's debt. Those who have shared in the bearing of Christ's Cross will some day share in the wearing of Christ's crown.

PETER'S TRAGEDY

Luke 22: 31-38 *and* 54-62

" Simon, Simon," Jesus said, " Look you, Satan has been allowed to have you that he may sift you like wheat. But I have prayed for you that your faith may not wholly fail. And you—when you have turned again—strengthen your brothers." He said to Him, " Lord, I am ready to go with you to prison and to death." " Peter," He said, " I tell you, the cock will not crow to-day before you have three times denied that you know me."

And He said to them, " When I sent you out without purse or wallet or shoes, did you lack for anything? " They said, " For nothing." But He said to them, " But now, let him who has a purse take it, and so with a wallet; and let him who has no sword sell his cloak and buy one. For I tell you that this which stands written must be fulfilled in me—' And he was reckoned with the lawbreakers '—for that which was written of me is finding its fulfilment." They said, " Lord, here are two swords." He said to them, " It is enough." . . .

So they seized Jesus and led Him away, and brought Him to the High Priest's house. Peter followed a long way away. When they had kindled a fire in the middle of the courtyard, and were sitting there together, Peter sat in the midst of them. A maidservant saw him as he sat in the firelight. She looked intently at him. " This man, too," she said, " was with Him." He denied it. " Woman," he said, " I do not know Him." Soon after another man saw him and said, " You, too, were one of them." Peter said, " Man, I am not! " About an hour elapsed and another insisted, " Truly this man, too, was with Him. I know it for he is a Galilæan." Peter said, "Man, I don't know what you are talking about." And immediately —while he was still speaking—a cock crew. And the Lord turned and looked at Peter. And Peter remembered what the Lord had said, that He said to him, "Before the cock crows to-day you will deny me three times." And he went out and wept bitterly.

WE take the story of the tragedy of Peter all in one piece. Peter was a strange paradoxical mixture.

(i) Even in spite of his denial Peter was fundamentally loyal. H. G. Wells once said, "A man may be a bad musician, and yet be passionately in love with music.' No matter what Peter did, however terrible his failure, he was nonetheless passionately devoted to Jesus. There is hope for the man who even when he is sinning is still haunted by goodness.

(ii) Peter was well warned. Jesus warned him both directly and indirectly. Verses 33-38 with their talk of swords is a strange passage. But what they mean is this— Jesus was saying, "All the time so far you have had me with you. In a very short time you are going to be cast upon your own resources. What are you going to do about it? The danger in a very short time is not that you will possess nothing; but that you will have to fight for your very existence." This is not an incitement to armed force. It is simply a vivid eastern way of telling the disciples that their very lives are at stake. No one could say that the seriousness, and the danger of the situation, and his own liability to collapse were not presented to Peter.

(iii) Peter was over-confident. It is an odd and a warning thing to remember that if a man says, "That is one thing I will never do," that is the very thing against which he must most carefully guard. Again and again castles have been captured because the attackers took the route which seemed unattackable and unscalable, because, at that very spot, the defenders were off their guard. Satan is subtle. He can attack at the point at which a man is too sure of himself, for there the man is likeliest to be unprepared.

(iv) In all fairness it has to be noted that Peter was one of the two disciples (John 18: 15) who had the courage to follow Jesus into the courtyard of the High Priest's house at all. Peter fell to a temptation which could only have come to a brave man. The man of courage always runs more risks than the man who seeks a placid safety. Liability to temptation is the price that a man pays when he is adventurous in mind and in action. It may well be that it is better to fail in a gallant enterprise than to run away and not even to attempt it.

(v) It was not in anger that Jesus spoke to Peter, but in sorrow that He looked at Him. Peter could have stood it if Jesus had turned and reviled him; but that voiceless, grief-laden look went to Peter's heart like a sword, and opened the fountain of tears.

> I think I'd sooner frizzle up,
>   I' the flames of a burnin' 'Ell,
> Than stand and look into 'Is face,
>   And 'ear 'Is voice say—" Well? "

The penalty of sin is to face, not the anger of Jesus, but the heartbreak in His eyes.

(vi) Jesus said a very lovely thing to Peter. " When you have turned," He said, " strengthen your brothers." It is as if Jesus said to Peter, " You will deny me; and you will weep bitter tears; but the result will be that you will be better able to help your brothers who are going through it." We cannot really help a man until we have been in the same furnace of affliction, or the same abyss of shame, as he has been. It was said of Jesus, " He can help others who are going through it because He has been through it Himself." (Hebrews 2: 18, 19.) To experience the shame of failure and disloyalty is not all loss, because it gives us a sympathy and an understanding that otherwise we would never have won.

THY WILL BE DONE

Luke 22: 39-46

> Jesus went out, and, as His custom was, to the Mount of Olives. The disciples, too, accompanied Him. When he came to the place, He said to them, " Pray that you may not enter into temptation." And He was withdrawn from them, about a stone's throw, and He knelt and prayed. " Father," He said, " if it is your will, take this cup from me; but not my will, but yours be done." And an angel from heaven appeared strengthening Him. He was in an agony, and He prayed still more intensely, and His sweat was as drops of blood falling upon the ground. So He rose from prayer and came to His disciples, and found them sleeping from grief. " Why are you sleeping? " He said to them. " Rise and pray that you may not enter into temptation."

THE space within Jerusalem was so limited that there was no room for gardens. Many well-to-do people had private gardens out on the Mount of Olives. Some wealthy friend had given Jesus the privilege of using such a garden, and it was to it that Jesus went to fight His lonely battle. Jesus was only thirty-three, and no one wants to die at thirty-three. He knew what crucifixion was like; He had seen it. He was in an *agony*; the Greek word is used of someone who is fighting a battle with sheer fear. There is no scene like this in all history. This was the very hinge and turning point in Jesus' life. He could have turned back even yet. He could have refused the Cross. The salvation of the whole world hung in the balance as the Son of God literally sweated it out in Gethsemane; and He won.

A famous pianist said of Chopin's Nocturne in C sharp minor, " I must tell you about it. Chopin told Liszt, and Liszt told me. In this piece all is sorrow and trouble. Oh such sorrow and trouble!—until he begins to speak to God, to pray; then it is all right." That is the way it was with Jesus. He went into Gethsemane in the dark; He came out in the light—because He had talked with God.

He went into Gethsemane in an agony; He came out with the victory won, and with peace in His soul—because He had talked with God.

It makes all the difference in what tone of voice a man says, " Thy will be done."

(i) He may say it in a tone of helpless submission, as one who is in the grip of a power against which it is hopeless to fight. The words may be the death-knell of hope.

(ii) He may say it as one who has been battered into submission. The words may be the admission of complete defeat.

(iii) He may say it as one who has been utterly frustrated, and who sees that the dream can never come true. The words may be the words of a bleak regret or even of a bitter anger, which is all the more bitter, because it cannot do anything about it.

(iv) He may say it with the accent of perfect trust. That is how Jesus said it. He was speaking to one who was Father; He was speaking to a God whose everlasting arms were underneath and about Him even on the Cross. He was submitting, but He was submitting to the love that would never let Him go. Life's hardest task is to accept what we cannot understand; but we can do even that if we are sure enough of the love of God.

> God, Thou art love! I build my faith on that . . .
> I know Thee, who has kept my path, and made
> Light for me in the darkness, tempering sorrow
> So that it reached me like a solemn joy:
> It were too strange that I should doubt Thy love.

Jesus spoke like that, and when a man can speak like that, he can look up and say in perfect trust, " Thy will be done."

THE TRAITOR'S KISS

Luke 22: 47-53

While Jesus was still speaking—look you—there came a crowd, and the man called Judas, one of The

Twelve, was leading them. He came up to Jesus to kiss Him; but Jesus said to him, " Judas, is it with a kiss that you would betray the Son of Man? " When those who were around Him saw what was going to happen, they said, " Lord, shall we strike with the sword? " And one of them struck the servant of the High Priest and cut off his ear. Jesus answered, " Let it come even to this! " And He touched the ear and healed him. Jesus said to the chief priests and the Temple captains, and to the elders who had come to Him, " Have you come out with swords and cudgels as against a brigand? When I was daily with you in the Temple you did not lift your hand against me; but this is your hour, and the power of darkness is here."

JUDAS had found a way to betray Jesus in such a way that the authorities could come upon Him when the crowd were not there. He knew that Jesus was in the habit of going at nights to the Garden on the Hill, and there he led the emissaries of the Sanhedrin. The Captain of the Temple, or the Sagan, as he was called, was the official who was responsible for the good order of the Temple; the captains of the Temple here referred to were his lieutenants who were responsible for carrying out the actual arrest of Jesus. When a disciple met a beloved Rabbi, he laid his right hand on the Rabbi's left shoulder and his left hand on the right shoulder and kissed him. It was the kiss of a disciple to a beloved master that Judas used as a sign of betrayal.

There are four different parties involved in this arrest, and their actions and reactions are very significant.

(i) There was Judas, the traitor. He was the man who had *abandoned God*, and who had entered into a league with Satan. It is only when a man has put God out of his life and taken Satan in that he can sink to selling Christ.

(ii) There were the Jews, who had come to arrest Jesus. They were the men who were *blind to God*. When God incarnate came to this earth, all that they could think of

was how to hustle Him to a Cross. They had so long
chosen their own way, and had so long shut their ears to
the voice of God, and their eyes to His guidance, that in
the end they could not recognise Him when He came.
It is a terrible thing to be blind and deaf to God. As
Mrs. Browning wrote,

> " I too have strength—
> Strength to behold Him and not worship Him,
> Strength to fall from Him and not to cry to Him."

God save us from a strength like that!

(iii) There were the disciples. They were the men who,
for the moment had forgotten God. Their world had fallen
in, and they were sure the end had come. The last thing
they remembered at that moment was God; the only thing
they thought of was the terrible situation into which they
had fallen. Two things happen to the man who forgets
God, and who leaves God out of the situation. He becomes
utterly terrified and completely disorganized. He loses
the power to face life and to cope with life. In the time of
trial life is unlivable without God.

(iv) There was Jesus. And Jesus was the one person
in the whole scene who *remembered God.* The amazing
thing about Jesus in the last days is His absolute serenity
once Gethsemane was over. In those days, even at His
arrest, it is He who seems to be in control; and even at
His trial, it is He who is the judge. The man who walks
with God can cope with any situation and look any foe
in the eyes, unbowed and unafraid. It is he, and he alone,
who can ultimately say,

> " In the fell clutch of circumstance,
> I have not winced nor cried aloud.
> Under the bludgeonings of chance
> My head is bloody, but unbow'd.
>
> It matters not how strait the gate,
> How charged with punishments the scroll,
> I am the master of my fate:
> I am the captain of my soul."

It is only when a man has bowed to God that he can talk
and act like a conqueror.

MOCKING AND SCOURGING AND TRIAL

Luke 22: 63-71

The men who were holding Jesus mocked Him and beat Him. They blindfolded Him and asked Him, " Prophesy! Who is it who hit you? " And many another insulting word they spoke to Him.

And when it was day, the assembly of the elders of the people came together, the chief priests and the scribes ; and they led Him away to the Sanhedrin, saying, " Tell us if you are God's Anointed One." He said to them, " If I tell you, you will not believe me; if I ask you, you will not answer. But from now on the Son of Man will be seated at the right hand of the power of God." They all said, " Are you then the Son of God? " He said to them, " You say that I am." They said, " What further evidence do we need? We ourselves have heard it from His own mouth."

THROUGHOUT the night Jesus had been brought before the High Priest. That was a private and unofficial examination. Its purpose was for the authorities to gloat over Him, and, if possible, to trip Him up in cross-examination, so that a charge could be formulated against Him. After that, He was handed over to the Temple police for safe-keeping, and they played their cruel jests upon Him. When the morning came He was taken before the Sanhedrin.

The Sanhedrin was the supreme court of the Jews. In particular it had complete jurisdiction over all religious and theological matters. It was composed of seventy members. Scribes, Rabbis and Pharisees, Priests and Sadducees, and elders were all represented on it. It could not meet during the hours of darkness. That is why they held Jesus until the morning before they brought Him before it. It could meet only in the Hall of Hewn Stone in the Temple court. The High Priest was the president of it. We possess the rules of procedure of the Sanhedrin. Perhaps they are only the ideal, which was never fully carried out; but at least they allow us to see, what the Jews, at their best, conceived that the Sanhedrin should be, and how far their actions fell short of their own ideals in the trial of Jesus. The court sat in a semi-circle, in which every member could see every other member. Facing the court there stood the prisoner dressed in mourning dress. Behind him there sat the rows of the students and disciples of the Rabbis. They might speak in defence of the prisoner but not against him. Vacancies in the court were probably filled by co-option from these students. All charges must be supported by the evidence of two witnesses independently examined. A member of the court might speak against the prisoner, and then change his mind and speak for him, but not *vice-versa*. When a verdict was due, each member had to give his individual judgment, beginning at the youngest and going on to the most senior. For acquittal a majority of one was all that was necessary; for condemnation there must be a majority of at least two. Sentence of death could never be carried out on the day on which it was given; a night must elapse so that the court might sleep on it, so that, perchance, their condemnation might turn to mercy. The whole procedure was designed for mercy; and, even from Luke's summary account, it is clear that the Sanhedrin when it tried Jesus was far from keeping its own rules and regulations.

It is to be very carefully noted that the charge that the Sanhedrin finally produced against Jesus was one of blasphemy. To claim to be the Son of God was an insult to God's majesty, and was therefore blasphemy, and punishable by death.

It is the tragic fact that when Jesus asked for love He did not even receive simple justice. It is the glorious fact that Jesus, even when He had emerged from a night of malignant questioning, even when He had been mocked and buffetted and scourged, still had the utter confidence that He would be set down at the right hand of God, and that His triumph was sure. His faith defied the facts. He never for a moment believed that men in the end could defeat the purposes of God.

TRIAL BEFORE PILATE AND SILENCE
BEFORE HEROD

Luke 23: 1-12

The whole assembly rose up and brought Jesus to
Pilate. They began to accuse Him. " We found this
man," they said, " perverting our nation, and trying
to stop men paying taxes to Cæsar, and saying that
He Himself is the Anointed One, a king." Pilate
asked Him, " Are you the king of the Jews? " He
answered, " You say so." Pilate said to the chief
priests and to the crowds, " I find nothing to condemn
in this man." They were the more urgent. " He is
setting the people in turmoil," they said, " throughout
all Judæa, beginning from Galilee to this place."
When Pilate heard this, he asked if the man was a
Galilæan. When he realised that He was under
Herod's jurisdiction, he referred Him to Herod, who
was himself in Jerusalem in these days. When Herod
saw Jesus he was very glad, because for a long time
he had been wishing to see Him, because he had
heard about Him; and he was hoping to see some sign
done by Him. He questioned Him in many words;
but He answered him nothing. The chief priests and
the Scribes stood by vehemently hurling their accusations against Him. Herod with his soldiers treated
Jesus contemptuously, and after he had mocked
Him and arrayed Him in a gorgeous dress, he referred
Him back again to Pilate. And Herod and Pilate
became friends with each other that same day, for
previously they had been at enmity with each other.

THE Jews in the time of Jesus had no power to carry out
the death sentence. Such sentence had to be passed by
the Roman governor and carried out by the Roman
authorities. It was for that reason that the Jews brought
Jesus before Pilate. Nothing better shows their conscience-
less malignity than the crime with which they charged
Him. In the Sanhedrin the charge had been one of
blasphemy, that He had dared to call Himself the Son of
God. Before Pilate that charge was never even mentioned.
They knew well that it would have carried no weight with
Pilate, and that he would never have proceeded on a

charge which would have seemed to him a matter of Jewish religion and superstition. The charge they levelled against Jesus was an entirely political charge, and it has all the marks of the minds and ingenuity of the Sadducees. It was really the aristocratic, collaborationist Sadducees who achieved the crucifixion of Jesus, in their terror lest He should prove a disturbing element and produce a situation in which they would lose their wealth, their comfort and their power. Their charge before Pilate was really three-fold. They charged Jesus (*a*) with seditious agitation; (*b*) with encouraging men not to pay tribute to Cæsar; (*c*) with the assuming the title king. Every single item of the charge was a lie, and they knew it. They resorted to the most calculated and malicious lies in their well-nigh insane desire to eliminate Jesus.

Pilate was not an experienced Roman official for nothing; he saw through them; and he had no desire to gratify their wishes. But neither did he wish to offend them. They had dropped the information that Jesus came from Galilee; this they had intended as further fuel for their accusations, for Galilee was notoriously "the nurse of seditious men." But to Pilate it seemed a way out. Galilee was under the jurisdiction of Herod Antipas, who, at that very time, was in Jerusalem to keep the Passover. So to Herod, Pilate referred the case of Jesus. Herod is one of the very few people to whom Jesus had absolutely nothing to say. Why did Jesus believe that there was nothing to be said to Herod?

(i) Herod regarded Jesus as a sight to be gazed at. To Herod, Jesus was simply a spectacle. Jesus was not a sight to be stared at; He was a king to be submitted to. Epictetus, the famous Greek Stoic teacher, used to complain that people came from all over the world to his lectures, to stare at him, as if he had been a famous statue, but not to accept and to obey his teaching. Jesus is not a figure to be gazed at but a master to be obeyed.

(ii) Herod regarded Jesus—quite bluntly—as a joke. He jested at Him; He clothed Him in a king's robe as an imitation king. To put it in another way—Herod refused to take Jesus seriously. He would show Him off to his court as an amusing curiosity, but there his interest stopped. The plain fact is that the vast majority of men still refuse to take Jesus seriously. If they took Him seriously they would pay more attention than they do to His words and to His claims.

(iii) There is another possible translation of verse 11. "Herod with his soldiers treated Jesus contemptuously." That could be translated, "Herod, with his soldiers behind him, thought that Jesus was of no importance." Herod, secure in his position as king, strong with the power of his bodyguard behind him, believed that this Galilæan carpenter did not matter. There are still those who, consciously or unconsciously, have come to the conclusion that Jesus does not matter, that He is a factor which can well be omitted from life. They give Him no room in their hearts and no influence in their lives and believe that they can easily do without Him. To the Christian, so far from being of no importance, Jesus is the most important person in all the universe.

THE JEWS' BLACKMAIL OF PILATE

Luke 23: 13-25

> Pilate summoned the chief priests, and the rulers, and the people and said to them, "You brought me this man as one who was seducing the people from their allegiance; and—look you—I have examined Him in your presence, and, of the accusations with which you charge Him, I have found nothing in this man to condemn; and neither has Herod; for he sent Him back to us. Look you—nothing deserving death has been done by Him. I will therefore scourge Him and release Him." All together they shouted out, "Take this man away! And release Barabbas for us." Barabbas had been thrown into prison

> because a certain disorder had arisen in the city, and
> because of murder. Again Pilate addressed them,
> because he wished to release Jesus. But they kept
> shouting, " Crucify, crucify Him! " The third time
> he said to them, " Why? What evil has He done?
> I have found nothing in Him which merits sentence
> of death. I will chastise Him and release Him."
> But they insisted with shouts, demanding that He
> should be crucified; and their voices prevailed. So
> Pilate gave sentence that their demand should be
> granted. He released the man who had been thrown
> into prison for disorder and murder, the man they
> asked for, and Jesus he delivered to their will.

THIS is an amazing passage. One thing is crystal clear—
Pilate did not want to condemn Jesus. He was well aware
that to do so would be to betray that impartial justice
which was the glory of Rome. He made no fewer than
four attempts to avoid passing sentence of condemnation.
He told the Jews to settle the matter themselves. (John
19: 6, 7.) He tried to refer the whole case to Herod. He
tried to persuade the Jews to receive Jesus as the prisoner
who was granted release at the Passover time. (Mark 15: 6.)
He tried to effect a compromise, saying that he would
scourge Jesus and then release Him. It is clear that
Pilate was cœrced into sentencing Jesus to death. How
could a Jewish mob cœrce an experienced Roman governor
into sentencing Jesus to death? It is literally true that the
Jews blackmailed Pilate into sentencing Jesus to death.
The basic fact is that, under impartial Roman justice,
any province had the right to report a governor to Rome
for misgovernment, and such a governor would be severely
dealt with. Pilate had made two grave mistakes in his
government of Palestine. In Judæa the Róman headquarters were not at Jerusalem but at Cæsarea. But in
Jerusalem a certain number of troops were quartered.
Roman troops carried standards which were topped by
a little bust of the reigning emperor. The emperor was
at this time officially a god. The Jewish law forbade any
graven image, and, in deference to Jewish principles,

previous governors had always removed the imperial images before they marched their troops into Jerusalem. Pilate refused to do so. He marched his soldiers in by night with the imperial image on their standards. The Jews came in crowds to Cæsarea to request Pilate to remove the images. He refused. They persisted in their entreaties for days. On the sixth day he agreed to meet them in an open space surrounded by his troops. He informed them that unless they stopped disturbing him with their continuous requests the penalty would be immediate death. " They threw themselves on the ground, and laid their necks bare, and said they would take death very willingly rather than that the wisdom of their laws should be transgressed." Not even Pilate could slaughter men in cold blood like that, and he had to yield. Josephus tells the whole story in *The Antiquities of the Jews*, Book 18, chapter 3. Pilate followed this up by bringing into the city a new water supply, and financing the scheme with money taken from the Temple treasury, a story which we have already told in the commentary on Luke 13: 1-4. The one thing the Roman government could not afford to tolerate in their far-flung empire was civil disorder. Had the Jews officially reported either of these incidents there is little doubt that Pilate would have been summarily dismissed. It is John who tells us of the ominous hint the Jewish officials gave Pilate, when they said, " If you let this man go you are not Cæsar's friend." (John 19: 12.) The Jews compelled Pilate to sentence Jesus to death by holding the threat of an official report to Rome over his head.

Here we have the grim truth that a man's past can rise up and confront him and paralyse him. If a man has been guilty of certain actions and conduct there are certain things which he has no longer the right to say. If he says them his past will be flung in his face. We must have a care not to allow ourselves any conduct which will some day despoil us of the right to take the stand we know we ought to take, and which will entitle people to say, " You of all men, have no right to speak like that."

But if such a situation should arise there is only one thing to do—to have the courage to face it and its consequences. That is precisely what Pilate did not possess. He sacrificed justice rather than lose his post; he sentenced Jesus to death in order that he might remain the governor of Palestine. Had he been a man of real courage he would have done the right, and taken the consequences, but his past made him a coward.

THE ROAD TO CALVARY

Luke 23: 26-31

> As they lead Jesus away, they took Simon, a Cyrenian, who was coming in from the country, and on him they laid the cross to carry it behind Jesus.
>
> There followed Him a great crowd of the people and of women who bewailed and lamented Him. Jesus turned to them. " Daughters of Jerusalem," He said, " do not weep for me, but weep for yourselves, and for your children, because—look you—days are on the way in which they will say, ' Happy are those who are barren, and the wombs that never bore, and the breasts which never fed a child.' Then they will begin to say to the mountains, ' Fall upon us!' and to the hills, 'Cover us!' For if they do these things when the sap is in the wood, what will they do when the tree is dry? "

WHEN a criminal was condemned to be crucified, he was taken from the judgment hall and set in the middle of a hollow square of four Roman soldiers. His own cross was then laid upon his shoulders. And he was marched to the place of crucifixion by the longest possible route. He was made to march by every road and street, and lane and alley, while before him there marched another soldier bearing a placard with his crime inscribed upon it, so that he might be a terrible warning to anyone else who was contemplating such a crime. That is what they did with Jesus. He began by carrying His own Cross (John 19: 17); but under the weight of it His strength gave out, and He could carry it no farther. Palestine was an occupied country, and any citizen could be immediately impressed into the service of the Roman government. The sign of such impressment was a tap on the shoulder with the flat of the blade of a Roman spear. When Jesus sank beneath the weight of His Cross, the Roman centurion in charge looked round for someone to carry it. Out of the country into the city there came Simon from far off Cyrene, which is the modern Tripoli. No doubt he was a Jew who all his life had scraped and saved so that he might be able to eat one Passover at Jerusalem. The flat of the Roman spear touched him on the shoulder and he found himself, willy-nilly, carrying a criminal's cross. Try to imagine the feelings of Simon. He had come to Jerusalem to realise the cherished ambition of a lifetime, and he found himself walking to Calvary carrying a cross. His heart was filled with bitterness towards the Romans and towards this criminal who had involved him in His crime. But if we can read between the lines the story does not end there. J. A. Robertson saw in it one of the hidden romances of the New Testament. Mark describes Simon as the father of Alexander and Rufus. (Mark 15: 21.) Now you do not identify a man by the name of his sons unless these sons are well-known people in the community to which you write. There is general agreement that Mark wrote his gospel to the Church at Rome. Now turn to Paul's letter to the Church at Rome. Amongst the greetings at the end he writes, " Salute Rufus, chosen in the Lord, and his mother and mine." (Romans 16: 13). So in the Roman Church there is Rufus, so choice a Christian that he can be called one of God's chosen ones, with a mother so dear to Paul that he can call her his mother in the faith. It may well be that this Rufus is the same Rufus who was the son of Simon of Cyrene, and his mother was

Simon's wife. It may well be that as he looked on Jesus Simon's bitterness turned to wondering amazement and finally to faith; that he became a Christian; and that his family became some of the choicest souls in the Roman Church. It may well be that Simon from Tripoli thought he was going to realize a life's ambition, and that he was going to celebrate the Passover in Jerusalem at last; that he found himself sorely against his will carrying a criminal's cross; that, as he looked, his bitterness turned to wonder and to faith; and that in the thing that seemed to be his shame he found his Saviour.

Behind Jesus there came a band of women who were weeping for Him. He turned and bade them weep, not for Him, but for themselves. Days of terror were coming. In Judæa there was no tragedy like a childless marriage; in fact childlessness was a valid ground for divorce. But the day would come when the woman who had no child would be glad that it was so. Once again Jesus was seeing ahead the destruction of that city which had so often before, and which had now so finally, refused the invitation of God. Verse 31 is a proverbial phrase which could be used in many connections. Here it means, If they do this to one who is innocent, what will they some day do to those who are guilty and who deserve it?

THERE THEY CRUCIFIED HIM

Luke 23: 32-38

Two others who were criminals were brought to be put to death with Jesus. When they came to the place which is called the place of a skull, there they crucified Him, and the two criminals, one on His right hand, and one on His left. And Jesus said, " Father, forgive them, for they do not know what they are doing." And, as they divided His garments, they cast lots for them. The people stood watching.

and the rulers gibed at Him. " He saved others,"
they said. " Let Him save Himself if He really is
the Anointed One of God, the Chosen One." The
soldiers also mocked Him, coming and offering vinegar
to Him, and saying, " If you are the King of the Jews
save yourself." There was also an inscription over
Him, " This is the King of the Jews."

WHEN a criminal reached the place of crucifixion his
cross was laid flat upon the ground. Usually it was a
cross shaped like a T with no top piece against which the
head could rest. It was quite low, so that the criminal's
feet were only two or three feet above the ground. There
was a company of pious women in Jerusalem who made it
their practice always to go to crucifixions and to give the
victim a drink of drugged wine which would deaden the
terrible pain. That drink was offered to Jesus and He
refused it. (Matthew 27: 34). He was determined to
face death at its worst, with a clear mind and senses un-
clouded. The victim's arms were stretched out upon the
cross bar, and the nails were driven through his hands.
The feet were not nailed, but only loosely bound to the
cross. Half way up the cross there was a projecting piece
of wood, called the saddle, which took the weight of the
criminal, or the nails would have torn through his hands.
And then the cross was lifted and set upright in its socket.
The terror of crucifixion was this—the pain of that terrible
process was bad enough, but it was not enough to kill a
man, and the victim was left to die of hunger and of thirst
beneath the blazing noontide sun and the frosts of the
night. Many a criminal was known to have hung for a
week upon his cross until he died raving mad.

The clothes of the criminal were the perquisites of the
four soldiers among whom he marched to the cross. Every
Jew wore five articles of apparel—the inner tunic, the
outer robe, the girdle, the sandals and the turban. Four
were divided among the four soldiers. There remained

the great outer robe. It was woven in one piece without
a seam. (John 19: 23, 24.) To have cut it up and divided
it would have ruined it; and so the soldiers gambled for
it in the shadow of the Cross. It was nothing to them that
another criminal was slowly dying in agony.

The inscription which was set upon the cross was the same
placard as was carried before a man as he marched through
the streets to the place of crucifixion.

Jesus said many wonderful things, but He rarely said
anything more wonderful than, " Father, forgive them,
for they know not what they are doing." Christian forgiveness is an amazing thing. When Stephen was being
stoned to death he too prayed, " Lord, lay not this sin
to their charge." (Acts 7: 60.) There is nothing so
lovely, and there is nothing so rare, as Christian forgiveness.
When the unforgiving spirit is threatening to turn our
hearts to bitterness, let us hear again our Lord praying for
forgiveness for those who crucified Him, and let us hear
His servant Paul saying to his friends, " Be ye kind to one
another, tender-hearted, forgiving one another, even as
God for Christ's sake hath forgiven you." (Ephesians 4: 32).

The idea that this terrible thing was done in ignorance
runs through the New Testament. Peter said to the
people in after days, " I know that, through ignorance,
you did it." (Acts 3: 17.) Paul said that they crucified
Jesus because they did not know Him. (Acts 13: 27.)
Marcus Aurelius, the great Roman Emperor and the
Stoic saint, used to say to himself every morning, " To-day
you will meet all kinds of unpleasant people; they will
hurt you, and injure you, and insult you; but you cannot
live like that; you know better, for you are a man in
whom the spirit of God dwells." Others may have in their
hearts the unforgiving spirit; others may sin in ignorance;
but we know better; we are Christ's men and women; and
we must forgive as He forgave.

298

THE PROMISE OF PARADISE

Luke 23: 39-43

> One of the criminals who were hanged kept hurling insults at Jesus. " Are You not the Anointed One? " he said. " Save yourself and us." The other rebuked him. " Do you not even fear God? " he said. " For we too are under the same sentence and justly so, for we have done things which deserve the reward that we are reaping; but this man has done nothing unseemly." And he said, " Jesus, remember me when you come into your Kingdom." He said to him, " This is the truth—I tell you—to-day you will be with me in Paradise."

IT was of set and deliberate purpose that the authorities crucified Jesus between two known criminals. It was deliberately so staged to humiliate Jesus in front of the crowd, and to rank Him with robbers. Legend has been busy with the penitent thief. He is called variously Dismas, Demas and Dumachus. One legend makes him a Judæan Robin Hood who robbed the rich to give to the poor. The loveliest legend tells how the holy family were attacked by robbers when they fled with Jesus, as a little child, from Bethlehem to Egypt. Jesus was saved by the kindness of a youth who was the son of the captain of the robber band. The little baby Jesus was so lovely that the young brigand could not bear to lay hands on Him but set Him free, saying, " O most blessed of children, if ever there come a time for having mercy on me, then remember me and forget not this hour." So, they say, that the robber youth who had saved Jesus when He was a baby, met Him again on a Cross on Calvary; and this time Jesus saved Him.

The word Paradise is a Persian word meaning *a walled garden*. When a Persian king wished to do one of his subjects a very special honour he made him a companion of the garden, and he was chosen to walk in the garden with the king. It was more than immortality that Jesus promised the penitent thief. He promised him the honoured place of a companion of the garden in the courts of heaven.

Surely this story tells us above all things that it is never too late to turn to Christ. There are other things of which we must say, " The time for that is past. I am grown too old for that now." But we can never say that of turning to Jesus Christ. So long as a man's heart beats, the invitation of Christ still stands. As the poet wrote of the man who was killed as he was thrown from his galloping horse,

> " Between the stirrup and the ground,
> Mercy I asked, mercy I found."

For us it is literally true that while there is life there is hope.

THE LONG DAY CLOSES

Luke 23: 44-49

By this time it was about midday, and there was darkness over the whole land until 3 o'clock in the afternoon, and the light of the sun failed. And the veil of the Temple was rent in the midst. When Jesus had cried with a great voice, He said, " Father, into your hands I commend my spirit." When He had said this He breathed His last. When the centurion saw what had happened, he glorified God. " Truly," he said, " this was a good man." All the crowds, who had come together to see the spectacle, when they saw the things that had happened, went home beating their breasts. And all His acquaintances, and the women who had accompanied Him from Galilee, stood far off and saw these things.

EVERY sentence of this passage is rich in meaning.

(i) There was a great darkness as Jesus died. It was as if the sun itself could not bear to look upon the deed men's hands had done. The world is ever dark in the day when men seek to eliminate and to banish Christ.

(ii) The Temple veil was rent in twain. The veil was the veil which hid the Holy of Holies, that place wherein there dwelt the very presence of God, into which no man might ever go except the High Priest, and he only once a year, on the great day of Atonement. It was as if the way to the secret of God's presence, hitherto barred to man, was thrown open to all. It was as if the heart of God, hitherto hidden, was laid bare to men. The coming of Jesus, the life of Jesus, and the death of Jesus, rent the veil which had concealed God from man. " He who hath seen me," said Jesus, " hath seen the Father." (John 14: 9.) On the Cross, as never before, and never again, men saw the love of God.

(iii) Jesus cried with a great voice. Three of the gospels tell us of this great cry. (cp. Matthew 27: 50; Mark 15: 37.) John, on the other hand, does not mention the great cry, but tells us that Jesus died saying, " It is finished." (John 19: 30.) In Greek and Aramaic *It is finished* is one word. *It is finished* and the great cry are one and the same thing. Jesus died with a shout of triumph on His lips. He did not say, " It is finished," as one who is battered to his knees and finally beaten, as one who admits defeat. He said it like a victor who has won his last engagement with the enemy, like one who has brought a tremendous task to its ultimate conclusion. Finished! It is the cry of the Christ, crucified and yet victorious.

(iv) Jesus died with a prayer on His lips. " Father, into your hands I commend my spirit." That is Psalm 31: 5 with one word added—the word *Father*. That verse was the first prayer that every Jewish mother taught her child to say last thing at night. Just as we were taught, maybe, to say, " This night I lay me down to sleep," so the Jewish mother taught her child to say, before the threatening dark came down, " Into thy hands I commend my spirit." And Jesus made it even more lovely for He began it with the word *Father*. Even on a Cross Jesus died like a child falling asleep in his father's arms.

(v) The centurion and the crowd were deeply moved as Jesus died. His death had done what even His life could not do; it had broken the hard hearts of men. Already Jesus' saying was coming true—" I, if I be lifted up from the earth, will draw all men unto Me." The magnet of the Cross had begun its work, even as He breathed His last.

THE MAN WHO GAVE JESUS A TOMB

Luke 23: 50-56

> Look you—there was a man named Joseph, a member of the Sanhedrin, a good and a just man. He had not consented to their counsel and their action. He came from Arimathæa, a town of the Jews, and he lived in expectation of the Kingdom of God. He went to Pilate and asked for the body of Jesus. He took it down, and wrapped it in linen, and laid it in a rock-hewn tomb where no one had ever yet been laid. It was the day of preparation, and the Sabbath was beginning. The women, who had accompanied Jesus from Galilee, followed and saw the tomb and how His body was laid in it. Then they went back home and prepared spices and ointments. And they rested on the Sabbath day according to the commandment.

IT was the custom that the bodies of criminals were not buried at all, but were left to the dogs and the vultures to dispose of; but Joseph of Arimathæa saved the body of Jesus from that indignity. There was not much time left that day. Jesus was crucified on the Friday; the Jewish Sabbath is our Saturday. But the Jewish day begins at 6 p.m. That is to say by Friday at 6 p.m. the Sabbath had begun. That is why the women had only time to see where the body was laid and to go home and prepare their spices and ointments for it and to do no more, for after 6 p.m. all work became illegal.

Joseph of Arimathæa is for us a figure of the greatest interest.

(i) Legend has it that in the year A.D. 61 he was sent by Philip to this country. He came to Glastonbury. With him he brought the chalice that had been used at the Last Supper, and in it the blood of Christ. That chalice became the Holy Grail, which it was the dream of King Arthur's knights to find and see. When Joseph arrived in Glastonbury they say that he drove his staff into the ground to rest on it in his weariness, and that the staff budded and became a bush which blooms every Christmas Day. St. Joseph's thorn still blooms at Glastonbury and, to this day, slips of it are sent all over the world. The first church in all England was built at Glastonbury, and the church, which legend links with the name of Joseph, is still a mecca of Christian pilgrims.

(ii) There is a certain tragedy about Joseph of Arimathæa. He is the man who gave Jesus a tomb. He was a member of the Sanhedrin; we are told that he did not agree with the verdict and the sentence of that court. But there is no word that he raised his voice in disagreement. Maybe he was silent; maybe he absented himself when he was powerless to stop a course of action with which he disagreed. What a difference it would have made if he had spoken! How it would have lifted up Jesus' heart if, in that grim assembly of bleak hatred, one lone voice had spoken for Him! But Joseph waited until Jesus was dead, and then he gave Him a tomb. It is one of the tragedies of life that we place on people's graves the flowers we should have given them when they were alive. We keep for their obituary notices, and for the tributes paid to them at memorial services and in committee minutes, the praise and thanks we should have given them when they were alive. Often, often we are haunted because we never spoke. A word to the living is worth a cataract of tributes to the dead.

D—11   303

THE WRONG PLACE TO LOOK

Luke 24: 1-12

> On the first day of the week, at the first streaks of dawn, the women came to the tomb, bearing the spices which they had prepared. They found the stone rolled away from the tomb. They entered in, but they did not find the body of the Lord Jesus. While they were at a loss what to make of this— look you—two men stood by them in flashing raiment. They were afraid, and they bowed their faces to the ground. But they said to them, " Why are you looking for Him who is alive among the dead? He is not here; He is risen. Remember how He said to you, while He was still in Galilee, that the Son of Man must be betrayed into the hands of sinful men and that He must be crucified, and that on the third day He would rise again." Then they remembered His words; and they returned from the tomb and brought the news of all these things to the eleven and to the others. Mary Magdalene was there, and Joanna, and Mary, the mother of James. They, and the other women with them, kept telling these things to the apostles. But their words seemed to them an idle tale, and they refused to believe them. But Peter rose up and ran to the tomb; and he stooped down and saw the linen clothes lying all by themselves; and he went away wondering in himself at what had happened.

THE Jewish Sabbath was our Saturday; it was the last day of the week, and it commemorated the rest of God after the work of creation. The Christian Sunday is the first day of the week, and commemorates the Resurrection of Jesus. So on this first Christian Sunday, the women went to the tomb, as they thought, to carry out the last offices of love for the dear dead, and to embalm and anoint Jesus' body with their spices. In the east tombs were often carved out in caves in the rock. The body was wrapped in long linen strips like bandages, and then laid on a shelf in the rock tomb. The tomb was then closed by a great circular stone like a cart-wheel which ran in a groove across the opening. When the women came, the stone was rolled away. Now, just here, we have one of these discrepancies in the accounts of the Resurrection of which the critics and opponents of Christianity make so much. In Mark the messenger in the tomb is a young man in a long white robe (Mark 16: 5); in Matthew he is the Angel of the Lord (Matthew 28: 2). Here it is two men in flashing raiment; and in John it is two angels (John 20: 12). It is true that the differences are there; but it is also true that, whatever the attendant description, *the basic fact of the empty tomb never varies*, and that is the fact that matters. No two people ever described the same episode or incident in the same terms; nothing so wonderful as the Resurrection ever escaped a certain embroidery as it was repeatedly told and recounted. But at the heart of the story that one all-important fact of the empty tomb remains. The women returned with their story to the rest of the disciples, and they refused to believe them. They called it an idle tale. The word the rest used to describe it is a word that is used in Greek medical writers to describe the babbling of a fevered and insane mind. Only Peter went out to see if it might not possibly be true. The very fact that Peter was there says much for Peter. The story of his denial of his Master was not a thing that could be kept silent; and yet Peter had the moral courage to face those who knew his shame. There was something of the hero in Peter, as well as something of the coward. The man who was a fluttering dove is on the way to becoming a rock.

The all-important and the challenging question in this story is the question of the messengers in the tomb, " Why are you looking for Him who is alive among the dead? " There are many of us who still look for Jesus among the dead.

(i) There are those who regard Jesus as the greatest man and the noblest hero who ever lived, as one who

305

lived the loveliest life that has ever been lived on earth and who then died. That will not do. Jesus is not dead; He is alive. He is not a hero of the past; He is a living presence to-day.

> Shakespeare is dust, and will not come
> To question from his Avon tomb,
> And Socrates and Shelley keep
> An Attic and Italian sleep.
>
> They see not. But, O Christians, who
> Throng Holborn and Fifth Avenue,
> May you not meet in spite of death,
> A traveller from Nazareth?

(ii) There are those who regard Jesus as a man whose life must be studied, and whose words must be examined, and whose teaching must be analysed. There is a tendency to think of Christianity and Christ in terms of something to be studied. The tendency may be seen in the quite simple fact of the extension of the study group and the extinction of the prayer meeting. Beyond a doubt study is necessary; but Jesus is not only someone to be studied; He is someone to be met and lived with every day in life. He is not only a figure in a book, even if that book be the greatest book in the world; again, He is a living presence.

(iii) There are those who see in Jesus the perfect pattern and example. He is that; but it remains true that a perfect example can be the most heart-breaking thing in the world. For centuries the birds gave men an example of flight, and yet not till modern times could man fly. We may remember that when we were young we were presented at school with a writing book. At the top it has a line of copperplate writing; below it had blank lines on which we had to copy it. How utterly discouraging were our efforts to reproduce that perfect pattern! But then the teacher would come and, with her hand, would guide our hand over the lines and we got nearer to it. That is what Jesus does. He is not only the pattern and the example. He helps us, and guides us, and strengthens us to follow that pattern and example. He is not simply a model for life; again, He is a living presence to help us to live.

It may well be that our Christianity has lacked the essential something, because we too have been looking for Him who is alive among the dead.

THE SUNSET ROAD THAT TURNED TO DAWN

Luke 24: 13-35

Now—look you—on that same day two of them were on the way to a village called Emmaus, which is about seven miles from Jerusalem; and they talked with each other about all the things which had happened. As they talked about them, and discussed them, Jesus Himself came up to them and joined them on their way. But their eyes were fastened so that they did not recognize Him. He said to them, "What words are these that you are exchanging with each other as you walk?" And they stood with faces twisted with grief. One of them, called Cleopas, answered, "Are you the only visitor in Jerusalem who does not know the things that happened in it in these days?" "What kind of things?" He said to them. They said to Him, "The story of Jesus of Nazareth, who was a prophet mighty in deed and in word before God and all the people; and how our chief priests and rulers handed Him over to sentence of death and how they crucified Him. As for us—we were hoping that He was the one who was going to rescue Israel. Yes—and to add to it all—this is the third day since these things happened. Yes and some women of our number astonished us, for they went early to the tomb, and, when they did not find His body, they came saying that they had seen a vision of angels, who said that He was alive. And some of our company

went to the tomb and found it just as the women had
said—but they did not see Him." He said to them,
" O foolish ones and slow in heart to believe in all the
things that the prophets said! Was it not necessary
that the Anointed One should suffer and enter into
His glory?" And beginning from Moses and all the
prophets, He expounded to them the things concerning Himself in all the scriptures. As they came
near the village to which they were going, He made
as if He would have gone on; and they pressed Him.
" Stay with us," they said, " because it is towards
evening, and the day is already far spent." So He
came in to stay with them. When He had taken His
place at table with them, He took bread, and blessed
it and broke it, and gave it to them; and their eyes
were opened and they recognized Him; and He
vanished out of their sight. They said to each other,
" Was not our heart burning within us while He was
talking to us on the road, as He opened the scriptures
to us?" And they arose that very hour and went
back to Jerusalem and found the eleven gathered
together and those with them, and found that they
were saying, " It is a fact that the Lord has risen,
and He has appeared to Simon." So they recounted
all that had happened on the road, and how He was
known to them in the breaking of bread.

THIS is another of the immortal short stories of the world.

(i) It tells of two men who were walking towards the
sunset. It has been suggested that that is the very reason
why they did not recognize Jesus. Emmaus was west of
Jerusalem. The sun was sinking, and the setting sun so
dazzled them that they did not know their Lord. However
that may be, it is true that the Christian is a man who
walks not towards the sunset but to the sunrise. Long
ago it was said to the children of Israel that they journeyed
in the wilderness towards the sunrising. (Numbers 21: 11.)
The Christian goes onwards, not to a night which falls,
but to a dawn which breaks—and that is what, in their
sorrow and their disappointment, the two on the Emmaus
road had forgotten.

(ii) It tells us of the ability of Jesus to make sense of things. The whole situation seemed to these two men to have no explanation. Their hopes and dreams were shattered. There is all the poignant, wistful, bewildered regret in the world in their sorrowing words, " We were hoping that He was the one who was going to rescue Israel." They are the words of men whose hopes are dead and buried. And then Jesus came and talked with them, and the meaning of life became clear to them, and the darkness became light. A story-teller makes one of his characters say to the one with whom he has fallen in love, " I never knew what life meant until I saw it in your eyes." It is only in Jesus that, even in the bewildering times, we learn what life means.

(iii) It tells us of the courtesy of Jesus. He made as if He would have gone on. He would not force Himself upon them; He awaited their invitation to come in. God gave to men the greatest and the most perilous gift in the world, the gift of free-will; and we can use it to invite Christ to enter our hearts or to allow Him to pass on.

(iv) It tells how He was known to them in the breaking of bread. This always sounds a little as if it meant the sacrament; but it does not. It was at an ordinary meal in an ordinary house, when an ordinary loaf was being divided, that these men recognized Jesus. It has been beautifully suggested that perhaps they were present at the feeding of the five thousand, and, as He broke the bread in their cottage home, they recognized His hands again. It is not only at the communion table we can be with Christ; we can be with Him at the dinner table too. He is not only the host in His Church; He is the guest in every home. Fay Inchfawn wrote,

> " Sometimes, when everything goes wrong;
> When days are short and nights are long;
> When wash-day brings so dull a sky
> That not a single thing will dry.

And when the kitchen chimney smokes,
And when there's naught so " queer " as folks!
When friends deplore my faded youth,
And when the baby cuts a tooth.
While John, the baby last but one,
Clings round my skirts till day is done;
And fat, good-tempered Jane is glum,
And butcher's man forgets to come.
Sometimes I say on days like these,
I get a sudden gleam of bliss.
Not on some sunny day of ease,
He'll come . . . but on a day like this! "

The Christian lives for ever and everywhere in a Christ-filled world.

(v) It tells how these two men, when they received their own joy, hastened to share it. It was seven miles' tramp back to Jerusalem, but they could not keep the good news to themselves. The Christian message is never fully ours until we have shared it with someone else.

(vi) It tells how, when they reached Jerusalem, they found others who had already shared their experience. It is the glory of the Christian that he lives in a fellowship of people who have had the same experience as he has had. It has been said that true friendship only begins when people share a common memory and can say to each other, " Do you remember? " Each one of us is one of a great fellowship of people who share a common experience and common memory of their Lord.

(vii) It tells us how Jesus appeared to Peter. That must ever remain one of the great untold stories of the world. But surely it is a lovely thing that Jesus should make one of His first appearances to the man who had denied Him. It is the glory of Jesus that He can give the penitent sinner back his self-respect.

IN THE UPPER ROOM

Luke 24: 36-49

While they were still speaking, Jesus stood in the midst of them, and said to them, " Peace to you!" They were terrified and afraid, because they thought that they were seeing a spirit. He said to them, " Why are you troubled? And why do the questions arise in your heart? See my hands and my feet—that it is I—myself. Handle me and see, for a spirit has not flesh and bones as you see that I have." And when He had said this He showed them His hands and His feet. When they still thought it too good to be true, and when they were astonished He said to them, " Have you anything to eat here?" They gave Him part of a cooked fish, and He took it and ate it before them.

He said to them, " These are my words which I spoke to you while I was still with you—that all the things which stand written about me in the law of Moses, and in the prophets, and in the psalms must be fulfilled." Then He opened their minds so that they understood the scriptures; and He said to them, " Thus it is written, that the Anointed One should suffer and should rise from the dead on the third day; and that repentance in His name and forgiveness of sins should be proclaimed to all nations, beginning from Jerusalem. And—look you—I send out the promise of my Father upon you. But stay in this city until you will be clothed with power from on high."

HERE we read of how Jesus came to His own when they were gathered in the Upper Room. In this passage certain of the great notes of the Christian Faith are resonantly struck.

(i) It stresses *the reality of the Resurrection*. The Risen Lord was no phantom or ghost or hallucination. He was real. The Jesus who died was in truth the Christ who rose again. Christianity is not founded on the dreams of men's disordered minds, or the visions of their fevered eyes, but on one who in actual historical fact faced and fought and conquered death and rose again.

(ii) It stresses *the necessity of the Cross*. It was to the Cross that all the scriptures looked forward. The Cross was not forced on God; it was not an emergency measure when all else had failed and when the scheme of things had gone wrong. It was part of the plan of God, for the Cross is the one place on earth, where in a moment of time, we see the eternal love of God.

(iii) It stresses *the urgency of the task*. Out to all men had to go the call to repentance and the offer of forgiveness. The Church was not left to live forever in the Upper Room; it was sent out into all the world. After the Upper Room there came the world-wide mission of the Church. The days of sorrow were past and the tidings of joy must be taken to all men.

(iv) It stresses *the secret of power*. They had to wait in Jerusalem until power from on high came upon them, until Pentecost had come. There are times when the Christian may seem to be wasting time, when he must wait in a wise passivity. Action without preparation must of necessity fail. There is a time to wait on God and a time to work for God. Fay Inchfawn writes of the days when life is a losing contest with a thousand little things.

> " I wrestle—how I wrestle!—through the hours.
> Nay, not with principalities and powers—
> Dark spiritual foes of God's and man's—
> But with antagonistic pots and pans;
> With footmarks on the hall,
> With smears upon the wall,
> With doubtful ears and small unwashen hands,
> And with a babe's innumerable demands."

And then, even in the business, she lays aside her work to be for a moment with God.

> " With leisured feet and idle hands, I sat.
> I, foolish, fussy, blind as any bat,
> Sat down to listen, and to learn. And lo,
> My thousand tasks were done the better so."

The quiet times in which we wait on God are never wasted times; for it is in the time when we lay aside life's tasks that we are strengthened for the very tasks we laid aside.

THE HAPPY ENDING

Luke 24: 50-53

> Jesus led them out as far as Bethany; and He raised His hands and blessed them; and as He was blessing them He parted from them, and was borne up into heaven. And when they had worshipped Him they returned to Jerusalem with great joy; and they were continually in the Temple praising God.

THE Ascension must always remain a mystery, for it attempts to put into words what is beyond words and to describe what is beyond description. But that something such should happen was essential. It was unthinkable that the appearances of Jesus should grow fewer and fewer until finally they petered out. That would have effectively wrecked the faith of men. There had to come a day of dividing, when the Jesus of earth finally became the Christ of Heaven. But to the disciples the Ascension was obviously three things.

(i) It was *an ending*. One stage was past and another had begun. The day when their faith was faith in a flesh and blood person, and when it depended on the presence of that person's flesh and blood were ended. Now they were linked to someone who was forever independent of space and time.

(ii) But equally it was *a beginning*. The disciples did not leave the scene heart-broken; they left it with great joy. They left it so, because now they knew that they had a Master from which nothing could separate them any more.

> I know not where His islands lift
>   Their fronded palms in air;
> I only know I cannot drift
>   Beyond His love and care.

" I am persuaded," said Paul, " that nothing—nothing in life or in death—can separate me from the love of God in Christ Jesus my Lord." (Romans 8: 38, 39.)

(iii) Still, further, the Ascension gave the disciples the certainty that they had *a friend, not only on earth, but in heaven.* Surely it is the most priceless thing of all to know and to feel that in heaven there awaits us that self-same Jesus who on earth was wondrous kind. To die is not to go out into the dark; it is to go to Him.

So they went back to Jerusalem, and they were continually in the Temple praising God. It is not by accident that Luke's gospel ends where it began—in the House of God.